BAGS TO RICHES

Ed —
Perhaps my words
will trigger
pleasant memories
of Izzi.

[signature]

I. J. "Izzi" Wagner
1915–2005

Why would anyone want to read about *me*? I am just a "bag man." In ten years or so, no one will remember I. J. Wagner. After all, the younger generation does not remember the movie stars I knew, or the presidents, or the governors. Most passers-by see a name on a building, and they don't know who that person was or why the building bears his name. But that's okay. It's more important for each generation to look ahead than to dwell too much on the past.

—I. J. Wagner, 2004

BAGS TO RICHES

———◆———

The Story of I. J. Wagner

by
Don Gale

Foreword by
Ted Wilson

The University of Utah Press
Salt Lake City

The Defiance House Man colophon is a registered trademark of the University
of Utah Press. It is based upon a four-foot-tall, Ancient Puebloan pictograph
(late PIII) near Glen Canyon, Utah.

10 09 08 07 06   5 4 3 2 1

LIBRARY OF CONGRESS CATALOGING-IN-PUBLICATION DATA

Gale, Don, 1933–
    Bags to riches : the story of I. J. Wagner / by Don Gale ; foreword by Ted Wilson.
        p. cm.
    Includes index.
    ISBN-13: 978-0-87480-885-8 (cloth : alk. paper)
    ISBN-10: 0-87480-885-5 (cloth : alk. paper)   1. Wagner, I. J. (Irving Jerome), 1915–
2005.   2. Paper bag industry—Utah—Salt Lake City.   3. Businessmen—Utah—Salt
Lake City—Biography.   I. Title.
    HD9839.P282W344 2006
    338.7'67633092—dc22   2006028282

With appreciation to

Rose Yuddin Wagner
and
Jeanné Rasmussen Wagner

The author did not have opportunities to meet either woman,
but their influence in shaping the life and thoughts of I. J. Wagner
was apparent in everything he did and said.

Contents

Foreword

---·•·---

Izzi Wagner burst into my life when I was twelve years old. My father's business was a stone's throw from Wagner Bag Company. I remember Izzi as a young, swaggering type of fellow with a wide smile and a bow tie. He would sashay into my dad's enterprise with a cheerful countenance and with a suggestion or two on how to run an awning shop. After Izzi left, my dad would disdainfully say, "Just like that S.O.B. Izzi to walk in and tell me how to run my business." But my dad still enjoyed a beer with Izzi at the Circle Inn across the street or a burger at the corner café of the Miles Hotel as they chewed the fat about Salt Lake City. Dad understood the two sides to Wagner's character. He was "busy Izzi" to some of his critics, but to the observant—my father included—he was "busy" because he cared.

Izzi Wagner loved Salt Lake City. Always a busy bee, his love swarmed the entire hive. He was an irrepressible downtown businessman, a member of the city planning and zoning board, a charter member of the airport authority, a major contributor to the arts and sports and physical fitness, and an active nonpartisan in politics.

Wagner could be an enormous challenge to a biographer. In order to capture the whole Izzi, it would require a breadth of discovery not usually given to traditional historical analysis. A more appropriate approach in this case would be to depend on the flow of the man's life, the pace of his presence, and the enormously wonderful stories of his existence.

Don Gale's account of Izzi Wagner does just that. Gale's narrative of Izzi Wagner's life depends not so much on detailed research methodology as on capturing the essence of a life. Gale understands that exploring Wagner's character is more an art form than a scientific exercise.

Gale's motif and title—*Bags to Riches*—bring Izzi's life into focus from the near to the far. Born into an impoverished immigrant family, he earned money as a boy by running errands for prostitutes and delivering coffee and sandwiches from Rex Drug. As an adult, he campaigned for the city's new symphony hall, and he made it possible to build a new Jewish Community Center, with its focus on recreation. It is fair to say that Izzi Wagner appreciated life because he saw it from all sides.

This breadth of appreciation gave Wagner a perspective that would serve him well as a community builder. He was the first to demand elimination of the pay toilets at the airport. A significant source of revenue be damned, he said, it is immoral to make one pay to go to the bathroom. In return, Izzi grinned and endured an oft-repeated joke about how the mambo was invented so Izzi could get into a pay toilet. His humble beginnings prompted his humble demands. Others joked about seeing Izzi at the self-service pump filling his Rolls-Royce with gasoline (long before all pumps were self-service). I'm told he smiled as he saved a few pennies at the gas pump, knowing his action would fuel not only his car but his jokester friends as well. (I wouldn't be surprised if he repeated the joke himself...and laughed loudest at it.)

This was Wagner—a humble man who understood the use of money. He used his money to build a business that employed many Salt Lake workers, to create the Rose Wagner Performing Arts Center, to develop Trolley Square, and to improve many city buildings. He was dedicated to making the city he loved better. And the city loved him in return.

Gale's account is a delightful journey through the life of a second-generation immigrant who magnified the love of America and his community. Gale's remarkable achievement cascades the reader with Izzi Wagner stories and ventures.

Izzi was a Jew in a strange land where Jews are called "gentiles." He broke the religious barrier of the country club and other "exclusive" organizations. Once inside the walls of such places, he was not above begging for dollars for the boys' and girls' clubs, for the downtrodden on the streets, and for artistic endeavors sometimes overlooked by the privileged few.

Gale shows that Wagner loved partnerships. His strength was in teaming with others, including Roy Simmons of Zions Bank fame. Simmons, the Mormon, and Wagner, the Jew, built an empire by understanding the strengths from both sides—indeed, all sides—of the community spectrum.

Gale also gets at a current and pressing need of our community, if indirectly. Wagner's undaunted mixing through all segments of society exemplified a style of personal integration with community and place that is too often forgotten today as the community struggles over what has come to be called "the religious divide."

Gale's biography is a good and warm read. The book fits nicely in the lap on a cool evening near the fireplace. One can happily revel in the past of Salt Lake City. It is comfort reading for the Salt Lake City aficionado.

But warmth and style easily transform to importance when one considers Wagner for what he was—an icon of inclusion, of entrepreneurship, and of community building. Those three traits are richly needed in the modern city of Wagner's dreams.

—Ted Wilson
Mayor of Salt Lake City
1976–1985

Preface

N O H I S T O R Y O F T W E N T I E T H - C E N T U R Y Utah would be complete without the story of Irving Jerome Wagner, better known as I. J. Wagner or, simply, "Izzi."

Early in the twentieth century—shortly before Izzi was born—Salt Lake City was considered one of the ugliest cities in the United States, according to historian Thomas Alexander. The city had more railroad tracks inside city limits than any other city in the land. It ranked near the bottom in miles of water pipe per capita, and even lower in miles of sewer line per capita. Many city streets were still unpaved or poorly paved. In other words, the city's economic climate was dismal. That would change dramatically during Wagner's lifetime—thanks, in part, to his influence. Dramatic changes were already under way when Izzi was born in 1915. Before he died, ninety years later, he would be instrumental in moving the city forward.

Isadore Wagner came into the world in a small adobe house near the center of downtown Salt Lake City. The house had no running water and no sewer line. He grew up in the same house, surrounded by bars, houses of prostitution, poverty, corruption, and discrimination. Many of those conditions would also change for the better during his lifetime. Again, I. J. Wagner would play a significant role in bringing about the changes.

Hard, sometimes brutal, physical labor was part of life during his formative years. World War I, Prohibition, the Great Depression, radio, and movies helped shape his philosophy, just as they helped shape the "philosophy" of the city and the nation. The early death of his father dropped tremendous responsibilities on his teenage shoulders. Close encounters with death as a

World War II Marine added to Izzi's sense of citizenship responsibility. So, too, did worldwide communication, depression, and war inundate state and city leaders with heavy responsibilities, obligations I. J. Wagner would share during the second half of the twentieth century.

Always the handsome romantic, Izzi found the mate who turned youthful romance into a lifelong love story. He also had romantic notions about people from different backgrounds living together peacefully and productively. With considerable help from a wise mother, he learned as a child to build bridges. He carefully and deliberately expanded his circle of influence to include Jews, Mormons, Catholics, atheists...Japanese Americans, African Americans, Latinos...laborers, managers, bankers...political leaders, church leaders, business leaders...and representatives from many other groups. He made no distinction from one individual to another; all were welcome at his table. Izzi also helped the community around him build bridges during a period when bridges were sorely needed.

Beginning in poverty, Wagner used wise management and indomitable optimism to build a fortune for himself, plus fortunes for many others. (He rarely entered any business deal without a partner.) Along the way, he gave much to those in need—often quietly. When life forces began to fade, he gave most of his fortune back to the community. And he worried that he had not given back enough, that he might leave the world before his account was in balance.

In similar fashion, the city in which Izzi was born went from poverty to affluence during his lifetime. He drew satisfaction from that change, believing that he might have played a small role in the transformation. He also gained satisfaction from knowing that he played a modest part in seeing that the state and the city "gave back" to their citizens—especially those in need.

And so the story of Izzi Wagner's life is something of a metaphor for the twentieth-century story of the city, state, and nation he loved. The story began in far-off lands.

Wagner's parents, Rose and Harry, were Jewish immigrants from Latvia and Ukraine, respectively. They met and married in Boston, and they eventually came to Utah in 1913. Izzi was born in Salt Lake City on March 31, 1915, the second of three Wagner children—Abraham, Isadore, and Leona.

The family experienced all the anti-Semitic prejudice typical of that period in the United States and Utah, but Rose taught her children how to deal appropriately with prejudice, both personally and socially. Izzi—always slight of build but handsome—learned to box in order to protect himself. He eventually won three "professional" bouts before deciding against a pugilistic career. He developed an outgoing, jovial personality that made him popular with his classmates...and would later serve him well in business. He even became sports editor of the high school newspaper.

Shortly after Izzi enrolled at the University of Utah—planning to become an attorney—Harry Wagner died suddenly. Izzi had to withdraw from the university in order to help his mother run the family business. At the time, Rose told Izzi that the Wagners were part of the great American success story, because they had arrived in Salt Lake with less than three dollars and were now six thousand dollars in debt.

It was the middle of the Great Depression. Settling that six-thousand-dollar debt seemed an unreachable goal. But Rose, Izzi, and Abe went to work. They renegotiated their debts, consolidated their resources, turned their home at 144 West Third South into a combined business and living quarters, and focused on a single line of business activities—burlap bags.

In earlier days, the Wagners bought and sold everything from bottles to batteries. Commerce in used bags grew faster than the trade in other items on their buy-sell list. At the time, Utah potato farmers and onion growers needed bags to get their produce to market. The Wagners bought used bags, cleaned them, repaired them, and sold them either to wholesalers or directly to produce growers. Before his death, Harry had dealings with new and used bag suppliers on the West Coast. Soon, the bag business occupied the largest share of the family's time and effort. And Wagner Bag Company was born.

The company grew from a firm dealing with rags and used bags into a sizable manufacturing facility, still at the Third South location. Under Izzi's guidance, the company expanded until it was buying its own raw burlap from India, printing it, and turning it into bags. Wagner Bag Company's line of products grew to include cotton bags for sugar and flour, paper bags for retailers, and plastic bags imported by the millions from Taiwan.

In the late 1950s, Wagner Bag built a new, modern 140,000-square-foot manufacturing plant in the southwest sector of Salt Lake City. In 1959, the family sold Wagner Bag to St. Regis Paper Company for millions in cash and stock.

Rose frequently told her children how fortunate they were to live in the United States of America. When World War II came along, Izzi felt obligated to forego a good chance for military deferment in order to join the U.S. Marine Corps. After boot camp, he married Jeanné Rasmussen (from a Utah Mormon family), then shipped off the next day to Guadalcanal. After their three-year wartime separation, the couple would be inseparable until Jeanné died in 1996.

Both felt a strong responsibility to work toward improvements in the community, state, and nation. They were active politically, socially, and, when their resources permitted, philanthropically. For most of his life, Izzi was the first in line at his district voting place on election day.

Even as a very young man, Izzi formed partnerships with different individuals to buy and sell businesses and properties, much as he bought and sold bags—a restaurant in Los Angeles, a nightclub in Salt Lake, commercial buildings in Salt Lake and Ogden, industrial property, parking lots, and many other investment properties.

When St. Regis purchased Wagner Bag Company, Izzi became the western representative for St. Regis Paper. The company provided an office in one of the city's newest buildings at Main and South Temple in the heart of downtown Salt Lake. Izzi, with his gregarious personality, continued to build relationships within the business-social structure of the city and state. He met almost daily at breakfast or lunch with various small groups of "power brokers." They often discussed problems facing the city and state, and then worked to solve those problems.

The effectiveness of Izzi's small leadership groups was an expression of the times. Today, attempts to deal with community problems usually generate organized community-action groups. Both the strength and the weakness of so-called community action groups are that they require balanced representative membership, open meetings, and mostly sterile discussions. The power brokers of the mid-1900s—including Izzi Wagner's groups—rejected such formalities. They met quietly to determine courses of action for the city and state. Then they used their considerable influence to make sure the media, elected officials, and others turned their plans into reality. Many of the state's more important laws, structures, and events originated with these concerned citizens working quietly but effectively—including Symphony Hall (now Abravanel Hall), the Salt Palace, downtown malls, freeway configurations, airport expansion, the Utah Stars professional basketball team, the Utah Jazz, and many more important additions or improvements.

Izzi Wagner played an important role in many of these developments. He had the time, the resources, and the contacts. He was not directly associated with recognized power centers—such as The Church of Jesus Christ of Latter-day Saints (LDS), political parties, or various de facto groups—and so he was able to act as unofficial mediator in many situations. He became a close friend to church leaders, governors, mayors, senators, business leaders, social activists, and others. These friendships gave him easy access to those who would be called upon to implement actions suggested by unofficial city and state leaders working quietly behind the scenes.

Over the years, Izzi was named to leadership positions in many government, civic, and social service organizations, including the Salt Lake Planning and Zoning Commission, Salt Lake Airport Authority, Convention and Visitors Bureau, Utah Manufacturers Association, Salt Lake Rotary, Arthritis Foundation, and many more. But his effectiveness was always most pronounced when working outside formal power structures.

Izzi was a leading voice and behind-the-scenes force to eliminate overhanging street signs and billboards in downtown Salt Lake City, to expand and modernize the Salt Lake City Airport, and to build the Salt Palace Convention Center, among other civic contributions.

The Wagners made generous contributions to charitable organizations, even though Izzi firmly believed that the responsibility for health care research and care of the ill and indigent belonged with government, not charity. He was convinced that the government should make sure no one in the United States goes hungry or homeless, and that government should be more involved in research to find answers for serious diseases, such as arthritis, cancer, diabetes, heart disease, and so on.

When Jeanné died, Izzi began looking for ways to memorialize her, as well as his mother, Rose, and his sister, Leona. (Jeanné was a dancer on the vaudeville circuit at the time she met Izzi.) When he moved his business from Third South, he sold much of the property to Salt Lake County. Now, he dreamed of establishing a memorial to his mother, his wife, and his sister on the site of the original Wagner home. He worked with Salt Lake County to plan and build a performing arts center on that site. When county-owned property proved inadequate, Izzi once again bought property he had owned earlier; he then donated it to the county. He also donated money for planning and construction costs. Thus came into being the Rose Wagner Performing Arts Center. Inside are the Jeanné Wagner Theatre auditorium and the Leona Wagner Theatre. The building houses the Gina Bachauer Piano Competition, Ririe-Woodbury Dance Company, and Repertory Dance Theater, among others. The auditorium provides a much appreciated venue for performances by resident dance companies and visiting artists who prefer a five hundred–seat hall over the larger auditoriums operated by Salt Lake County.

Izzi also made contributions of almost fifteen million dollars to enable the Jewish Community Center to purchase and completely remodel a building that once served as headquarters for the Fort Douglas Country Club. That facility, located adjacent to the University of Utah Health Sciences Center, is now called the I. J. and Jeanné Wagner Jewish Community Center. It includes two swimming pools, four tennis courts, a basketball court, a fully equipped exercise complex, meeting rooms, and other facilities. Izzi insisted that membership be open to all who wish to join (limited only by the facility's capacity), and so the center has become a favorite for families living in the area, as well as personnel at the medical center.

Thus, there is little doubt that I. J. Wagner—who started as a rag dealer early in the twentieth century—became a major influence in the development of Salt Lake City and its environs. Salt Lake City had little to recommend it when Izzi was born in 1915, but it ended the century as a thriving, successful metropolis, thanks in part to his efforts. His contributions of work, energy, wisdom, and resources will continue to benefit Utah citizens throughout the twenty-first century and beyond.

The story of his life is also the story of the city he loved. He always found ways to work through the negatives and focus on the positives in his environment. To him, problems were welcome challenges, not feared impediments.

Izzi often said that what he accomplished would not be remembered long. That's the way it should be, he believed, because future generations should be thinking ahead, not dwelling on the past. "No one wants to read the story of my life," he said. "I'm just a bag man."

The nature of history is that, with few exceptions, physical structures survive only a few generations. And the names attached to such structures are forgotten even before the buildings undergo the inevitable changes. (Izzi sometimes recited a list of famous names he said young people had already forgotten.)

Words are more permanent than structures. Words become part of the historical record. Many decades from today, historians will try to piece together an understanding of the twentieth century from their own perspectives, but their viewpoints will necessarily be grounded in different experiences, different lifestyles, and different information sources. It is important that the record include at least one assessment from today—a "real-time" history, if you will.

The words on the following pages seek to capture the experiences of one man whose background and influence went far beyond the ordinary. The words are filtered through the subject's memory and the interpretations of a fascinated listener. Both are selective—limited by the passage of time and the imprecision of human curiosity. This book is not intended to be a definitive chronicle. It is not so much about history as it is about the character of those who molded the history of the twentieth century—specifically, the character of one such individual. It is a series of verbal snapshots "taken" by one man—Izzi Wagner—over a period of almost one hundred years. He would not consider requests for formal interviews or tape-recorded conversations. The following words are words relayed in hundreds of conversations with Izzi at breakfast, at lunch, and in his office. His memories were recorded on paper soon after the conversations took place. Follow-up questions in the same informal settings were used to establish accuracy and clarify meaning. He also agreed, hesitantly, to transmit what few records he maintained through the author to the University of Utah Library, providing opportunities for the author to look through the materials before turning them over to the university. Finally, sources reported here include words conveyed in conversations with many of his friends. Indeed, all those who knew him seem to have memories, anecdotes, and stories they are eager to share. (Mention the name of Izzi Wagner to any of his many acquaintances, and his or her eyes light up, a smile appears, and he or she feels obliged to retell one or more of Izzi's oft-told jokes.) A few photographic snapshots from Izzi's haphazard collection are also included to add visual recollections of a fascinating individual and a fascinating period of time. Few of the photos were dated, but fortunately the author was able to ask Izzi about identities and dates. Izzi also had a chance to read the first draft of the manuscript before he died. He said, with a smile, "Where did you find all those lies about me…and why would anyone care?"

The following pages answer those questions. The primary source was I. J. Wagner himself. And although this book is not a history in a purely academic sense, no record of Utah can be complete without it.

A Note about Sources

Through a period of more than five years, I met with Izzi Wagner almost daily over morning tea and lunch and on other occasions. Our offices were adjacent, and so we frequently exchanged visits. When we parted, I turned to my computer to make notes about our conversations, thinking they might someday be useful for an article or column. I asked him on more than one occasion if he would consent to the use of a tape recorder during our conversations. He always declined with emphasis. The pile of notes grew over the years. Sometimes, he showed me letters, photos, and other documents. I asked if I could make copies, and he often consented. As the project began to take shape, I asked Izzi's secretary, Dora Bailey, for files of clippings and other items. She found most of what I requested—always with Izzi's permission.

When Izzi died, hundreds of photos and other items were earmarked for the trash bin. With Dora's help, I sorted through the photos to find those most relevant. All of these items, including my notes, were donated to the J. Willard Marriott Library at the University of Utah, where they will be housed in Special Collections.

BAGS TO RICHES

1

From Eastern Europe to Utah

———◆———

ROSE YUDDIN WAGNER was born January 21, 1883, in Kraslava, Latvia, about one hundred miles southwest of the capital city of Riga. Her ancestors had migrated to that area from Spain many years earlier. The family name, Yuddin, probably originated from references to the family's Jewish heritage. Her birth name was probably Rachel, although on a Russian passport issued in 1907 she is listed in German as "Rachlia Judin" and in French as "Rochle Judin." (In correspondence, she later signed her name as "Rachelle Wagner.")

Herschel Wigrizer (Harry Wagner) was born in Vilna Goberna, a small city near Kiev in the Ukraine. The exact date of his birth is somewhat uncertain. The Ukraine was under control of the Russian czar. Herschel had six sisters. Unfortunately, little is known about the Wigrizer family history, because Harry died at a relatively young age, long before he had the time or inclination to relate much information about his parents and ancestors.

During the early 1890s, Herschel married a beautiful young woman from a well-to-do family named Susman. Modern family records call her Polly, although that was probably not her birth name. In 1900, Herschel and Polly had a son named Morris. Soon after the birth of Morris, Herschel decided to seek new opportunities in America. He landed at the port of Boston, and he found work at Lawrence, Massachusetts, as a laborer, unloading ships. He later worked in a fruit store and may have opened his own fruit cart or fruit store in Lawrence. Soon, his wife and son came to the New World to join Herschel. But Polly did not adjust well to life in America. Herschel earned only a few cents a day, and life was difficult. Polly longed for the good life of her early years, not knowing that anti-Semitism was on the increase in the Ukraine. In about 1908, Polly and her son, Morris, left Boston to return home. Apparently, they encountered severe persecution in the Ukraine. Morris was badly wounded in anti-Jewish riots. He carried scars the rest of his days. Family legend has it that an uncle built a false wall in his house in order to hide Morris from protesters. The uncle could feed Morris only bread and milk for many months.

It is unlikely that Herschel heard from Polly for several years following her departure from America. However, in about 1920, Morris—now a young man—returned to Lawrence to work. Over a long period, he saved enough money to bring his mother, Polly, back to the United States. However, by that time, Herschel had moved on with his life. He would not see Polly again until he returned to Boston for Morris's wedding in 1926. He probably assumed either that Polly and Morris were killed in the anti-Semitic pogroms or that Polly had elected to end their marriage.

Rose Yuddin's homeland of Latvia was also part of czarist Russia. Jews were not allowed to own land, and so the family farmed part of an estate owned by a local Russian baron. As Rose told it later, the baron exacted his tribute by simply arriving at the household, unannounced, and demanding major portions of the output from the land, including crops, animals, and money. (The family was able to earn a little money each year by placing tables and chairs outside their house and selling sandwiches and homemade vodka to Russian soldiers passing through the area.)

Life was extremely difficult for Rose and her parents, three sisters, and three brothers. But like most Jewish families, the Yuddins were close-knit, and they found ways to build enjoyment into their difficult circumstances, often through music and education. In order to successfully navigate her many relationships, Rose learned to speak four languages: Hebrew, Yiddish, Russian, and German. Later, she would also learn English.

The Yuddin women worked as hard as any men, but living conditions continued to deteriorate for the family. No doubt, the hard work contributed to the early death of their mother, who died while Rose was still a teenager.

Rose's older sister (called Mary in later years) married a young man from the area named Abe Karras. He was soon conscripted into the Russian army. Jews were not allowed to rise above the rank of private. After his first six years of military service, Mary's husband was notified that he would be required to serve another six years. At great personal risk, he went AWOL. The couple left their families and everything they knew to seek a new life in the

United States of America. They had heard the many stories circulating about opportunities in America. Some of the stories came from Mary's uncle, who was already in Boston. He promised the young couple a place to stay until they could find their own way in the new land.

The Yuddins' Russian landowner reacted to the departure of family members by making life even more difficult for the remaining Yuddins. The Russian Revolution created more difficulties and disruptions. The army needed food and resources. Soldiers passed back and forth through the area, often without much regard for local inhabitants. Yuddin family members and friends were conscripted into the Russian military. Some lost their lives or were wounded. When soldiers came through Kraslava, they asked locals whether they were "white" or "red," symbols for the two warring factions in the revolution. "Reds" were acceptable; "whites" were treated with disdain, sometimes beaten or murdered. Anger, unrest, and distrust were added to the list of discomforts already affecting all aspects of life in Latvia. At times, the Yuddin children hid in a cellar to keep themselves safe from marauding Bolshevik soldiers.

At one point, Rose's brother Jacob was arrested. He spent several days in jail because local officials objected to something he had said or done. He was drafted into the Russian army as soon as he came of age. (All three of Rose's brothers were eventually killed by the Nazis during World War II.)

Rose's sister Mary wrote on several occasions, urging Rose and her younger sister, Ethel (her American name), to come to Boston, where life was much better than in Latvia. She promised them a place to stay, and said she would help them find work. Rose and Ethel decided it was time to leave home. By that time, their mother had died. They said good-bye to their father, Abe; their oldest sister, Shifra; brothers Jacob, Zussman, and Michael; and their friends, none of whom they would ever see again. In 1907, they made contact with what amounted to an underground network in order to secure Russian passports.

Rose and Ethel Yuddin arrived at the port of Boston sometime in the late spring of 1908. Rose was twenty-five years old. They were among almost ten million immigrants who came to the United States during the first decade of the twentieth century. (Herschel Wigrizer was also part of the wave of immigrants.)

After their difficult journey by sea from Latvia to Boston, Rose and Ethel moved in with their sister until they could find jobs and an apartment of their own. The apartment in which they eventually located consisted of a one-room, walk-up flat in the Jewish section of Boston, not far from significant historical landmarks in that city. They found jobs at a shoe factory in Jamaica Plain, a Boston suburb. They worked twelve hours a day, six days a week, for a weekly salary of three dollars. The factory made button shoes. Rose marked the location for the buttons, and her sister sewed them in place. The factory was owned by a man of the Catholic faith. He believed in a "day of rest," and so his factory was one of the few that closed on Sundays, giving the two sisters a day off. One of their favorite pastimes was to make sandwiches of bread and mayonnaise, spend a nickel each for the subway, and go to Boston Commons to listen to free concerts. Rose especially loved all kinds of music, from popular to classical. Somehow, she also found time to go to night school and learn English.

As noted above, during these same years, Herschel Wigrizer was seeking his fortune in the Boston area. He worked on the docks. He moved freight for local business. He even tried opening his own fruit stand. But the season was short, and his entrepreneurial efforts were disappointing. Herschel was hard-working, but he was always dreaming of schemes to increase his income. Sometimes those opportunities worked out, and sometimes they resulted in disappointment. He moved often. He eventually ended up in the same boardinghouse where Rose and Ethel lived. That's how Rose Yuddin and Herschel Wigrizer met. Herschel had not heard from his wife or son. Soon the friendship between Herschel and Rose turned to courtship. They were married in about 1911. Rose almost certainly knew about Polly and Morris before the wedding.

At some point during this period, Herschel Wigrizer changed his name to Harry Wagner. There seems to be no official record of the change, and so it is doubtful that Harry went through the necessary steps to make his name change legal. He probably decided that "Harry Wagner" was more American than "Herschel Wigrizer." (He was not alone; many immigrants of the period Americanized their names.)

The couple soon established themselves in the community. Harry—always outgoing and gregarious—became friendly with a man named Henry Harris. The two had business dealings, although the nature of those dealings is unclear. Before long, Harris heard that the western United States was a land filled with opportunities. He moved to Portland, Oregon. Within a few weeks, he wrote to Harry and Rose, urging them to join him. He said that Portland offered many business opportunities.

Harry had been out of work for a while, and so it wasn't long before Rose and Harry were on the train to Portland. It was a struggle to save enough money for the train tickets. They packed their meager belongings into a couple of boxes, and once again, Rose Wagner said good-bye to family and friends to begin yet another adventure in yet another new land.

They found the promised opportunities in Portland. Harry rented a horse and wagon to begin transporting luggage for the many newcomers arriving in the city. Rose soon became pregnant, but she lost the baby in a miscarriage. Before long, Harry's restless friend, Henry Harris, sought new opportunities. He moved once again—this time to Salt Lake City. As before, he wrote to Harry and Rose, urging them to join him in Utah. It wasn't long until the Wagners were again on a train, heading for another unknown land. Rose and Harry arrived in Salt Lake City in 1913. Harry had about three dollars in his pocket.

They first moved in with Henry Harris at an adobe house he was renting located at 144 West Third South. Soon, Rose and Harry found a small apartment of their own near Fourth South and Fifth East Streets. Rose talked a nearby grocer into giving her credit so she could buy enough to eat. Harry went to work, helping his friend move baggage and other materials from place to place around the city. While they were at the Fifth East location, Rose gave birth to their first child, Abraham Wagner.

Before long, Harry was able to lease a cart and a horse of his own. He found that most of his business revolved around the comings and goings of trains at the Denver and Rio Grande (D&RG) Railroad station located at the foot of Third South Street. His former partner, Henry Harris, was once again planning to move on, this time to California. Harry and Rose decided not to follow Harris. Instead, they moved into the little adobe house on west Third South formerly occupied by Harris. It was much more roomy than their apartment, the rent was reasonable, and it was located close to the railroad station where Harry did most of his business. The little house had several rooms, one or two heated by Franklin stoves. The water supply came from a faucet in the front yard. An outhouse was located at the end of a walkway in the rear. During the winter, they wrapped the outdoor water spigot with burlap to keep it from freezing, but there was no way to keep the outdoor "facility" from reaching temperatures far below freezing.

Lilac bushes grew in front of the house, and when the lilacs were in bloom, Rose sold the flowers for five cents a bunch. (A nickel would buy a loaf of bread; a quart of milk cost a dime.)

The second Wagner son was born in that small adobe house on March 31, 1915. The Wagners named their second son Isadore. The name appears on his school records and other documents of his early years. As he grew older, childhood playmates naturally began calling him "Izzi," a nickname that would stay with him for the rest of his life. (When he was an adult, Izzi often told friends that his mother named him "Irving Jerome" after her two favorite composers, Irving Berlin and Jerome Kern. But Kern and Berlin did not make their marks in popular music until a few years later. Izzi himself chose the name, probably in the mid-1930s when he was thinking about becoming a movie star. He probably changed his name legally, because he was able have "Isadore" replaced on his birth certificate with "Irving Jerome" when he applied for a passport in 1962. When he became a successful businessman, Izzi shortened both "Irving" and "Jerome" to call himself "I. J. Wagner." He used the initials only for the most formal documents. Few acquaintances had any idea what the *I* and the *J* stood for. Most called him Izzi, and anyone who knew anything about Salt Lake City recognized the name and the individual it described.)

Harry continued to move various goods around town. As soon as possible, he bought the horse and wagon. He also had success in picking up passengers and their luggage from the railroad station and delivering them to one of several hotels along Second and Third South Streets in downtown Salt Lake City. Many arriving passengers were from the coal mines in south-central Utah. They came to the capital city whenever they could to have a good time and spend what little money they earned. Harry eventually bought a secondhand truck. He kept the horse—named Queenie—and bought a buggy to use as a family conveyance for trips to the synagogue, picnics, and other outings.

Harry made a two-sided sign for the truck. On one side it said "Baggage," on the other side "Passengers." When a freight train arrived, he flipped the sign to "Baggage." When the train schedule listed a passenger train, he turned the sign to "Passengers." He was always able to find strong young men in the neighborhood to help with the heavy lifting for a few cents. One of them was a young tough named Jack Dempsey, who would later go on to become the heavyweight boxing champion of the world.

On one occasion, Harry was helping a nearby grocer move his fixtures and inventory to a new location. When almost everything was moved out, Harry found a stack of empty burlap bags that had once been used for potatoes, onions, and other produce. Harry asked the owner if he wanted the empty bags moved to the new location. The owner said no. He told Harry he could have the bags, and he suggested that a local junk dealer would buy the bags for two cents each. At the end of the day, Harry threw the empty bags on the truck and took them home.

Rose, always insightful, asked if there was a market for used bags. Harry told Rose about the junk dealer who might buy them. Rose shook out the bags, sorted them, and bundled them up. Harry sold them for a total of about four dollars—more than he made in a day picking up passengers and luggage.

Rose encouraged Harry to check with other grocers to see if they might have empty bags needing to be recycled. She figured they could make a small profit from buying and selling used bags, even if it meant paying a penny or so for each of them. Harry found that grocers and others were happy to save the trouble of storing, sorting, and transporting the used bags to the junk dealer. Each individual grocer had relatively few bags—hardly enough to make the process worthwhile for the grocer—but gathering used bags from many grocers led to a sizable accumulation. Before long, the bag business was much more productive than "Baggage" and "Passengers" put together.

Soon, Rose had another of her many business insights. One day, Harry returned from delivering a truckload of bags to the junk dealer. Rose asked him how much the dealer had paid. Harry said his buyer paid two cents per bag. Then Rose asked what the dealer did with the bags. Harry said the junk dealer sold them to potato and onion farmers in northern Utah and even Idaho. Rose asked how much the bags were worth to farmers. Harry said they sold for about three cents. Rose said if the wholesaler could sell them for three cents, then Harry could easily sell them to farmers for two and a half cents. Wagner Bag Company was about to become a reality. Rose and Harry would buy and sell almost anything, but they focused on burlap bags.

Harry operated his transport business from a small building on west South Temple Street, across the street from where the Delta Center is now located. The building provided a place for Harry to keep his horse and other business equipment. Nearby was the old Devereaux House, which had become a boardinghouse.

Through correspondence with her younger sister, still in Boston, Rose knew that Ethel was managing a small boardinghouse. She wrote to urge Ethel to come to Utah, where Rose knew similar work was readily available. Ethel joined the Wagners in Utah, and she soon found work in Salt Lake as the manager of several boardinghouses, including the Devereaux House. She leased the buildings from their owners. The Devereaux House would become a favorite getaway place for Izzi and his friends when they were growing up. Aunt Ethel could always find cookies for her nephew and his friends.

One of Ethel's boarders was a bootlegger. He operated a still in his room on the top floor of the house. One day, the still blew up, blowing a hole in the roof and causing a considerable amount of damage. The building owner blamed Ethel for renting to such outlaws. He canceled Ethel's lease. She then took over the Boston Hotel, directly across the street from the Wagner house. (The Boston Hotel is now Squatter's Pub, but a sign painted high on the side of the building still proclaimed "Boston Hotel" until it was painted over in 2003.)

In the meantime, Rose's older sister Mary and her husband went on to become successful entrepreneurs in Boston, operating a small retail store and investing in real estate. It would be thirty years before Rose would see Mary again. On that occasion, Mary arrived at the Wagner home unannounced. Izzi said he never heard so much screaming and crying as the day Rose opened the door to find Mary standing on the stoop.

When Harry's son, Morris, returned to the United States in the early 1920s, he contacted Harry and learned about Harry's new life. Harry invited Morris to Salt Lake and gave him a job. Morris stayed for about six months before returning to the East Coast. During that time, Morris met his step-brothers and stepsister—Abe, Izzi, and Leona Wagner. In 1926, Morris married a young woman named Jennie Tatelman. Harry went to Boston for the wedding, where he saw Polly for the first time in two decades. (Izzi remained in close touch with Morris and, later, with Morris's son, Leon Wigrizer, for the rest of his life.)

In this environment, Izzi Wagner spent his childhood. Salt Lake City was not much of a city during Wagner's childhood years. The population was growing, but it would not reach 150,000 until well into the 1930s. During the early part of the century, a national magazine ranked Salt Lake as one of the ugliest cities in the United States. However, by the time Izzi was born in 1915, a beautification movement was under way, spurred not by government but by private organizations such as the Ladies Literary Guild, the Chamber of Commerce, and various service groups. According to historian Thomas Alexander, the effort was a reflection of national movements called City Beautiful and City Practical. By the early 1920s, the city was busy planning more parks, moving railroad tracks, and improving water and wastewater systems.

Still, Salt Lake City was by far the largest city in the Intermountain West. The entire state of Utah had a population of less than half a million. The number of Jews in the state was probably fewer than one thousand—although their influence on Utah history would prove much greater than their numbers. The city's first synagogue was located in a hotel about half a block west of the Wagner residence. Segregation was an accepted social practice. Anti-

Semitism was the norm. Prostitution, drinking, gambling, and other vices were openly tolerated, sometimes providing under-the-table income for local officials.

It was not an easy life, but as Izzi grew up, he heard Rose say often, "I would rather sleep on the floor in America than on a silk bed in Russia."

2

The Childhood Years

———◆———

ISADORE WAGNER GREW UP in the little adobe house at 144 West Third South. Eventually, the family piped water inside the house and installed indoor bathroom facilities.

Behind the house, half a block away on Pierpont Street, was Salt Lake High School. When West High School opened, the old Salt Lake High School became the National Guard Armory; later, Western Newspaper Union, a printing paper supply house; and still later, a company called Twin Typographers that provided lead type for local printers. It is now home to two popular restaurants, Café Pierpont and Baci Trattoria.

Two blocks north was the Bamberger Railroad station, a small commuter line that ran between Salt Lake and Ogden. The Salt Lake terminal was below street level where Abravanel Hall is now located. The station for a second commuter line—the Garfield Railroad—was a few blocks west. Among other destinations, the Garfield line served Saltair, a resort on the banks of the Great Salt Lake. Both the Denver and Rio Grande and the Union Pacific railroad depots were within a few blocks. A freight rail line ran along what was then First West Street (now Second West) to serve manufacturing plants, warehouses, and other businesses located on both sides of the road. Railroad spurs ran east and west from the First West line, including a spur behind the Wagner house. J. G. McDonald's Candy Company and Sweet's Candy Company were within a block of Izzi's childhood home.

Across Third South from the Wagner house was a small hotel, the Bristol, which later became a bordello. Another small hotel and house of prostitution was directly east of the Bristol, and at least half a dozen other bordellos were located nearby. Izzi and his young friends called the prostitutes "window tappers," because they would sit provocatively at street-level hotel windows and tap on the glass with finger thimbles whenever potential "clients" walked by. During his preteen years, a favorite pastime for Izzi and his pals was to try to identify prominent men from the community as they walked surreptitiously down the alley to enter the back door of the Bristol Hotel. Izzi recalled when the city's mayor, the chief of police, and a prominent attorney were charged with taking under-the-table payoffs from houses of prostitution—and he produced newspaper clippings to prove it. The 1938 headline read, "Men Charged with Profiting from Earnings of Fallen Women." The three men were sentenced to jail terms ranging from six months to one year. (When World War II began, the federal government —not local officials—insisted that houses of prostitution be shut down in order to protect servicemen.)

Two or three small family-operated grocery stores were within a block of the Wagner home. Nearby West Temple was the site for many small businesses—mostly bars, pool halls, and assay offices—stretching from Fourth South to South Temple. At one time, Izzi sold Sunday newspapers each week outside a prominent bar on the corner of Second South and West Temple.

Pioneer Park, with two swimming pools and a baseball diamond, was a block and a half away. Central Park was on Second South near Third East. Fremont Elementary School was less than two blocks north and west. West Junior High (later Horace Mann) and West High School were within easy walking distance. Several small industrial plants were nearby, as were a number of grain and flour elevators. And the downtown business section of Salt Lake City's Main Street was little more than one block east.

On the southeast corner of West Temple and Third South was Rex Drug, where the boys could buy a phosphate or an ice cream cone if they could coax a nickel out of their father. When they asked for the nickels, Harry always lectured them about the value of money and told them they would be better off eating bread and onions...but he usually gave them nickels.

A Buddhist church was located on First South, two blocks away, and a small Japanese community surrounded it. The new Jewish synagogue was three or four blocks east. African Americans found living quarters west of nearby railroad stations. A grocery store across Third South served the Italian community. Swedish immigrants congregated north of West High School. Greeks and eastern Europeans came to central Utah as miners. They often stayed in nearby hotels when visiting the city—especially on weekends. In

1925, a new Greek Orthodox Church was constructed about a block west of the Wagner home.

And so Izzi Wagner grew up not only near the literal center of the Salt Lake business district but also near the center of its vice district, on the fringes of many ethnic communities, and adjacent to the city's primary transportation corridors.

Young Izzi could never have imagined that one day he would own the land where many of his childhood landmarks stood, including most of the block where he lived (now the Rose Wagner Performing Arts Center), the Bristol Hotel (now a parking lot for the Rose Wagner Center), Rex Drug, many business properties along Main Street, and numerous other pieces of land throughout the city. Years later, he formed various partnerships with his many friends to buy and sell buildings the way he learned to buy and sell all manner of goods while growing up in the Wagner household.

His mother, Rose, was the greatest influence in his life. She was self-educated, but her wisdom far exceeded that of many individuals boasting years of academic achievement. She loved music and theater, and she passed those interests on to her children. Discipline was imposed not by the stick but by her words and her behavior. She insisted on high standards of behavior, and when her children did not meet her standards, they soon learned of her displeasure. She was given to making terse philosophical pronouncements about behavior and relationships. Her advice often consisted of only a few well-chosen words, partly because she was still learning English and partly because she knew short sentences have the strongest impact. The children spoke English and some Yiddish or Hebrew around the house, but when Rose and Harry wanted to say something privately, they spoke in Russian so the children could not understand. Rose was an excellent cook, and she was always willing to share what limited food they had with those who had even less. The family raised chickens in the backyard, and so meals often included eggs or chicken.

Izzi's father, Harry, exerted less influence over his children than their mother. Harry worked long hours. When he was home, he was likely to be asleep. He had a large circle of friends, and when time allowed, he liked to gather with friends to play poker. Harry also liked to fish, and once in a while he took his sons fishing—usually for carp in what was called "the surplus canal," west of town near the Jordan River. Harry died suddenly when Izzi was seventeen, and so Harry did not have much time to share with his children such things as the Wagner (Wigrizer) family history, or his advice, or his disciplinary effort. His interests were directed almost entirely toward his business. He liked baseball, but he did not understand it. One day when Izzi and Abe came home from school, they found their father listening to the World Series on radio. Abe asked the score, and Harry said the score was five to three. Abe asked who was winning, and Harry said, "The one with five."

The family could not afford a radio, but on at least one occasion—perhaps the occasion mentioned above—Harry took advantage of offers from local appliance dealers to deliver radios "on trial" for the World Series. Users could then return the radios if they did not want to buy them—no questions asked. The dealers expected the free trial period to generate buyers, but Harry returned his "trial" radio after the series ended.

Much of what we know about Izzi's childhood comes from anecdotes he remembered and repeated often to anyone who would listen. Telling these stories with obvious delight was part of the irresistible Wagner charm.

In the early years, there was no hot water in the Wagner house except what could be heated on the stove, and so once a week Rose walked her children to a boardinghouse two blocks away where they could bathe in a copper tub. The children took turns...at twenty-five cents for each tub of water. Rose was always the last to bathe. The boardinghouse was operated by a Japanese man, and it catered to a Japanese clientele. There was a pool table on the first floor, and while the children waited their turns for bathing, they watched and listened as the Japanese patrons chattered in language totally foreign to the youngsters. The owner befriended the Wagner children, and Izzi came to appreciate still another culture. He became lifelong friends with the son of the boardinghouse operator, Fugio "Fudge" Iwasaki, who eventually owned and operated one of Salt Lake's best-known restaurants, the Pagoda. Later, Izzi helped Fudge establish his restaurant business, and for the rest of his life, Izzi Wagner never received a bill when he ate at the Pagoda. Eventually, Izzi would be the first non-Japanese Utahn to become a lifetime member of the Japanese-American League.

The Wagner family was a hardworking group. Both Izzi and Abe began earning money while still in elementary school. One day when Izzi, then about six years old, was at the railroad station with his father, he watched newsboys walking up and down beside a passenger train that had stopped temporarily at the Salt Lake station to discharge a few passengers and take on others. The newsboys waved their newspapers as they walked alongside the waiting train. Every now and then, a passenger opened the train window, took a paper, and handed the boy a nickel. Izzi knew his mother saved newspapers, and so the next day he took a handful of old newspapers and waved them in front of train windows. Some unsuspecting passengers took a paper and handed Izzi a nickel. By the time they discovered the newspapers contained yesterday's news, the train was already on its way. When Rose found out what had happened to the missing newspapers, she scolded Izzi and offered a lesson about honesty in business—a lesson he never forgot. I. J. Wagner often regretted the incident. He said he would have liked to find the passengers he had cheated so he could return not only their nickel but appropriate interest as well.

Not many years later, Izzi earned money as an errand boy for the women at a neighborhood brothel. He took sandwich orders from the women, then ran across the street to Rex Drug to fill the orders. The prostitutes paid him well, and he got to know the woman who ran the Bristol Hotel, Kitty. She and her husband, Sam, had come to Salt Lake from San Francisco. No one knew Sam's last name, but everyone called him "Sam Spiegel" because he spent so much time looking in the mirror. ("Spiegel" is Yiddish for "looking glass.") Kitty could not read or write, and so she sometimes called on Izzi to help her with mail and other paperwork. Kitty sent money each month to her mother in the East, telling her mother that she had a fine job managing a hotel. Some years later, Izzi and Rose were going to Boston to visit Rose's sister. Kitty asked them to stop in New York to see her mother. She gave the Wagners money to take to her mother, and she told Rose to tell the woman how well Kitty was doing as manager of the hotel. When Izzi and Rose found Kitty's mother in New York, she and Rose conversed for a long while, mostly in Yiddish. Izzi did not know exactly what they were saying. He hoped Kitty's message was conveyed to her mother. On another occasion, Kitty's brother stopped in Salt Lake to tell Kitty that their mother had passed away. When he found out that Kitty was running a house of prostitution, he grew angry and left town.

Immediately east of the Bristol Hotel was a smaller hotel that provided rooms to African American guests, mostly railroad porters and waiters from nearby restaurants, including those located in the Hotel Utah, a facility owned and operated by the Mormon Church. On the ground floor of the little hotel across from the Wagner home was the Black Elks Lodge and a barbershop where the customers were African American. Sam Spiegel liked the barber in that particular barbershop and always went there to have his hair cut. But he insisted that the barber pull down the shades so no one could see him patronizing the shop. Such was the sad climate of the times. (Izzi would eventually own both the Bristol Hotel and the little hotel east of it. He tore them down to create a parking lot "in perpetuity" for the Rose Wagner Performing Arts Center.)

Kitty played a role in another incident a few years earlier. Izzi and a friend went to see a silent movie featuring a cowboy named Black Bart. Black Bart always wore a mask to keep his identity secret, and so when the boys paid their nickels to get in, they were given paper masks like Black Bart's. The five-cent ticket price allowed them to sit on a small chairless platform at the side of the theater. When the movie ended, the boys walked the two blocks home, still wearing the masks. It was dusk, and the lighted sign in front of the Bristol Hotel shone brightly. The sign was made up of many small incandescent electric lights. The boys decided to practice their Black Bart shooting skills by using rubber bands to shoot bent straight pins at the lights. The lights popped loudly when they were hit. Soon, the madam came running from the building, chasing the boys. She could not catch them.

But when Izzi arrived home a short time later, his mother confronted him about the vandalism. She said Kitty named Izzi as one of those involved. Izzi said, "How could she know it was me? I was wearing a mask." Of course, Rose used the occasion to teach yet another lesson about respecting the property of others.

Baseball was a popular summer sport. However, Izzi and his friends could not afford real baseballs, and so they made their own. They saved string, rolled it into tight balls roughly the size of baseballs, and then wrapped the balls with black electrician's tape. When Izzi was about nine, he and a friend made a tight ball of string, but they did not have either tape or money to buy tape. They went to a nearby five-and-dime store. Izzi pretended to accidentally knock a roll of tape from the display to the floor. Then he walked away. The friend followed, picked up the tape from the floor, and put it in his pocket. They thought no one would see their clever deception. But a clerk witnessed the entire caper. He collared the two boys and called the manager. Izzi was "scared to death." He later said he was convinced he was on his way to prison for life. The manager dressed down the two boys, then took them home to report the incident to their parents. Izzi said he could not remember whether his mother was angry or disappointed or both, but Rose let him know, in no uncertain terms, that stealing was wrong. She could deliver more punishment with a few choice words—including some in Yiddish—than with a willow or a leather belt. Izzi said the electrician's tape incident was the first and last time he took anything from anyone.

The fact that the Wagner children were not at all anxious to kindle Rose's displeasure was evidenced in another incident. Izzi and his friends were riding bicycles—secondhand bikes, of course. Izzi fell and broke his arm. The boys rushed him to the doctor's office, about a block from the Wagner home.

The doctor set the broken arm, but as Izzi left the office, his arm encased in an obvious plaster cast, he pleaded with the doctor, "Please don't tell Ma."

Izzi and his friends spent many hours at Pioneer Park, slightly more than a block west of the Wagner home. The park was surrounded by a three-foot-high hedge. The small pavilion in the park was the scene of regular band concerts. On summer evenings, youngsters sat on the grass to watch movies. The park had a baseball diamond and two swimming pools—one for boys, and one for girls. African Americans were not allowed to swim at public pools, and so some of Izzi's close friends did not swim with the gang. However, everyone played baseball together. (Not far away was the Jordan River, where there were no racial restrictions on swimming. In later years, the river became a hangout for Izzi and his friends, even though Rose discouraged her sons from swimming there because it was heavily polluted.)

Pioneer Park brought many memories to Izzi, and he often drove by the park in his later years. He commented about how the park had become a sad resting place for the homeless instead of the lively activity center he remembered, filled with children and laughter. His experiences at Pioneer Park would influence decisions he made later to encourage and generously support a similar activity center for children at another location in the city.

African Americans were required to sit in the balcony at movie theaters, and so when Izzi went to the movies with his African American friends, they separated in the lobby, then rejoined after the movie. Izzi did not think much about it until Rose eventually told him about the evils of segregation...and the related anti-Semitism she had experienced in her life. She told him he would surely experience discrimination and name-calling, but that he must never allow it to control his life. She also taught him to value all friendships, regardless of race, religion, or social background.

Izzi became close friends with a young Italian named Henri "Hank" Milano. Milano's mother managed the Elms Hotel on the corner of South Temple and Post Office Place. Hank and Izzi developed a friendship that would last seventy-five years. They participated in pranks together, formed business deals, traveled, and played practical jokes on one another.

During hot summer nights, the Wagner boys would sometimes crawl out their bedroom window, meet a few friends, go to Pioneer Park, climb the high fence around the swimming pool, and enjoy moonlight swims. In those days, law enforcement officials often "looked the other way" with regard to such childhood escapades. Izzi became an accomplished swimmer and baseball player. Each summer there was a city baseball league. Teams from the various city parks—Pioneer Park, Central Park, Liberty Park, and so on—competed.

The Pioneer Park team on which Izzi and Abe Wagner played usually did well in the competition. Abe was especially skilled on the baseball diamond, and he later played on semiprofessional teams. They never forgot the fun they had on the baseball diamond, and when Izzi took over Wagner Bag Company, the company always sponsored teams in the area's summer leagues.

Rose Wagner wanted her children to learn traditional Jewish values and customs. She sent Izzi to the synagogue school to learn Hebrew and the principles expounded in the Torah. He went faithfully for a couple of weeks, but one day the teacher humiliated him in front of other students and cracked his knuckles with a ruler. Izzi went home and told his mother he would never go back to the Hebrew school...and he didn't.

Rose loved show business and music. She instilled those same interests in her children. Whenever possible, she took them to vaudeville shows at the nearby Orpheum Theater (now the Capitol Theatre) or other venues around town. Downtown Salt Lake City was filled with theaters—more than a dozen of them, including the Pantages, the Gem, the Empire, the Lyric, the Bungalow, and the Empress. There were so many theaters along Third South that city officials eventually named the street Broadway. When Izzi was eight years old, Rose made sure he was at the casting call for a traveling vaudeville show called Poodles Hannefort Circus, appearing at the Orpheum Theater on Second South. Izzi was hired to come up on stage when Hannefort called for volunteers from the audience. Izzi was always the "volunteer" selected to stand on the back of a horse that ran around in a circle. He was secretly hooked to a wire, which allowed him to jump in the air, do somersaults, and perform other acrobatics, much to the delight of the audience. Izzi earned a dollar a day, but his showbiz career ended after a week or so, when school started. It would not be the end of Izzi's fascination with show business.

In those days, live stage performances were often preceded by silent movies. Then, in the late 1920s, movies added sound. Full-length movies, weekly movie serials, cartoons, and newsreels began to replace vaudeville. Izzi grew up with the movies. He would be a fan of movies and movie stars for the rest of his life.

Rose insisted that Izzi take violin lessons and, later, saxophone lessons. Izzi liked the saxophone better than the violin. He kept both instruments long after his music lessons ended, eventually pawning the saxophone to help pay the rent for an apartment he and his new wife moved into after World War II. The violin lessons cost one dollar each, and it was a considerable financial sacrifice for the Wagner family. Izzi defrayed some of the cost by helping his violin teacher post flyers on telephone poles. The flyers promoted concert performances by the teacher. The violin teacher was an especially popular performer in Utah County, and so Izzi sometimes rode down that way with his teacher on Saturdays to post flyers in American Fork, Pleasant Grove, and other areas. The flyers were stapled to wooden telephone poles. Each journey earned Izzi or his sister a free violin lesson.

Izzi recalled, sadly, that a few years later, during the Great Depression, this same violin teacher knocked at the Wagner door one day to see if he could do chores to earn enough money to buy himself a meal. Rose was happy to help the man. Rose Wagner was always as generous as possible to those who were down and out, finding ways to help without compromising the dignity of individuals needing assistance. When possible, she hired itinerants for a day or two to help at Wagner Bag Company.

Izzi's sister, Leona, took violin lessons and piano lessons. She eventually became a more accomplished musician than her brother. Rose often asked the children to perform for the family and visitors, but Izzi said their performances sounded more like scratching than music. He said he could easily pick out any melody he heard, but he had trouble keeping time.

Life in downtown Salt Lake City was always exciting for the Wagner brothers. They learned to swim, play baseball, shoot pool, and even box. The city's largest covered arena was about a mile away—the Hippodrome on Ninth South and Main Streets. A group of boys would pool their resources to buy one ticket for a boxing match, bicycle race, dance marathon, or some other event. The ticket holder would enter and make his way to the top level of the circular arena. He would open a window, and, one by one, the other boys—who had already climbed up onto the roof—would surreptitiously crawl through the window to join their friends. Again, officials were not overly aggressive in enforcing the rules…unless the arena was sold out.

In those days, it was not uncommon for small bars to stage boxing matches as a means of attracting customers and creating revenue. Participants were paid about five dollars to go into the ring and battle. Winners received a second five dollars at the completion of the match. Heavyweight champion Jack Dempsey got his start fighting barroom matches, sometimes in Salt Lake City.

When he was in his midteens, Izzi Wagner decided boxing was a good way to earn a few dollars, and so he learned to box. Besides, as he grew older, he found it necessary to defend himself against those who were intolerant of his ethnic background. He was short but well muscled and handsome. Rose did not like the idea of her son being a pugilist. She told Izzi to concentrate on learning the violin. "You can't get hurt playing the violin," she said. Izzi eventually had three "professional" fights, and he won all three. But he decided being pounded around the face and head was no way to make a living, and so he never boxed again except in self-defense.

When he was twelve years old, Izzi got a job helping at a nearby grocery store. He stocked shelves, bagged groceries, and performed other mundane duties. The store was owned by an Italian couple who were always fighting. One or the other would grow angry and storm out of the store for extended periods. The man often went over to Washington Square, three blocks away, to sit on the grass while his temper subsided. One day, both husband and wife stormed out at the same time. The man told Izzi he was in charge, which meant twelve-year-old Izzi was solely responsible for assessing charges, taking money, and making change. When he told his mother what had happened, Rose praised him for being able to handle the responsibility.

Young Izzi held other jobs during his early teens. He worked fourteen hours a day selling fruit from a stand on Ninth South and Main Streets. The pay was twelve dollars a week. The stand was owned by Moise Warshawski—who would change his name to Morris Warshaw when he founded Grand Central Market...and then to Maurice Warshaw when his Grand Central chain became one of the most successful retail establishments in the state. (Warshaw had been a member of the group that founded Clarion, Utah, in 1911. It was a community of Jewish farmers who came to Utah from central Europe via the eastern United States. Clarion was located near Gunnison in the central part of the state, but there was never enough water to make farming viable, and so many residents, including Warshawski, moved north to Salt Lake City.)

Izzi also worked for a summer at a food stand located on Third South Street between Main and State. The stand was operated by two men from Chicago. No one could understand how they could sell fruit and other produce so inexpensively. Izzi later learned that the Chicago pair were actually in the hijacking business. The two and their associates would hijack trucks in Wyoming or Nevada, transfer the truck contents to their own vehicles, and then sell the stolen goods from the Third South produce outlet. Izzi remembered that the two gangsters left town in a hurry when police were tipped off about the racket.

The Wagner family enjoyed activities together. Rose went to the synagogue almost every Saturday, but Harry and the children were not as steadfast in their religious responsibilities. Family outings were often centered around picnics in one of the city's parks, silent movies, live theater, and outings at Saltair or at a nearby "resort" called Beck's Hot Springs. Many Jewish families gathered at Beck's on Sundays for picnics and swimming. Mineral water at Beck's Hot Springs was as warm as bathwater. Harry and Rose were convinced that soaking in the water had medicinal value. The children didn't like the hot mineral pools, but they could swim in separate pools kept at lower temperatures. In the early days, these outings included hitching Harry's horse, Queenie, to an elaborate open buggy. Later, Harry bought a used Lincoln Town Car to serve as the family automobile.

In May 1925, Rose bought the little adobe house on which they had been paying rent for more than a decade. She paid sixty-five hundred dollars for the house. It was owned by the Peery family in Ogden. The family also owned what was then the Miles Hotel (now Peery Hotel) on the corner of Third South and West Temple. Rose paid five hundred dollars down and fifty dollars a month on the mortgage. The house was paid off in January 1932, and the deed was transferred to Rose Wagner. Harry's name does not appear on the transaction.

At some point during the mid-1920s, Izzi met his stepbrother, Morris Wigrizer. Morris came west to see his father, and Harry gave him a job for about six months. Morris then returned to Boston, where he married. Harry went to Boston to attend the wedding.

The Wagner children attended Fremont School at 153 South Second West (now Third West). The three-story stone building was built in 1891 at a cost of twenty-seven thousand dollars. It was one of the first schools constructed after formation of the Salt Lake School District in 1890. Fremont School was closed in 1938, partially reopened during World War II, and demolished in 1968. Izzi visited the school one last time shortly before the wrecking ball arrived.

After elementary school, the Wagner youngsters moved on to West Junior High School, three blocks north, and then to West High School. All were within easy walking distance from the Wagner house.

Izzi was on the West High baseball team, the football team, and the basketball team. He took classes in typing, shorthand, and journalism. During his senior year, he was named sports editor of the school newspaper, and he wrote a column called "They Say..." He remembered writing a column about the age of one football player. The athlete claimed to be of driving age (sixteen years), but readers of "They Say..." learned he was only fifteen. The football player was not happy about the column. He threatened Izzi with bodily harm, but Izzi stood up to him—as he always did—and the football player backed down.

Isadore Wagner's 1932 West High School report card (his senior year) shows that Izzi earned B grades in English and advanced law, C grades in psychology and Latin, and "one hundred" merit awards during each quarter through the year. Those who knew him best find his Cs in psychology to be not only ironic but humorous as well. According to his friends, Izzi Wagner knew more about human behavior and psychology than most of the professionals in the field, let alone his high school teacher. Perhaps the Cs originated from something other than academic performance.

During his high school years, Izzi learned how to take care of himself in the face of ethnic insensitivity. Only one or two other students at West High were Jewish. Sometimes, callous students would call him names—egged on, no doubt, by racist parents. His mother taught him throughout his growing years never to back down but never to initiate confrontation. His short stature may have helped more than it hindered, because few expected someone his size to be tough, feisty, and fully able to take care of himself. He remembered defending himself at least three times against anti-Semitic classmates. One day, he came home from school with blood on his shirt. Rose was concerned. Izzi said, "Don't worry, Ma. It isn't my blood; it's the other guy's." Rose's concern transformed into a reprimand for fighting. She encouraged him to settle differences with words and humor, not fists.

In high school, Izzi also developed his facile wit, his outgoing personality, and his ability to get along with anyone and everyone. These characteristics would serve him well throughout his life. He was never intimidated by rank, position, or accomplishments. He approached everyone as a friend, and he expected to be treated as a friend in return.

Because of his outgoing personality and his handsome looks, Izzi became popular with the young women in his school. It was a time of band music and school dances, and Izzi attended most of them. During the summer months, there was also dancing at Saltair on what the resort billed as "the largest dance floor in America." The dance floor had a roof, but it was open on three sides to the cool night air coming off Great Salt Lake. Dating young men and women could get on the open-air train that connected the city to the lakeside resort, spend the evening on the dance floor, and ride the late train home. Well-known big bands and vocalists often made weekend appearances at Saltair. One night a week was "stag night." Young women would line up in front of the bandstand, and young men would ask, "May I have this dance?" This same practice was repeated at other local dance venues during winter months. Izzi used the stag-night tradition to expand his circle of female friends.

In the days of the Great Depression, school districts were always short on funds. One strategy used to conserve school resources was to eliminate a year of high school. The school district combined seventh and eighth grades into a one-year term called Articulating Unit. Thus, after two years of high school education, Izzi graduated from West High School when he was barely seventeen years old. He decided to become a lawyer, with Rose's encouragement. In the summer of 1932, Isadore Wagner enrolled at the University of Utah.

3

Taking Charge

———◆———

Izzi's experience with higher education did not last long—less than two weeks.

On August 4, 1932, Harry Wagner died, apparently from stomach cancer. He was fifty-three, according to the obituary published in local newspapers. He had suffered from stomach problems for some time, but on the afternoon of August 3, the pain was so severe that he could hardly walk. Izzi and Rose helped Harry into the backseat of the family's Lincoln Town Car. Izzi drove him to St. Mark's Hospital, then located across from Wasatch Springs on north Second West (now Third West). The family expected Harry to be treated and released, as had happened before. Izzi picked up a girlfriend and took her swimming at Wasatch Springs before returning home for the night. At about two in the morning on August 4, the doctor called from the hospital to tell Rose that Harry had passed away. His death was totally unexpected.

Harry had been a successful businessman, but he had a weakness for gambling—mostly poker with his friends and horse racing through local bookie establishments. He spent many hours around a poker table, and bookies operated in nearby bars or even at barbershops. Harry lost much of the money he worked so hard to earn. According to Izzi, Harry was occasionally victimized by local cardsharps.

After the funeral, Rose called her family together. She told them—perhaps with a forced smile—that theirs was the typical American success story. She and Harry had arrived in Utah with total resources of three dollars, and now the family was six thousand dollars in debt. It was the height of the Great

Depression; prospects were grim. As usual, Rose was optimistic. She was certain they could find a way to succeed. After all, she said, this is America.

They decided Abe should continue going to college, at least through the current year, but that Izzi would have to drop out to concentrate on helping Rose run the business. Leona was still in high school, but Rose felt the environment around the Wagner house was not appropriate for a young lady such as Leona. Rose said she would have little time to care for Leona because she would have to devote more time to the business than in the past. Rose said she would contact her sister in Boston to see if Leona could live with her during Leona's final year in high school.

Much of the six-thousand-dollar debt was accounts payable—money owed to suppliers. Rose was appalled to learn that they were in debt to business friends, those with whom she hoped to continue doing business. One of Izzi's first assignments was to visit creditors and mend fences. He was remarkably well equipped for the job. His friendly, outgoing personality made him a natural for the assignment.

One thing Harry left—which he owned, free and clear—was a 1927 Lincoln seven-passenger sedan. (The seventh passenger sat on a small jump seat in the spacious rear passenger area.) When he drove the huge automobile, Izzi felt like a chauffeur, but it was the only transportation he and Abe had until Izzi was able to buy a used Pontiac a year or two later.

Next, Rose, Abe, and Izzi went to visit a local bank owned by The Church of Jesus Christ of Latter-day Saints, the Utah Home Loan Savings Bank. They called it the "Mormon bank." The Wagners desperately needed a line of credit to keep them in business, and they were told the Utah Home Loan Bank was the most likely source of the funds they needed. After hearing about the family's plans for the business, a sympathetic bank officer agreed to extend credit. Izzi never forgot that the "Mormon bank" helped the Wagners through the most desperate time of their business operation. The experience would influence positively his relationships with his Mormon neighbors for the rest of his life. (Years later, a new manager at the bank refused to extend credit for Wagner Bag on a Friday when Izzi needed to meet payroll. Izzi immediately transferred the Wagner Bag account to another local bank. Izzi did not readily tolerate what he considered breaches of trust. Still, he often mentioned the vital role played by the "Mormon bank" in rescuing Wagner Bag during the Depression.)

In essence, the Wagners had operated two separate businesses. Harry's business—H. Wagner Bag Company—operated out of an old warehouse near the corner of what was then Fifth West and South Temple Streets. It was west of the boardinghouse (Devereaux House) managed by Rose's sister. Rose also operated her own small business—Wagner Bag Company—out of the adobe house on Third South. She bought and sold everything—bottles, clothing, furniture, and whatever else she could locate. Neighborhood youngsters gathered bottles to sell to Rose. She greeted them with a smile and friendly banter. The youngsters used the money to buy candy or tickets to movie westerns. She called them "candy cowboys."

The two-business arrangement existed because Harry sold bags only in bales. Two or three times a year, he took the train to California to buy large quantities of new and used bags. But Harry did not want to deal with small lots of thirty to one hundred bags. However, many area farmers did not need and could not afford more than a few bags at a time. Also, Harry did not open his business until eight o'clock, and farmers who sold their produce at the farmers' market would come into town very early in the morning with truckloads of produce. They needed to purchase bags and fill them before the market opened for business. Rose Wagner opened her business anytime a customer knocked on her door, and she sold bags in any quantity—usually cash and carry. But she also sold bags on credit to farmers who had no cash. Many were Japanese truck farmers, and they always paid up after the farmers' market closed for the day. When Izzi asked how she decided who got credit, Rose said, "If they come in a big car, it's cash. But if they have dirt under their fingernails, they get credit."

Shortly before Harry died, he had closed down his operation on South Temple Street. Depression-era business was so bad he could no longer pay the rent. At that time, the Wagners divided the adobe house on Third South. The west side became Wagner Bag Company, and the east side became the Wagner residence. The former family living room was converted into an office. Izzi and Abe moved tons of heavy bales of burlap bags from Harry's warehouse into what had once been bedrooms.

Izzi claimed the family would have been rich if Harry had not gambled away so much of what the business earned. But after Harry's death, they were far from rich. One Friday afternoon, the telephone bill was due. If the money didn't reach the telephone company by five o'clock, the company would turn off the phone service. Rose said they couldn't do business without a telephone. She scrounged every cent she could find, but it still was not enough to pay the bill. In desperation, she finally had to walk across the street and borrow ten dollars from Kitty, the "manager" of the Bristol Hotel brothel. It was a painful thing for Rose to do—first, to admit she needed the money, and second, to ask the madam for the loan. She sent Izzi running all the way to the telephone company office in order to beat the five o'clock deadline.

Eventually, they were able to hire two out-of-work miners to help with the heavy work. Rose paid the men one dollar a day plus room and board. They slept on cots in a spare room at the back of the house.

The Wagner home was a favorite stopping place for the many transients passing through town on their way to what they hoped would be jobs in California or Washington or Colorado. Sometimes, they stopped to work a few hours to earn meals and a little money. They knew Rose Wagner would work them hard and feed them well. They could even earn a dollar or two. Often, there wasn't much food, but Rose shared whatever the family had. Rose's compassion and generosity continued throughout her life, and it "rubbed off" on Izzi and his siblings. (Later, when Jews were trying to establish the State of Israel, Hasidic Jews would come knocking on the door to ask for contributions to help create the new nation. They wore hats, long black coats, prayer shawls, and beards. Rose always contributed, but her contributions varied from person to person. One day Izzi asked, "Ma, why do you give some five dollars, some ten dollars, and some fifteen dollars?" Rose responded, "Vell, if the beard is short, they get five dollars. If the beard is halfway to the belt, I give ten dollars. But if the beard reaches the belt, I know some of the money will actually go to Israel, and I give fifteen dollars.") During the Great Depression, merely surviving required great effort, resourcefulness, and innovation.

Rose taught her children to love and appreciate the United States. Shortly before Harry died, Rose learned, much to her surprise, that she was not an American citizen. She apparently assumed that when she married Harry (a citizen) she automatically became a citizen, too. As soon as she learned that was not true, she began studying American history to prepare herself for the citizenship examination. Her studies continued after Harry died, often late into the night, until she eventually earned citizenship. As usual, Rose's learning experience turned to a teaching experience for her children. She quizzed them about the information she learned in her studies. She wanted to make sure they were learning these marvelous things in school. Soon, the children knew as much as she did about American history and traditions. She also read the newspaper every day, and she told her children that they had a responsibility to improve the world.

Izzi and Abe learned valuable lessons about buying and selling from

Rose and—before his death—Harry. During Prohibition, they learned where illegal liquor was being sold. Bootleg alcohol was available through enterprising bellmen at most hotels. (That included the Hotel Utah, owned and operated by the Mormon Church.) Izzi and Abe made the rounds of local hotels, where they purchased empty bottles. Then the Wagners washed the bottles and resold them to bootleggers. A printer doing business in the basement of a nearby hotel provided fake labels reading Scotch, whiskey, gin, and so on, but the contents for every brand usually came from the same still. The bottles were filled, sold to dealers, picked up by bellmen, and sold to consumers. The same bellmen then collected empty bottles from hotel rooms, and sold them back to the Wagners for another round of washing, filling, and circulation. Harry found a place to buy corks by the gross, and the Wagners sold the corks to bootleggers.

Bootleggers also bought scraps of burlap from the Wagners. The illegal liquor salesmen wrapped filled and labeled bottles with burlap and sprinkled the burlap with salt water. When the burlap dried, it was covered with white salt crystals. The bootleggers told their customers the salt was from the wind and salt air on the ship coming from Scotland or England.

The best stills were made with copper. When police raided a bootleg production facility, they used axes to put holes in the stills. In the early days of Prohibition, the Wagners picked up the ruined stills and sold the copper to junk dealers. Then they learned how to repair the stills and sell them back to the bootleggers. Eventually, Harry became an honorary sheriff's deputy. He went along on some of the raids, and he would talk the police into putting fewer and smaller holes in the confiscated boilers, making it easier to repair the damaged stills for resale.

The Wagners also sold barrels. Wooden barrels were often used to store illegal alcohol. The Wagners would buy used barrels, number the barrel stays, take the barrels apart, clean them up, and sell the pieces to bootleggers. The bootleggers could hide a dismantled barrel or two in the trunk of a car and drive to a hidden location without fear of detection. Then they would assemble the barrel according to the numbered stays. They first filled the barrel with water, which caused the wood to expand and seal itself; then the bootleggers filled the barrel with distilled spirits for storage and transport.

Wagner says it's a good thing he never acquired a taste for alcohol, because he certainly had opportunities to do so during his formative years. Prohibition was never effective—in Salt Lake City or anywhere else. Alcohol was always available. Izzi and his teenage friends would occasionally split a

quart of beer, but it never became a habit. And Rose always kept wine and
"spirits" in the house. She added whiskey and honey to tea as a treatment for
colds and other maladies.

The Depression made everyone conscious of what we would now call
"recycling." The Wagners recycled countless items in order to generate income. Used merchandise was available from many sources, because so many
individuals lost jobs and income, suffered mortgage foreclosures, and were
forced to sell household goods. Among other things, the Wagners recycled
bottles, clothing, furniture, and, of course, bags of all kinds. Automobile batteries were full of lead, and there was a good market for lead, so the Wagners paid cash for old batteries, which they sold to junk dealers. Later, they
found a local mechanic who could actually rebuild the batteries to make
them usable once again. He paid a few pennies more for discarded batteries
than lead merchants offered.

The Wagners bought empty beer bottles by the thousands, washed them,
and sold them back to Fisher Brewery, Becker's Brewery, and other local
breweries. They bought used ketchup bottles from restaurants, washed them,
boxed them by the hundreds for transport, and sold them to local canneries,
such as Del Monte. They bought empty fruit jars. Rose sold the fruit jars to
consumers from a display in front of the house on Third South.

Through these and other childhood experiences, Izzi learned there is a
market for everything; the challenge is to find the highest price and the most
reliable buyers.

Of course, the Wagners bought used bags from granaries, flour mills,
potato chip makers, grocers, and other sources. When used bags came in,
Abe and Izzi developed a way to quickly turn them inside out using two
broomsticks. The few kernels of wheat or barley remaining in a used bag
were collected. Not a single kernel was wasted. When the collected grain
became enough to fill a bag, it was sold to local farm suppliers for hog and
poultry feed.

They could not wash burlap bags, because burlap shrinks excessively.
They found other ways to clean used bags as much as possible. And even
badly torn bags were salvaged. Burlap from torn bags was used to repair
bags less seriously damaged. And the railroads bought thousands of pounds
of burlap scraps. They used it to stop leaks at the bottoms of coal cars, where
dump doors did not fully close. The burlap kept coal from dribbling out as
the train moved toward its destination. Other scraps of burlap were bundled
into large bales and sent to carpet manufacturers in California, where the
scraps were used to make padding for carpet.

Torn cotton bags were sold to a local laundry supply house to be bleached and become dish towels and cleaning cloths. The Wagners arranged with the Utah State Prison—then located in Sugarhouse—to buy discarded denim shirts and jeans formerly worn by prisoners. These, too, were sold to a local laundry, where the denim became industrial cleaning cloths.

All of these ventures were learning experiences for Izzi. He learned how to locate goods, how to negotiate purchases, how to find markets for practically any type of goods, and how to sell goods profitably.

He also learned a few painful negative lessons. Wagner Bag Company needed storage space to keep thousands of bags waiting to be sold. They often bought large quantities of bags after the early California harvest and held them until the Utah-Idaho harvest later in the year. Izzi located three empty storefront properties on West Temple. He paid fifty dollars per month rent for the storage space. One night, a fire destroyed the West Temple buildings and most of the Wagner inventory. Abe was distraught, but Rose said, "Ve came here with three dollars. So long as ve have more than three dollars, ve are successful." From that sad experience, Izzi learned the value of insurance. He would never again buy or rent a facility without also buying comprehensive insurance.

The fire led to another valuable learning experience. After the fire, Abe and Izzi built a corrugated tin shed behind the adobe house to serve as storage space. They had no idea that such buildings had to be approved by the city and had to meet city building codes. The building inspector threatened to force the Wagners to remove the shed because it was not an approved structure. Izzi used his considerable skills to talk the inspector out of it. He agreed to bring the little shed up to code and to meet building permit requirements in all future construction. He also made a one-hundred-dollar-contribution to the political party then in power at city hall. The building inspector never returned. The experience influenced Izzi's decision years later to serve on the city zoning board, a position he held for many years and one that allowed him to literally change the look of downtown Salt Lake City. The experience also convinced him that he would be wise to know and support political candidates with whom he agreed.

After Harry's death, Rose continued as company bookkeeper, but also took on the role of chairperson and conscience of the company. Abe and Izzi divided up other duties. Each had a list of customers and suppliers for which they were responsible. Izzi's responsibilities included many out-of-town customers. It was not unusual for him to drive to Ogden in the morning, negotiate a sizable order for bags from one of the large flour mills, return to Salt

Lake, load up the truck, and make a second trip to Ogden to deliver bags to a different customer.

On one of his first trips to the largest flour mill in Utah, Globe Mills, Izzi was ushered into the office of the manager. It was, to Izzi, a huge office, and the man had a separate office outside for his secretary. For one of the few times in his life, Izzi was intimidated by the surroundings. When he got home, he told Rose he had been uncomfortable in those spacious and well-appointed surroundings. Rose said, "Remember, ve all go to the bathroom the same way. When someone makes you uncomfortable, just imagine him sitting on the throne with his pants down, and you won't be uncomfortable anymore." Izzi said he was never again uncomfortable around executives, officials, or celebrities.

Rose sometimes invited select customers to her home for dinner, and they usually came, because even during Prohibition she always had wine and other beverages in the house to augment her excellent cooking. On one occasion, Rose asked Izzi to pick up a customer and bring him to dinner. When Izzi arrived at the customer's office, the man also brought with him his secretary. It was obvious the relationship was more than a boss-employee situation. Later, Izzi asked Rose about the impropriety of facilitating the get-together. Rose said, "Sometimes it is wise not to ask too many questions."

One day, Izzi and Abe took Rose to Ogden to meet with a customer there. After securing a sizable order, they went for a celebration dinner at an upscale restaurant. The restaurant provided finger bowls, complete with a slice of lemon floating in the shallow water. It was the first time any of them had seen such dining amenities. Rose dipped a spoon into the finger bowl and tasted the contents. "Feh!" she said. "They call this soup?"

Izzi was a natural salesman. He got along well with everyone he met. The skills he had acquired while growing up were the very skills needed for a successful salesman and negotiator. He enjoyed being around people, interacting with them, and assessing their needs. He also enjoyed helping them meet those needs.

Rose told him that the way to be a great salesman was to determine the customer's "Achilles' heel." She did not use the term in the sense it is normally used these days. For Rose, the term *Achilles' heel* did not mean weakness or vulnerability, as it did in Greek mythology. Instead, it meant an "opening" or a point of entry into the individual's real self. She believed that business people, by necessity, erected barriers between their deeply held concerns and their day-to-day business dealings. She believed a good salesperson must get through those barriers if he or she wants to make a meaningful connection with the individual.

Izzi said that sometimes a customer's Achilles' heel was playing golf on an exclusive golf course. Sometimes it was having a chance to meet and talk with a certain celebrity. Sometimes it was a small gift that the individual wanted but would not likely purchase for himself or herself. He cited as an example the many times he tried to see an important potential customer in a large eastern city. He had never been able to meet with the person, face-to-face, but he continued to visit the man's office, hoping for an audience. One day, the man's secretary told Izzi that the individual he wanted to see was out of the office for the day. As Izzi chatted with the secretary, he learned that her boss was attending a birthday party for his five-year-old son—the most important person in the boss's life, according to the secretary. Izzi saw an opening, an Achilles' heel. He went to a nearby department store, bought a tricycle, and had it delivered to the potential customer's office as a birthday gift for the son. The next time Izzi asked for an appointment, he was given access to this important buyer. Before long, the man was dealing exclusively with Wagner Bag as his company's source for thousands of burlap and cotton bags. The company became a very welcome long-term customer.

Wagner Bag could always undersell its competitors because it was a family-owned business and the company office and the family home were the same. Company expenses were less than expenses for competing companies. As Izzi put it, "We all ate off the same table and lived in the same house, while our competitors dined at the country club." He added, "We always had something to eat. We were always clean. Mother's pride and joy were her children, followed closely by her citizenship."

Rose's home was filled with music and laughter. She listened to music on the radio or the phonograph, and when no music was playing, she sang Russian folk songs. It was a happy environment, but Rose also focused on making the business a success. Nevertheless, Izzi claimed Wagner Bag never spent a dime on advertising; instead, the company used its resources to build strong person-to-person relationships with customers and suppliers.

I. J. Wagner (his new business name) thrived on his assignment. He truly enjoyed meeting new individuals, getting to know them, telling a few jokes, and suggesting how Wagner Bag could help companies of all sizes succeed. His repertoire of humorous stories grew until he became one of Utah's most adept raconteurs. Some of his contacts represented very large companies, and he learned to appreciate the symbols of success—large offices, staff support, new cars, and club memberships.

Because of his Jewish heritage, it would be many years before I. J. Wagner was allowed to join most of Utah's golf and social clubs. He was welcomed at the Ogden Country Club—thanks to one of his customers—but Salt Lake City's "exclusive" Alta Club rejected him. He could not join the Ambassador Club, another watering hole and gathering place for those seeking relief from Utah's stringent liquor laws. And the Fort Douglas Country Club did not allow Jewish members. (Years later, Wagner bought the Fort Douglas Club social center and donated it to the Jewish Community Center. It is now known as the "I. J. and Jeanné Wagner Jewish Community Center." He claimed his early rejection by the club did not influence his later purchase of the same club, but friends don't necessarily agree.)

When friends asked him to join the Salt Lake Country Club in the 1950s, he learned that the club did not accept Jewish members. He told his friends not to advance his name, since it would be rejected one way or another. One longtime friend—a prominent Salt Lake attorney and political operative—said, "We'll see about that." The attorney threatened to publicly withdraw his own membership unless the board accepted I. J. Wagner. Izzi soon became a member of the country club, where he played golf often and ate lunch almost every Saturday throughout the rest of his life.

Izzi's experience with buying and selling soon led him to buying and selling business establishments and properties. He traveled often to San Francisco and Los Angeles to meet with suppliers who provided the burlap and cotton used to make bags...and to develop new customers. He would drive straight through—journeys that usually took sixteen to twenty hours. When he became tired, he would pull over to the side of the road and lie down on the gravel shoulder for a short nap. There wasn't much traffic to disturb a sleeping traveler. In those days, highways were two-lane roads. The speed limit was sixty miles per hour. Even the best cross-country highways went through every small town along the way, usually right down the main street. Small cities restricted speed from city limit to city limit, and most towns felt obliged to place at least one traffic signal on the highway. Travel was tedious. One did well to average forty or forty-five miles per hour over the course of a day.

Automobiles did not have air-conditioning. Travelers rode with the windows open in the summer. During winter weather, snow often froze on the windshield when inefficient wipers could not keep up. Engine cooling systems did not work well in summer heat or on long uphill stretches, and so drivers often hung water bags on the front bumpers so they would have cooling water when the car boiled over. Gasoline was inexpensive—about twenty cents a gallon—but extremely low mile-per-gallon performance required frequent refueling stops. Neither engines nor tires were as reliable as they are today, and travelers were sometimes fleeced by clever service station operators who sold unneeded tires, belts, hoses, and other items. Izzi traveled at night during the summer to avoid the heat, and he learned to take care of his automobiles. He prized both reliability and good design in the cars he drove.

Izzi also grew up with the movies. He was fascinated with movie stars and other celebrities. He thought that he was just as handsome as most movie stars (and he was). He also had a very good voice, and he knew the words to most popular songs of the day. At some point during the 1930s, he decided he wanted to break into show business. As mentioned, he traveled often to Los Angeles and Hollywood. On one occasion, he put together a portfolio of photographs with the intent of submitting them to various Hollywood studios. It was probably during this period that he decided to change his name to one with more Hollywood appeal. He had never been fond of the name Isadore, and he was aware that many performers changed their names. (Years later, he frequently showed friends a list of stage names and original names for famous individuals. It was as if he was justifying his own name change, even though he never mentioned it specifically.) He chose the name Irving Jerome Wagner because Irving Berlin and Jerome Kern were big names in the music business, and because they were both favorites of his mother. Whether he talked to Rose about the name change is unclear. It is also unclear whether he went to court to officially change his name at that time or later. (He must have changed it officially at some point, because it shows up in his 1942 military records. Also, when he applied for a passport in 1962, he was able to officially amend his birth certificate to read Irving Jerome Wagner.)

Nothing came of Izzi's effort to become a movie star, but the name by which he became known in all his subsequent business dealings was I. J. Wagner. Through the rest of his life, he told friends his mother had named him Irving Jerome because of her love for music. Before long, he probably began to believe the story himself. Still, for anyone who had day-to-day dealings with the young man from Wagner Bag Company, he was always "Izzi."

On one of his many trips to California, Izzi took his friend Hank Milano.

Milano was an accomplished accordion player. They traveled to San Francisco, then down the coast to Los Angeles. They were in a hotel in Los Angeles when Izzi noticed an ad in the newspaper for an accordion teacher. He told Hank that he should apply for the job. Milano was shy, and so Izzi said he would go with Hank to investigate the opportunity. Izzi carried Hank's accordion. When they arrived at the address listed, the man in charge asked Izzi to demonstrate his skill on the accordion. Izzi said he did not play, but that he was Milano's agent. Hank played a few numbers, and he was hired on the spot. Izzi negotiated a good salary for his friend. When Izzi returned to Salt Lake, he told Milano's mother what had happened. She was upset that Izzi had taken her boy away from her, and she never forgave him. Ironically, Milano, a Catholic, remained in Los Angeles, met a Mormon girl there, converted to Mormonism, and married. They had six children, but the marriage eventually ended in divorce. Hank moved back to Salt Lake City, where he remarried. Hank Milano and Izzi Wagner were lifelong friends. They often talked on the telephone or got together for lunch.

On another trip in 1934, nineteen-year-old Izzi Wagner had purchased a used Pontiac for twenty-five dollars. He made it to Los Angeles, but the car "died" on a Los Angeles street. He called a junk dealer and sold the car for twenty-five dollars. Then he went to a small restaurant nearby for a cup of coffee. The address was 1415 West Ninth Street. The owner behind the counter complained about the lack of business. He said he would sell the place if he could find a buyer. Izzi asked him how much it was worth. The owner said he would sell the place to the first person who offered fifty dollars to cover one month's lease. Izzi said, "It's a deal." He did not have fifty dollars at the time, but he soon found a business partner. Charlie Zender was a cook Izzi knew at another restaurant. Charlie had recently retired from the U.S. Marine Corps, and he wanted to run his own restaurant. The two of them bought the restaurant, its fixtures, tables and chairs, and utensils. Izzi changed the name to Wagner's Restaurant and printed a new menu. He devised a system that allowed good customers to buy six dollars' worth of food vouchers for five dollars cash. He then concluded his business with clients in Los Angeles and caught a bus to Salt Lake City. Rose may not have been totally pleased with the idea of her son owning a restaurant in a faraway city, but she was supportive.

Izzi returned to the restaurant now and then to check up on the business and collect his meager profits. The menu for Wagner's Restaurant included the following items:

Ham or Bacon and Eggs with Potatoes,
Toast, Jelly and Coffee 35

Wheat Cakes, Syrup, Butter and Coffee. 15
Two Eggs, Any Style, Waffle, Toast, Jelly, Coffee 30

Wagner's Club Breakfast
Two Halves Grapefruit, Ham, Sausage or Bacon,
Two Eggs Any Style, Jelly, Coffee 40

25¢ SPECIAL LUNCH FROM 12 TO 4
ENTREE—Soup, Salad, Vegetable, Potatoes, Dessert and Drink

Wagner's Steaks and Chops
The price of Entree indicates the complete price of the meal.

COCKTAIL
Seafood — Shrimp — Fruit

SOUP
Chef's Choice — Choice of Salad

ENTREES
Wagner's Special Dinner Steak 40
    "   "   "   " with Onions 45
    "   "   "   " with Mushrooms 50
Wagner's 12-oz. T-Bone Steak 65
    "   16-oz.   "   " 75
    "   8-oz.   "   " 50
Two Center Cut Pork Chops and Baked Apple 50
Roast Sirloin of Beef, Brown Gravy 35
Wagner's Fried Rabbit, Hunter Style 55
Wagner's De Luxe Chicken Dinner. $1.00

DRINKS
Coffee — Tea — Milk or Buttermilk

DESSERTS
Baked Apple — Prunes — Mixed Fruits — Fruit Salad
Jello — Sliced Oranges — Ice Cream — Pie
Grapefruit — Peaches — Pineapple — Apricots — Pudding

Altogether, there were eighteen items on the breakfast menu, nineteen items on the dinner menu, and a lunch special—quite a variety for a small restaurant. Prices may be shocking to modern-day restaurant-goers, but it was the time of the Great Depression, and Americans felt fortunate to earn a dollar or two a day.

After a few months of absentee ownership, I. J. Wagner sold his share of the restaurant in Los Angeles to his partner for one thousand dollars.

Like most siblings, Izzi and his brother, Abe, sometimes disagreed about how to operate the business. On one occasion, they had a falling-out, and Abe left home to find work in California. On March 8, 1935, Rose wrote in Yiddish to a family friend in California. She told him that Abe and Izzi had a quarrel, and that Abe left home on a truck headed for California. She pleaded with the friend to buy Abe a bus ticket and send him back home. She promised she would make some money "the way I did before" and pay for the ticket. She also wrote that Izzi had been very sick and was in bed for three weeks. Whether the letter ever reached the friend in California is questionable, because it was found many years later in Izzi's custody. Apparently, he knew about the emotional letter from Rose, and it affected him deeply. He and Abe mended their differences and worked together on a variety of projects for more than fifty years.

A few years after Izzi's Los Angeles restaurant venture, Izzi and a friend named Gus Weiser were driving from Salt Lake to Los Angeles when they stopped in Las Vegas to gamble. (Gus was a partner with Izzi in a business called W & W Music Company. They placed jukeboxes and punchboards in various restaurants and bars around Salt Lake.) Izzi did not like to gamble, because he had seen his father lose so much money that way, but Gus insisted on stopping in Las Vegas. In those days, Las Vegas was little more than a "wide place along the road," with only one or two gambling establishments. It was their lucky day, because the two won more than four thousand dollars at the craps table—a great deal of money at a time when new cars cost less than a thousand dollars. They quit while they were ahead, and they left Las Vegas. By the time they had traveled a hundred miles or so down the road, Gus convinced Izzi that their luck was so good they should turn around, go back to Vegas, and win even more. They returned to Las Vegas, but they apparently left their luck on the desert. They lost not only the four thousand dollars they had won, but all the spending money they had with them. Credit cards did not exist in those days, and so Izzi had to make a collect call to a friend in Salt Lake. He didn't dare call his mother, and so he called the bartender in the bar across the street from the Wagner home, collect. The bartender did not speak much English, and he did not understand what "collect" meant. Izzi shouted, "It's Izzi. Just say 'okay.'" Then began the painful process of trying to explain to the bartender how to wire money. Finally, in desperation, Izzi told the bartender to wait for the next customer, then call back at the number he gave—a phone booth in Las Vegas. Before too long, the bartender called back and put his customer on the line. Izzi explained what had to be done. The bartender and the customer closed the bar, put a sign on the door, and went to Western Union to wire Izzi fifty dollars.

As mentioned, the bartender—an Italian immigrant named Sam Notti— managed the bar across the street from the Wagner home. The bar was always cold because the owner insisted on turning off the heat when no customers were present. Sam wore a heavy overcoat while tending the bar.

Izzi learned that another bar was for sale on Main Street, across from the post office. There was a bookie joint in the back room, and the bar was mostly a cover for the betting room. Izzi asked Sam to go in partnership with him to buy the bar on Main Street. The arrangement was for Izzi to put up the down payment and for Sam to run the operation. It took some talking before Izzi could convince Sam to give up a paying job during the Depression, but he finally agreed.

They closed down the bookie joint, and concentrated on operating a bar offering sandwiches and beer. The most popular song of the time was "The Beer Barrel Polka," sung by the Andrews Sisters...and many other vocalists. They decided to name the bar the Beer Barrel, and Izzi ordered a neon sign to put in the Main Street window. But city officials complained about the name of the establishment. They said it was illegal to advertise beer in Utah, and the sign was an advertisement for beer. Izzi argued that the name was simply a name; it had nothing to do with advertising beer. He called attention to the popular song played over and over again on every jukebox in every bar and restaurant in town. He won the case. It was his first confrontation with sign regulations, but it would not be his last. (As mentioned earlier, Izzi eventually became chairman of the Planning and Zoning Commission, where he led a successful campaign to remove billboards from downtown and eliminate overhanging signs on Main Street.)

A few years later, Wagner sold the Beer Barrel and bought a nightclub just around the corner on Fourth South Street. The club was in the basement of the New Grand Hotel. (It is now the Manhattan Club.) It had been the Officers Club for military personnel stationed in Salt Lake City, mostly at Fort Douglas on the east side of the city. It was one of the few places in town where alcoholic beverages could be served legally, but only to military

officers. A new Officers Club was opening at Fort Douglas, and so the downtown location was no longer needed. Izzi became involved when he heard
that the downtown club was selling its truck. He needed a truck for the Beer
Barrel. When he inquired about the truck, he learned that the New Grand
Hotel owned the Officers Club and everything in it—from the truck to the
fixtures. Hotel managers worried that when the Officers Club moved out,
they would lose the rental income from the club. Izzi offered to rent the facility for the same amount paid by the officers group. Hotel managers jumped
at the opportunity. Izzi's only out-of-pocket expense came from changing the
name and redecorating the place. He renamed the club the Chi Chi Club because he had visited a Chi Chi Club in Los Angeles and liked it. He even cop-
ied the Los Angeles club's decor by using split bamboo on the walls. Utah's
restrictive liquor laws helped make the Chi Chi Club a popular gathering
place. It was almost always full, especially on weekends. Military personnel
continued to frequent the Chi Chi Club because of its downtown location.
Even though the club could no longer sell alcohol (other than beer), patrons
brought their own liquor in brown paper bags, a common practice in Utah at
the time. The club provided mixers. The food at the Chi Chi Club was better
than at many places around town, and Izzi arranged for nightly music and
entertainment. He brought Sam Notti with him to help run the club.

During the years prior to World War II, Izzi Wagner was a popular "man
about town." He was exceptionally handsome, and so he dated many of the
eligible young women in the city. Since the population was largely Mormon,
most of the women he dated were of that particular faith, although their
adherence to the practices of Mormonism ranged over a broad spectrum.
Some attended church meetings regularly; some did not. On rare occasions,
Wagner accompanied a lady friend to a church service.

In the early days, most transportation to and from dates required streetcars, buses, and trolleys. Izzi would not drive the big Lincoln on dates. When
he was finally able to buy his own secondhand car, dating became easier
and more varied. A favorite dating activity during the summer was to spend
most of a day and evening on the shores of Great Salt Lake—swimming a
little in the salty water, but mostly sunning on the beach. (On at least one
occasion, Izzi and a friend swam all the way to Antelope Island and back, a
one-way distance of five miles or so.) The "big band" craze was in full swing
(pun intended), and many famous bands came to Saltair, an amusement park
and dance center on the shore of the lake. It was a popular dance destination for young people in and around the city. Izzi's fascination with show-
business celebrities was well satisfied by seeing most of the famous band

leaders, instrumentalists, and vocalists of the era. Local bands and traveling bands also played at the Coconut Grove and the Rainbow Rendezvous in downtown Salt Lake.

On one night a week, many dance venues offered a chauvinistic practice where women lined up in front of the bandstand and men selected their dance partners from the "lineup." The practice presented Izzi with many opportunities to meet young women from different backgrounds and different parts of the city. He did not hesitate to take advantage of those opportunities.

Wagner related many stories about the women he dated. Some should not be repeated. In one or two instances, parents forbade their daughters from dating Izzi when they learned he was Jewish. But more often than not, parents enjoyed his wit and charm as much as did their daughters. Throughout his life, he kept in touch with one or two of the women he dated during those years, making sure they were in good health.

During one of his many visits to Los Angeles, Izzi and Hank Milano were at the beach, stretched out in the California sun. Young women were playing volleyball nearby. Izzi was half asleep when a ball bounced off his head. One of the young women came over and said, "I'm sorry, sir. Are you okay?" Izzi looked up at the beautiful woman and said, "You can bounce a ball off my head any day." Then he closed his eyes again.

The next day, he and Hank were walking to lunch when they passed a burlesque theater. The theater poster featured a beautiful young woman named Dagmar. She was the star of the show. Izzi asked Hank if the woman on the poster looked like the same girl who had bounced the volleyball off his head the day before. Hank agreed, and they went inside to see the show. Dagmar was, indeed, beautiful. When they came out, Izzi asked the man at the box office where the dancers went for breaks. The man pointed to a nearby coffee shop. Izzi and Hank went in, bought coffee, and waited. Sure enough, the dancers soon arrived, including Dagmar. Izzi said to her, "Do you remember me?" She responded, "Aren't you the man I hit with the volleyball yesterday?"

That was all it took. Izzi soon arranged a date with Dagmar. From then on, he dated her almost every time he visited Los Angeles. Eventually, Dagmar was offered a role in the famous Minsky Burlesque in New York City. Izzi then dated her on the few occasions when he visited New York. When he stopped dating everyone except the woman he would eventually marry, he tore up the photographs he had of Dagmar, as well as those of other female friends. He did not hear from Dagmar again until some years later. By then, he was married and achieving some success in business. One night, he had a phone call from Dagmar. She said she was ill and needed medical treatment. She asked Izzi to loan her a few hundred dollars. He talked to his wife, and she said that by all means he should send Dagmar the money. He sent a money order, never expecting to see the money again. However, several months later, a letter arrived with a thank-you and a check for the full amount. He never saw or heard from Dagmar again, even though he visited New York at least once a month for almost thirty years.

When Izzi moved into his twenties, Rose encouraged him to find a wife. He came close to proposing marriage on several occasions, but his decision to do so usually faded before the critical moment arrived. One of his favorite dates was a beautiful young woman named Marjorie Brown. She was the daughter of a Mormon bishop, a lay leader of one of the many Mormon "wards" in Salt Lake City. Izzi got along well with Marjorie and her family, and on more than one occasion he planned to ask her to marry him. However, when the time came to propose, he always changed his mind. Many years later, he introduced the woman who had become his wife to Marjorie. They became good friends. Marjorie Brown lived in California, and during their senior years Izzi called her on the telephone almost weekly to make sure she was happy and in good health.

One evening in 1939, he was having dinner with a woman friend at the Hotel Utah—the city's most exclusive dining experience. The hotel provided a dance band and live entertainment. The entertainment that evening featured a dancer with the stage name of Jeanné Doré (her real name was Jeanné Rasmussen). She was beautiful, talented, and petite. Izzi was immediately attracted to her. He determined to arrange a meeting. He admits that he was probably rude to his date for the evening. He watched carefully for the appropriate time, excused himself from his companion, and "accidentally" bumped into Jeanné in the hallway near the coat-check stand. He complimented her on her performance, asked her name, and said he would call her. Of course, she gave him her stage name, thinking that would be the end of it. Izzi could not find the stage name in the phone book or the Polk Salt Lake City Directory.

The next week, he had a date with the same girlfriend; their relationship was serious. He asked her to go with him to the Chi Chi Club, but she declined. She was from a strong Mormon family, and she knew her father would not approve of the Chi Chi Club. Izzi went to the club on his own. To his surprise, Jeanné was there with a friend of Izzi's. He tapped on his friend's shoulder and asked if he could cut in. The friend had overimbibed and was looking for an excuse to sit down, and so the first dance turned into several more dances. Izzi told Jeanné about his futile effort to find her telephone number. She confessed she had given him her stage name, knowing he would be unable to track her down. The dance-floor conversation led to a date, and that date led to several more. Soon, Jeanné decided she would not go back on the vaudeville circuit but would stay in Salt Lake City. Izzi arranged a good job for her at the Chi Chi Club, where she could entertain and also earn substantial tips as a hat-check girl (everyone wore a hat in those days). And Izzi gave up his list of women friends to focus his attention on Jeanné.

Jeanné Rasmussen was a native Utahn. Her family was Mormon, but the degree of adherence to Mormon doctrine varied from family member to family member. Her father, Joseph Smith Rasmussen, was a railroad man, with minimal concerns about religion. Her mother, Rose Lister Rasmussen, was an active participant in the LDS Church. Her older sister was very active in her church. Jeanné favored her father's position.

While growing up, she studied dance—mostly tap and acrobatic dancing—and then became a professional dancer in vaudeville shows. For nine years before Izzi met her, Jeanné had been "on the road." She performed twice a day, often seven days a week, moving from city to city, for thirty-five dollars a week. Out of that meager income, she had to pay room and board and provide her own costumes. She formed a partnership with another female dancer to create an act that became popular in traveling vaudeville shows across the nation. She performed in all but two or three of the nation's then forty-eight states. When Izzi first met Jeanné, she had taken a short booking in Salt Lake City in order to spend a little time with her family. She intended to rejoin the vaudeville circuit after her Utah stay.

During Izzi's dating years, one place was out of bounds for him and his women friends—the Wagner home. He was not proud of his address across from the bordello…or the fact that his home was part residence and part factory…or that some of the rooms were used to house boarders who were often transients. When friends asked where he lived, he sometimes gave false addresses, and on a few occasions he walked long distances from a phony drop-off point rather than be driven directly to his home.

Izzi was determined to turn the old adobe house into a respectable-looking business building. Eventually, he bought a truckload of used brick (long before used brick became a popular construction material). He hired an out-of-work (and alcoholic) bricklayer for a dollar a day to construct a new facade on the old adobe house. Then Izzi himself painted a new sign for the building: Wagner Bag Company. It took him two weeks to paint the lettering on the building. Through much cajoling, Rose was able to rescue a few of her flowers in order to keep them growing in a narrow strip of soil between the building and the sidewalk.

The business continued to grow, especially the manufacturing component. More and more space was needed for storage of raw materials and finished products. Machinery—sewing machines, materials handling equipment, and so on—took up more and more space. In 1941, when Izzi was still in his midtwenties, he tore down the old building and replaced it with a new building. The new facility included offices, a large production area, a shipping department, and warehouse space. At the time, there was a sheet-metal company to the east, a parking lot, and the Miles Hotel on the corner (now the Peery Hotel). Several small businesses were located on the ground floor of the Miles Hotel, including Typesetting Service Company, a shop that provided cast-lead type to local printers. Wagner Bag would later expand to the east and west.

Izzi found machinery and equipment on the used machinery market, just as he had located so many other items in those early days. For example, he found a used bag-patching machine in storage at a local moving and storage company. There was no possibility that the owner would ever reclaim the item, and so Izzi bought it from the storage company for a dollar down and additional dollars "whenever we could get them." He found a used printing machine that could print on burlap bags. He found and purchased used burlap bags, turned them inside out, cleaned them, and printed the names of individual local farmers on the recycled bags. He learned to profitably produce very small orders. Larger companies wouldn't bother with such individualized small orders. Wagner Bag soon cornered almost all of the local market.

In about 1940, the business had grown so much that there was no longer room for family living space. Rose, Abe, and Izzi bought a house on Tenth East Street in Sugarhouse, across from Granite Furniture Company (Granite would later buy the house to make room for a parking lot). The Wagners purchased the house for thirty-five hundred dollars in 1940. They would sell it a decade or so later for thirty-five thousand dollars.

Rose, Abe, and Izzi lived in the house in Sugarhouse. The house was near a grocery store and almost directly across the street from a movie theater, which pleased Rose. By this time, Leona had left Salt Lake to live with Rose's sister in Boston. Several years later, Leona met and married an artist from California. The two of them moved to Salt Lake and lived in the basement apartment of the Sugarhouse home.

Rose did not drive, and so either Izzi or Abe took her to the office every day. But Izzi did not spend much time at home. He traveled a great deal, and he had time-consuming responsibilities at both Wagner Bag Company and the Chi Chi Club. He was also busy courting Jeanné.

At times, Izzi worked too hard. One day, he drove two blocks from Wagner Bag to the bank on Main Street to make a deposit. There were no parking meters, and he parked parallel in front of the bank. Inside, he ran into a neighbor. The two began talking. Izzi was so engrossed in the conversation that he walked with the neighbor two blocks back to the office, forgetting he had driven to the bank. Later, he went to his usual parking place beside Wagner Bag Company, and his car was not there. He called the police to report a stolen car. The police searched for two days—at least, they said they were searching for the car. Two days later, Izzi had to return to the bank. He saw his car parked in front of the bank, and he remembered what had happened. "Luckily," he said, "the police chief was a friend of mine. The chief arranged to remove the stolen car report from the records so I wouldn't be arrested for stealing my own car."

By the time World War II came along in 1941, the Wagners had repaid their debt, and the business was doing well. They were not wealthy, by any means, but they were out of debt, and they were making payments on valuable property in the heart of the city as they continued to purchase expansion property around the old homestead.

The primary sources of entertainment were radio and movies. Downtown Salt Lake housed more than a dozen movie theaters, some seating as many as eighteen hundred patrons. Sometimes, short vaudeville acts filled in between showings of the feature movie. One newspaper columnist years later wrote that Izzi Wagner sometimes entertained with his violin during intermissions, but that is highly unlikely. Movie theaters were elaborate structures, with ornate walls, columns, and ceilings. Uniformed ushers with flashlights guided ticket holders down the aisles. It was an environment totally different from the silent-movie venues of Izzi's childhood. Radio was such a popular and powerful force that movie theaters sometimes stopped the showing of a movie long enough to broadcast extremely popular radio programs over the theater loudspeakers. How often this happened is subject to discussion, but that it did happen now and then cannot be disputed.

The decade of the 1930s was a very heady decade for Izzi Wagner. He was a teenager who had to become an astute businessman in short order. He became suddenly independent, even though he enjoyed the benefit of an extremely wise mother. He watched radio and movies become dominant features of American culture, displacing vaudeville and traveling theater. Like most Americans, he idolized movie and radio celebrities. He witnessed historic events in the making, as movie newsreels brought theater audiences realistic pictures of news around the world. And he listened to live radio reports of history-making events in distant places.

He both saw and heard the tragedy of war developing in Europe, its effects reaching ever closer to Salt Lake City. He heard about the persecution of the Jews in Germany and about the deaths of his own relatives (including his mother's brothers) at the hands of the Germans. The war was a great change agent for everyone, including the Wagners. Wartime rationing and scarcities added to the economic pressures every family experienced during the Great Depression. Those who were adept at "recycling"—as the Wagners had learned to be—became valuable resources for families, friends, neighbors, and the community. At the same time, everyone became more patriotic, more unified, and more willing to accept the sacrifices required by war.

4

Marriage and War

———•———

Izzi continued to operate the Chi Chi Club in the New Grand Hotel at Fourth South and Main. Jeanné was the hostess and also operated the coat room—important parts of any nightclub at that time. On most days, Izzi worked at the club until twelve thirty or one (the law required closing at midnight); then he slept a few hours before going to Wagner Bag at six thirty to put in a full days' work there. He had incredible amounts of energy, but he also had the ability to sleep under almost any conditions. He could grab a catnap whenever circumstances allowed—an ability that would come in handy later when he would end up in a foxhole on Guadalcanal.

Wagner could probably have applied for and received an exemption from military service because both the Wagner family and the Wagner Company were dependent on him. However, he was anxious to do his patriotic duty. By that time, everyone in the Jewish community knew what Adolf Hitler was doing to the Jewish people in Europe. Izzi wanted to join the fight against the brutal Nazis. (Rose had already learned or would soon learn that all three of her brothers had been killed by the Germans.)

The U.S. Marine Corps recruiting office was just around the corner from the Chi Chi Club. Izzi says he was attracted by the handsome dress-blue uniform of the Marines. Chances are his attraction to the Marines was driven more by the image of the Marines—considered the premier fighting force for the nation—than by the image of the uniform itself, especially when he found out that dress blues were not standard issue; if he wanted the dress uniform, he would have to buy one.

On February 14, 1942—two months after the Japanese attacked Pearl Harbor on December 7, 1941—I. J. Wagner walked around the corner and joined the United States Marines. His height—five feet, six inches—barely exceeded the minimum limit for that branch of the military service, but he was accepted. He asked for and received a short delay before reporting for duty, and it didn't take him long to acquire a handsome dress-blue uniform (which he wore on appropriate occasions). Then he concentrated on getting his business and personal affairs in order.

His full load of responsibilities required that he make sure all his business operations were either sold or in good hands before he went off to the uncertain future of military life. He had to make sure the bag business—and especially his customers—would be well taken care of during his absence. He visited with each of them. They applauded his patriotism and assured him they would continue to deal with Wagner Bag Company. Of course, the business would be in the capable hands of Rose and Abe, and wartime shortages would allow the two remaining Wagners to capitalize on their "recycling" skills.

After careful consideration, Izzi decided to sell the Chi Chi Club. He felt that wartime pressures and the heavy influx of servicemen and -women into the Salt Lake area would create operational problems that would be impossible for an absentee owner to manage. He worried about undesirable elements and activities coming into the club and giving it a bad name. He also worried about how club managers might react to the inevitable influx of servicemen and -women in transit to battles in Europe and the Pacific. Military conscripts were easy targets for the unscrupulous. (His concerns proved to be well founded.) Izzi had no trouble selling the club for a reasonable profit, even though he had owned it only a short time. ("I always made a profit in business transactions," he said. He didn't include the times he bought property and then gave it away for charitable purposes...or bought and sold property for no profit in order to help friends or to facilitate community improvement.)

Perhaps the most important thing he had to do before going off to war was to make sure his growing interest in Jeanné would be "protected" during his absence. He was confident of his ability to retain her affection in person, but he did not know what might happen while he was far away and out of communication for months at a time. When he sold the Chi Chi Club, he made sure Jeanné would continue to have a job there. He warned her of the potential dangers, and the two of them talked about how she might respond. (Her standard response to soldiers who approached her for dates was: "I can't. I have a husband and baby at home.") When all those details were settled, Izzi asked Jeanné to marry him—not right away, but as soon as his military schedule allowed. This was a dramatic step for one of the most eligible bachelors in town. (As mentioned earlier, he had often come close to marriage, but he always changed his mind before the question was finalized—usually with a sigh of relief.)

Apparently, Jeanné also continued to perform at the club. The new owners changed the name from the Chi Chi Club to the Brass Rail. A flyer promoted the new club:

TONIGHT'S THE NIGHT

JACK EVERETTE
and his
MANHATTAN CLUB BAND
start at the
BRASS RAIL
under the THE NEW GRAND HOTEL

A real entertaining band, featuring that
East of the Mississippi Rhythm
so popular in the better night clubs.
Direct from 16 weeks at the Manhattan Club in Detroit.

Also the newest dances by
JENNE DORE.

Cover Charge 50¢   Wasatch 10203

Between the time he signed up for the Marines and the time he left for boot camp, Private Wagner tied up all the loose ends he thought needed attention. Now and then, he appeared around town in his dress blues, always accompanied by Jeanné. But he would have few occasions to wear anything other than standard-issue uniforms over the next three years.

In March 1942, Private I. J. Wagner left Salt Lake City for San Diego and the Camp Elliott Marine boot camp. The intense training of boot camp was not a pleasant experience for Izzi. It was not the physical stress; he was tough enough to handle that easily—tougher than most fellow enlistees. The problem was putting up with the psychological and social abuse that was so much a part of basic training. A necessary part of military training is to focus not on the individual but on the group, the team. In some cases, that meant replacing individuality with subordination. It meant tearing down personal impulses in order to substitute group impulses.

Izzi was used to being in charge, not taking orders—especially from those for whom he had little respect. He recalled vividly the first words from his drill sergeant: "Youse guys don't know nuthin' no-how nowhere!" The new Marine from Salt Lake City disliked the sergeant's crudeness and his general ignorance about language and about everything else outside the drill manual and Marine life. Izzi's experience with business, his leadership skills, and his general knowledge exceeded that of many of his fellow recruits...and most of his military superiors. He did not like boot camp, but he persevered, and he became if not a model recruit at least an acceptable one.

During one of the most stressful periods, Izzi and another recruit were on a lunch break, eating C rations—a small can of "mystery meat," a small can of fruit, a cracker designed to expand in the stomach to give the impression of fullness, and a sweet of some kind. They saw in the distance an outcropping of land. They estimated that it was four or five miles away. Both were strong swimmers, and they knew they could swim across the bay to the landing in the distance. They fantasized about fleeing boot camp. But after further consideration, they realized that what they saw in the distance was a U.S. Navy camp. They would be escaping boot camp only to end up at a busy navy base. They laughed about it and went back to training. That was the first and only time Izzi considered going AWOL.

"Youse guys have fifteen minutes for the three s's," the sergeant would yell at five o'clock each morning. And the recruits would roll out of bed to shower, shave, and take care of personal needs before beginning another long day of training.

It didn't take Izzi long to make friends among his new associates—sixty men of the 249th Platoon of the United States Marine Corps, San Diego, California. He remembered a few of their names for half a century. Many became casualties during the war. At some point during boot camp, a call went out for Marines who could type and take shorthand. Izzi had learned both skills at West High School, and so he volunteered. He was moved from a rifle company to headquarters company. The new assignment gave him a little more freedom to move about the base and "work the system." He was also the driver for an officer, and so he would sometimes take the officer to San Diego, drop him off at his destination, and have a few hours on his own.

On April 10, 1942, he wrote to his mother:

Dear Mother:

I received the money by wire and I appreciate it very much. I am now doing typing and clerical work and I like it very much. Up to date the work has been quite easy for me. I really don't have too much to do but the work will become harder I imagine as I go along. Everything is going along very nicely and I feel good. I went to Los Angeles last nite and talked to Mr. Shuken over the phone. He said something about some kind of a celing [*sic*] on bags. My address is Private Irving J. Wagner, 2-H-6, Camp Elliott, Calif. I get to go down town quite often and it makes you feel a lot better when you can eat a good steak and take your time eating it. I saw Max Zemen again yesterday and he is doing a very good business. His sister Sophie is working in the shop with him. Leona is leaving today for Los Angeles and I probably will see her Saturday nite which is tomorrow. Tell Abie to be sure and keep the books in good shape and keep all the records right and that is very impor-tant now. Don't speculate on anything that you have not got sold regardless of how scarce bags are because the market has to go down sometime and we are sitting pretty good now and there is no sense in losing what we have. Keep my insurance payments up. I may be able to come home in about two weeks for a couple of days. How is Ethel. Is Dale still working for us. Tell Moran hello and also Sam Notti. How is Pat and Sam getting along now? It is raining today and I don't have anything to do but type a leter [*sic*] home and listen to the radio. I will send you a good picture of me next week when I get my new uniform. Well that's about all of the news for now and I will write more later.

Love, Izzi

Obviously, Wagner Bag Company was always on Izzi's mind. So, too, was he concerned about friends and relatives. As always, his thoughts were about the future, even as he found ways to enjoy the challenges of the day.

Izzi made contact with an old friend, Ed Allem. Ed was from Salt Lake City. He was a corporal in the fire battalion on the Marine base. (Allem would later go on to found the Cinegrill, still one of Salt Lake City's most popular eating establishments.) Izzi spent time with Ed whenever possible. Ed taught him some of the "ropes," and they sometimes arranged overnight passes to have fun in San Diego.

On July 4, 1942, I. J. Wagner was promoted to private first class. An en-listed man's pay at the time was well under fifty dollars a month, regardless of rank, and so the promotion made little difference in Wagner's income.

Izzi called Jeanné whenever his schedule allowed. Once or twice, she took the bus to San Diego when Izzi had weekend passes. They liked to go dancing, especially at the Latin Quarter. Izzi urged Jeanné to marry him before he went overseas. He told her he would not know where he was going until shortly before his group left, but that he would surely be in combat. Those who know Izzi believe he probably also said something about the ten-thousand-dollar life-insurance policy issued to every military serviceman. It would not have been unlike Izzi to say something like: "At least you'll have ten thousand dollars to remember me by if I should get killed." Jeanné agreed to marry him. She was as much in love with Izzi as he was with her. She didn't want to take any chances that he might "get away."

However, the Marines did not allow leave time at the end of boot training. Troop movements were top secret, and the military wanted to minimize chances that personnel on leave might inadvertently tip off the enemy about troop deployment plans. Of course, most of the time the troops had a good idea where they were going, thanks to the pervasive "rumor mill." But trainees were scheduled to board ship within a day or two after completion of boot camp.

Izzi was not going to let the rules stop him from marrying Jeanné on his, not the military's, schedule. He worked out a scheme with his friend Ed Allem. The night before Izzi's company was to leave, Ed smuggled Izzi off base on a fire truck. They met Jeanné at a nearby hotel. The first task was to find a wedding ring. They found a gold-plated band in a pawn shop. It cost four dollars. Izzi did not have four dollars, and so Jeanné paid for the ring. (Years later, she said, "I wore it for two or three years. It turned my finger quite green.") Next, they found a minister. His name was Reverend Anger. Izzi and Jeanné were married in what Izzi said was "the shortest ceremony on record." (One of Izzi's oft-repeated lines was: "We were married by Anger.") Ed Allem was best man. It was August 13, 1942. After the ceremony, they went to the Latin Quarter to celebrate. The couple had only a few hours before Corporal Allem made sure Private First Class Wagner got back to camp.

The next day, Izzi boarded ship to sail for his next destination—a staging point for the invasion of the island of Guadalcanal. The bride and groom would not see each other again for two years. Izzi was twenty-six years old. His bride was five years older, although she told him she was younger. (He discovered her real age years later when they applied for passports. He asked her why she had lied to him about her age, and Jeanné responded, "I was afraid you might get away from me.")

After the wedding, Izzi called Rose to tell her he and Jeanné were married and that he would be leaving the next morning for combat duty. Rose said, "She's a nice young lady. Now don't get yourself shot." The following Saturday, Rose and her good friend Mrs. Gust were on their way to synagogue. Rose told Mrs. Gust the news about Izzi getting married. Mrs. Gust said, "That's wonderful. And which nice Jewish girl did your Izzi marry?" Rose responded, "He didn't marry a Jewish girl." Mrs. Gust said, incredulously, "How could you let a handsome boy like Izzi marry a shiksa?" Rose gently put her hand on Mrs. Gust's arm and explained: "Ven I got married, I didn't ask advice from my children. Vy should they come to me for marriage advice?"

Izzi's ship joined a task force headed for the New Hebrides Islands, a staging area for the U.S. invasion of Guadalcanal. His headquarters battalion was assigned to the Second Marine Division. The official embarkation roster for the "Advance Echelon, Headquarters Battalion, Second Marine Division, Camp Elliott, San Diego, California" listed twelve officers (including a major general), thirty-three sergeants, seventy-three enlisted men, and five navy personnel. (Izzi kept the mimeographed roster and occasionally used it to track down some of the personnel listed. Many would lose their lives during the war.) Despite his rank and his assignment, Izzi knew that in battle, every Marine was a rifleman.

Guadalcanal was the first amphibious landing by U.S. forces in World War II. It was the first of a string of island invasions up through the Solomons, Gilberts, Marshalls, Marianas, and Philippines to secure a route to Japan for American ships and planes. At the time, no one in the U.S. military had experience with island-to-island fighting, and no one knew quite what to expect.

Guadalcanal was selected because it had an airfield that, with a little work, would be able to handle large bombers. It would be renamed Henderson Field in honor of Major Lofton Henderson, who lost his life in the naval battle of Midway.

The invasion of Guadalcanal took place on August 7, 1942, when the First Marine Division went in. It was a success, but troops soon learned their equipment was not well suited for jungle warfare. Supply ships were sunk or damaged by Japanese planes and submarines. Torrential rain made every movement difficult. Marines eventually moved inland, where they captured Japanese trucks and Japanese food stores to replenish their own diminishing supplies. They secured the airfield on August 17, and they began making needed improvements, using the one bulldozer they had and the captured Japanese trucks. The rain made the field a sea of sticky black mud. On August 20, twelve navy dive-bombers arrived, followed the next day by fifteen fighter planes. The airplanes were able to provide some relief for troops on the ground from the constant bombing and strafing of Japanese planes…and to make it possible for a destroyer serving as a supply ship to unload much needed supplies.

However, victory on Guadalcanal was not to come easily. Japan's military leaders knew the battle over Guadalcanal would be a critical point in the war. They sent more troops, more planes, and more ships to join the campaign. It would rage on for six months, and more naval battles would be fought off that small island in six months than were fought by the British Navy throughout all of World War I. So many ships went down off the coast of Guadalcanal that the area was dubbed "Iron Bottom Sound."

Guadalcanal was a key battle for both sides. It was the first offensive battle for the Americans. Commanders were convinced the outcome at Guadalcanal would set the tone for a planned string of island encounters. Japanese leaders knew that if they lost Guadalcanal, it would likely be the beginning of the end for their ambitious military plans. They continued to throw men and equipment into the battle, even when it became clear they could not emerge victorious.

Japanese forces pushed toward Henderson Field. The Marines were in danger of losing it, and so the Second Marine Division was called in. Izzi was promoted to corporal on September 1, and his headquarters battalion landed on Guadalcanal on September 21. They took up positions on the beach near the Tenaru River. Their primary goal was to protect Henderson Field, but everyone realized that the final outcome would require virtually pushing the Japanese forces into the sea. The outcome was far from a foregone conclusion. In early October, the U.S. secretary of the navy told reporters, "Everybody hopes that we can hold on."

The Marines dug foxholes on or near the beach. Air raids came one after another. It was not uncommon for Marines—including Corporal Wagner— to be stuck in their foxholes for twelve to fourteen hours at a time while planes roared overhead and artillery shells screamed their deadly warnings. The troops ate only if they had C rations with them, and any natural bodily functions had to occur in place. Whenever the bombing stopped, troops ran for the river or the beach to strip down and clean themselves and their clothes as much as possible.

Latrines consisted of fifty-gallon drums planted in the sand. One Marine was suffering from the ever present diarrhea when an air-raid siren sounded. He could not leave the latrine to make his way to a foxhole, and so when the bombs started falling, he simply dropped into the drum. When the malodorous Marine finally headed for the river, his "buddies" found it an excuse to laugh. They never let him forget the incident.

Years later, Izzi recalled his introduction to combat during an interview with a Salt Lake City news writer:

> In combat, nobody's brave. Not like in the movies. You climb down the side of a ship that's the size of Hotel Utah. You climb down a rope ladder, and you've got your pack with everything you own in it, including your rifle, your ammunition, and your grenades. If you slip and fall, you'll break your neck. Then you get into a Higgins boat. You crouch down. You hit the beach, and you dig a foxhole. People are shelling. You don't know whether the shells are coming from your people or the enemy. Now, let me tell you how brave you are. You have two choices: Either you go forward and take a chance of getting shot, or you go backward and drown. So what do you do? You're brave. You go forward.

Life on Guadalcanal was incredibly difficult. Supplies failed to arrive because supply ships were sunk at sea or could not get close to the beach. The first mail came in October—more than two months after the invasion. Japanese bombing attacks continued without letup. The battle over the airfield went back and forth as reinforcements arrived on both sides. Transport planes could not land with supplies. The troops heard the large guns of ships battling in nearby sea-lanes. Friends died all around . . . or failed to return from daily combat patrols. Years later, Izzi told a friend: "We lost about one-fifth of our company. It was terrible. There were so many losses that we lost track."

American forces were terribly "green." With few exceptions, none had been in battle before. The climate was oppressive. The heat and humidity drained energy, and rain often came down like the torrents at the bottom of a waterfall. The island smelled of decaying vegetation—to which was soon added the stench of decaying bodies, mostly Japanese. American commanders knew so little about jungle warfare that at one point they asked even noncommissioned officers and enlisted men to make written recommendations about how to improve battle procedures. Their written comments were sent to Washington, compiled, edited, and printed in a small pamphlet distributed to officers. Commissioned and noncommissioned officers were encouraged to use suggestions from their own troops to make adjustments to the operating procedures they had learned in training. That training had not included jungle combat with out-of-date weapons, limited supplies, and ineffective heavy equipment. For example, Japanese snipers often hid high up in the fronds of palm trees. They waited for patrols to pass by, then began picking off the stragglers, one by one. Shooting into the palms was a waste of scarce ammunition, since few bullets ever found their targets. One enlisted man suggested that they get hold of shotguns and fire buckshot into the palms. Sure enough, whenever a pellet hit a sniper, he would invariably let out a yelp, giving away his position so rifle shots could bring him down.

Izzi Wagner disliked the idea of shooting at other human beings, especially young men he did not know. He was never able to forget the first time he stepped over a fallen log only to place his foot on the dead body of a Japanese soldier. It sickened him. He picked up the soldier's wallet, thinking he would turn it over to the Red Cross so they could contact the dead soldier's family. The wallet contained photos of a young woman and a couple of children. Again he was sickened. He saw fellow Marines pick up "souvenirs" from fallen enemy troops—helmets, knives, guns, jewelry—and he recoiled at the evils of war.

As mentioned earlier, Wagner was the first non-Japanese lifetime member of the Utah Japanese-American League. Yet he was forced, out of necessity, to kill what he thought of as relatives of his Utah friends. He remembered seeing many bodies of young Japanese men. "They looked fifteen or sixteen," he said. "They had photos of mothers and fathers and girlfriends. It was a gruesome business. But we had little choice. It was kill or be killed."

Eventually, the Marines solidified their foothold on the island. U.S. fighter planes, operating from aircraft carriers, forced Japanese planes to cut back or eliminate air raids. Troops erected a small tent for the headquarters company in which Wagner served. He was assigned as battalion clerk.

V-mail was a World War II precursor of e-mail. Military personnel in distant lands wrote letters on a special single-sheet V-mail form. Letters were read by military censors before being scanned by a facsimile machine and then transmitted by radio to a Stateside receiver where the facsimile was printed out to be mailed to the recipient. Censors were strict. To get around the censors, many servicemen prearranged signal words with their loved ones. One of Izzi's V-mails to Jeanné survived the years. It was dated "About Jan 30, 1943":

> Dearest wife Jeanne:
> I am still on an island in the Pacific. We are in contact with the front lines everyday and everything seems to be in our favor. This island is covered with cocoanut [*sic*] trees and in peace time I imagine quite beautiful. Of course

the mosquitos, flies, bugs, land crabs etc. don't seem to add any particular beauty to the place but they are bearable as are the continuous rains. The natives here are very cooperative and friendly although they speak a very limited amount of English. I am in good health and getting along very well under the circumstances. Our food is good and *we are getting plenty to eat everyday.* Darling, I haven't heard from you for quite sometime. This is probably due to the fact that ships only dock here to bring in supplies and sometimes it seems as though they will never get here. I miss you more than words can describe darling and I do wish that it were possible for me to be with you—but this is part of war. We are here for a good cause; and when the war is over we will not have to be parted again. Ed is not with me anymore, but I hope to see him in the next few months. *How is Helen?* We get the press news from the States every morning and also hear the radio short wave broadcasts. The natives are very small people; some of them look like pigmies [*sic*]; some have read [*sic*] hair. They can really scurry up a cocoanut tree. A few daisy pushers are dropped occasionally but I generally sleep right through their raids. Although the news press say that the Marines have left this island; the enemy seem to have an entirely different opinion. I am certainly glad that I joined this branch of the service. The Marines always get what they go after (recruiting advertising). I haven't heard from home for sometime so please write me all of the news & don't forget to have a subscription of the Salt Lake paper sent to me at my address. Darling, when I get back we are going to build a new home. I don't know when that will be, but I think that I will be back within the next two years at the most. How are you getting along? Are your finances holding out all right? I am anxiously awaiting a letter from you and also a photograph. My snapshots of you are slowly fading due to the heat and perspiration. The office (or reasonable facsimile thereof) is quite different from Camp Elliott. Give my regards to Sammy, Max and any of the other members of the old gang you may happen to run into. How is my mother and brother. Tell them to write me. If you don't hear from me for a month or two please don't worry because I may be on the high seas. I am awaiting one day darling, and that is the day we meet again. You have proven yourself to be just the way I always thought you would be; brave, optimistic and the best wife in the world. I love you with all my heart and adore you feverishly. You are my ideal. Keep your chin up sweetheart and I know that everything will turn out for the best. Sgt Shuman sends his regards. Watch your health. Give my love to your family. And so my dear until my next letter, I will close with a million loads of kisses.

G'Nite, IRVING

Izzi underlined the two passages indicated. Underlining was part of the code
he had arranged with Jeanné. Underlining *"We are getting plenty to eat
everyday"* meant that just the opposite was true. And underlining *"How is
Helen?"* meant that he was simply finding a way to work "Helen" into the
letter. They did not know anyone named Helen. It was the code word they
had agreed on for Guadalcanal. Had he named the island, it would have been
excised by the censor. Thus, Jeanné knew that Izzi was on Guadalcanal and
that food supplies were limited.

The bloody battle of Guadalcanal went on for six months, ending in February 1943. Both sides suffered heavy casualties. All told, the Japanese had
sent forty thousand troops to Guadalcanal. Japanese forces referred to it
as "the island of death." Some twenty-three thousand of those troops lost
their lives, more from starvation and disease than from combat wounds.
Some drowned when the transport ships used to evacuate them were sunk
by American ships and submarines. The Japanese evacuation of Guadalcanal
began on the night of February 1, 1943. The last troops left the island on
February 9.

During his several months on Guadalcanal, Izzi grew a mustache and a
long beard. It was one of the defenses many adopted to ward off the ever
present swarms of mosquitoes. Long-sleeved shirts were necessary, even in
the tropical climate. Still, hundreds of Marines were afflicted with malaria,
brought on by the sting of mosquitoes.

In February, not long before troops of the Second Marine Division were
scheduled to leave Guadalcanal, one of the malaria-bearing mosquitoes made
its way through Izzi's defenses, and he contracted malaria. He was confined
to the hospital tent with others who were sick and wounded. His body temperature reached 106 degrees. Doctors wondered if he would survive, since
they had relatively limited medical resources. They gave him quinine and
tried to control his temperature as best they could in the oppressive climate.

Izzi's headquarters company shipped out without him. The division went
to another staging area to prepare for the next island invasion a few months
later. This one would be the battle of Tarawa, perhaps the bloodiest battle
of the Pacific war. U.S. casualties on Tarawa would be as high as 40 percent
killed or wounded, with twenty of every one hundred invading Marines giving their lives on that tiny speck of an island. But Izzi could not leave Guadalcanal. He was on the waiting list for transfer to a hospital in New Zealand,
and malaria cases were not at the top of the priority list for limited space on
hospital ships.

After sixty years of living with the memory of his close call at Tarawa, Izzi often said, with a smile, "That mosquito saved my life. That's why I never swat a mosquito. When one lands on me, I pet it."

In late February 1943, a feverish I. J. Wagner was loaded aboard a hospital ship bound for New Zealand. The trip took many days because the ship observed the zigzag protocol of wartime movement, trying to avoid the occasional Japanese bomber or submarine still patrolling the Coral Sea.

In the New Zealand military hospital, his temperature continued to fluctuate up and down. On occasion, it would soar into the 104–106-degree range. When the fever and the shaking of malaria left him, periodically, Wagner tried to rejoin his unit, but each time he tried, malaria fever laid him low. Medical science in those days did not have treatment regimens to deal effectively with malaria. Doctors controlled it with quinine and other medications, but many men who contracted malaria during World War II suffered from it for the rest of their lives.

Izzi was worried about his future. He did not know if he would ever get well, and he wondered if he would have enough energy to meet the demands of civilian life. But he was still president of Wagner Bag Company, and he had confidence that he could lead the company to continued success when and if he returned, provided he regained his health. He wrote to Rose to suggest that she prepare a will. He wanted to make sure that his brother and sister were well protected. Accordingly, Rose had an attorney prepare a one-page will in October 1943. It stipulated: "I give and bequeath unto my son, Isadore Wagner, the sum of Ten dollars ($10.00)." The remainder of the estate was to be divided equally between Abraham Wagner and Leona Wagner, and Abe was to be the executor of Rose's estate.

Izzi would remain in New Zealand for almost a year. On April 14, 1943, he was promoted to sergeant. He fulfilled military assignments in the New Zealand area whenever he was well enough to do so, but he spent much of the time in the hospital. He had more than forty attacks of malarial fever. For a few weeks in the fall of 1943, Izzi served as a clerk and driver for Major David M. Shoup. Shoup was promoted to colonel in November. Later that month, Colonel Shoup led the Second Marine Division in the invasion of Tarawa. His heroic action there earned him the Congressional Medal of Honor, as well as the British Distinguished Service Order. Years later, in 1959, General Shoup was named the twenty-second commandant of the United States Marine Corps. As Izzi did with so many other acquaintances throughout his life, he stayed in touch with Shoup through the years, and he arranged to have dinner with the retired commandant in the early 1980s. Shoup died in 1983 and was buried in Arlington National Cemetery. "He was a helluva guy," Izzi said. Some years later, at Izzi's request, Shoup's widow sent "Sgt. Wagner" a photograph of her husband, together with a note that said, in part: "I well remember how wonderful it was to have you and Jeanné with us. I wish we could repeat those happy days now. Semper Fi."

Eventually, orders put Izzi on another hospital ship early in 1944—this one on its way back to the United States. The ship landed at Long Beach. Patients were placed aboard a bus with three tiers of beds along the sides. But the bus was crowded with those more seriously injured than Wagner, and Izzi ended up lying on the floor for the trip to Corona Naval Hospital.

Corona Naval Hospital was a considerable improvement over previous medical facilities, and treatments there began to have a positive effect. Still, Izzi's temperature would sometimes reach 106 degrees. One day, he awoke from feverish unconsciousness to find a beautiful blonde woman kissing his forehead. It was movie star Joan Blondell, along with some of her associates on a USO tour, including Jane Wyman (soon to become the first wife of Ronald Reagan) and Chester Morris, the actor who played Boston Blackie in many movies. Sergeant Wagner, always starstruck, said he thought he had "died and gone to heaven."

One of the first things he did when he arrived at the hospital was telephone Jeanné. They had a great deal of "catching up" to do. Communication had been extremely limited during two years of separation. Izzi encouraged her to come to Corona, which she did frequently during the next few months. She was surprised when she saw him for the first time in the hospital. He had lost considerable weight, and the malarial fever caused him to lose much of his dark, wavy hair.

Jeanné would take the bus from Salt Lake to Corona, rent a room for a week or so, and visit the hospital whenever regulations permitted. Soon, Izzi was well enough to be allowed weekend passes. They enjoyed the beach and occasionally took the bus to nearby locations. As Izzi regained his strength, they sometimes went as far as Los Angeles to see a vaudeville show or visit a nightclub. On more than one occasion, they missed the last bus and had to hitchhike back to the hospital.

Izzi knew Los Angeles well because he had made frequent business trips before the war. He had owned the restaurant there, and, of course, he had several girlfriends in the area, including the vaudeville dancer named Dagmar.

Now, it was 1944. Izzi and Jeanné were walking along a street in the Los Angeles theater district. Izzi saw Dagmar's name on a theater poster. He told Jeanné all about Dagmar. She encouraged him to go inside and say hello to her. The two of them went through the front door and into the lobby. Then Izzi decided it wasn't such a good idea after all. He told Jeanné that the past should remain in the past. He told her that when he had met her, he had torn up and discarded all his photos of former girlfriends, and it was best that he discarded their memories as well.

After a few months in the Corona hospital, doctors declared Sergeant Wagner "fit for duty," so long as it was not combat duty. He had been helping out in the hospital supply detachment, where his resourcefulness and efficiency were often praised, and so he fully expected to be assigned to one of the navy's major supply depots in Seattle, Chicago, or another large supply center.

The captain called his group together and began reading names and assignments. Izzi's friends went to assignments all across the nation. When the captain got to the end of the alphabet, he called: "Wagner, I. J.—Clearfield Naval Supply Depot, Clearfield, Utah." Izzi could hardly believe his good fortune. He immediately called Jeanné with the good news, and he was soon on a troop transport train headed back to his hometown.

He and Jeanné first lived in a duplex owned by Jeanné's parents and next door to the Rasmussen home about two miles from downtown Salt Lake City. However, they soon found a small apartment in the Avenues section of Salt Lake City, slightly closer to Clearfield and quite a bit closer to Wagner Bag Company. The house—one of the early homes built in the city—was located, appropriately, between I and J Streets on Second Avenue. It was owned by an attorney who lived on the first floor. He had converted the second floor into two apartments. And so for the final year of his military service—and the first "together" year of his married life—Izzi Wagner lived in a Salt Lake City apartment, commuted thirty miles to Clearfield, and wore a Marine uniform to work every day.

Jeanné took over the household responsibilities, as she would do for the rest of her life. She was a talented designer and seamstress—skills learned while on the vaudeville circuit. She designed and made most of her own clothes. She also took classes at LDS Business College to improve her bookkeeping and business skills. She was always eager to learn new skills, and at one point she signed up for an upholstery class so she and Izzi could buy used furniture and restore it for use in their home.

Izzi had time to renew his association with Wagner Bag Company. He was able to work there on weekends, making sure the company was ready for the postwar boom everyone expected. Since the company's customers included large flour mills in Ogden, Utah, not far from Clearfield, it was common for the Marine sergeant to be seen at dinner with prominent Ogden businessmen.

Irving Jerome Wagner was honorably discharged from the United States Marine Corps on the twenty-sixth day of January 1945. The discharge certificate lists his character as "excellent."

I. J. Wagner's wartime experience changed him in a number of ways. First, it intensified his "joy of living" after having seen how fragile life can be, including his own. Second, Jeanné's loyalty to him over their long separation cemented his devotion to her. They would become virtually inseparable throughout her lifetime. Third, his successful dealings with the stresses of war and serious illness added to his self-confidence without increasing his sense of self-importance. Fourth, he developed a more sanguine attitude toward risk. He was now ready for the next dramatic change in his life.

5

Building Friendships and Business

———◆———

THE WAR ENDED IN August 1945, and for Sergeant I. J. Wagner, the transition back to civilian life was one of the most complete and expeditious on record. He did not enjoy military life because he did not like taking orders; he wanted to be in charge. (Later, when President Harry Truman fired General Douglas MacArthur, Rose saw the newspaper headline and told her two sons something they had already learned: "See vat I told you. Never vork for anyone; alvays be boss.") It didn't take long for the wartime sergeant to once again become a peacetime general. Over the coming years, Izzi would see one or two of his old Marine buddies again, but usually only when they came to him seeking work. He did not hire former Marine associates, because he felt the ones still looking for work months after the war ended were not very reliable. Besides, he did not want to be reminded of his military experiences, especially boot camp.

However, he did hire Japanese workers who had been confined during the war at Utah's Topaz internment camp. It was one of the so-called relocation camps used to house Japanese Americans arrested early in World War II. Izzi had great respect for his loyal and hardworking Japanese friends. He had been doing business with them for many years before the war. Some of those confined at Topaz remained in Utah to become successful and prominent citizens. Many became truck farmers, growing celery, onions, and other crops. Naturally, they bought bags from Wagner Bag Company.

In 1945, the postwar boom was still a few years away, but Izzi went to work creating an economic boom for Wagner Bag Company. One of the first things he did was design a trademark for the company. It was basically a burlap bag with hands, feet, and facial features. He called the trademark "Wagbag," and he registered it with the State of Utah on September 21, 1945. Later, he filed the trademark with the U.S. Patent Office. He had the Wagbag logo painted on company trucks. For a short while, company stationery featured the Wagbag logo.

Izzi soon reinstituted a practice he had begun before the war: daily lunches with customers, potential customers, business leaders, and politicians. Often, these gatherings also took place during breakfast, morning coffee break, and dinner. He never ate alone. Some mealtime meetings were weekly get-togethers with a fixed group of individuals; others were spur of the moment. If lunch on a particular day was not preplanned, Izzi got on the phone early to arrange a lunch group—sometimes one person, more often three or four. He always joked about who would pick up the check. ("The last time Joe picked up a check," Izzi often teased, "was when he stopped for a hitchhiker in Czechoslovakia.") But everyone knew that lunch would almost always be on Izzi Wagner's tab. This daily practice continued throughout his life, even during his later years when getting out to lunch was sometimes physically difficult. The locations changed from time to time, but the routine remained basically the same for more than half a century: a few jokes, a little small talk, and pointed questions about family, politics, and business. Once in a while, Izzi benefited from a "free ride" because the restaurateur remembered the business Izzi had brought during tough times...or a favor Izzi had done for the owner and his family years ago...or just because everyone liked Izzi Wagner. He neither wanted nor expected favors, but sometimes the cashier let him know the meal tab had already been paid.

Rarely did the mealtime meetings involve open sales pitches to customers or potential customers. Subjects for conversation included business conditions, politics, personal or family activities, and so on. Sometimes, Jeanné joined the evening dinner events, but more often than not, she preferred to let the activities go on without her. When Izzi joined friends for dinner and card games (usually gin rummy), Jeanné learned to expect a phone call late in the evening. Izzi would tell her that the card game might extend to early morning hours because so-and-so was losing, and Izzi knew he would have to keep playing until the "loser" had a change of luck or until the "loser's" own domestic demands dictated closure. Jeanné never complained; she simply went on with her own activities until Izzi came home. Then she expected him to fill her in on the evening's conversation.

According to Izzi, on one occasion, the steward at a local private club had not yet acquired a full command of English. The card game continued late into the evening. The wife of one of the card players phoned to ask if her husband was there—let's call him "Mr. Smith." The club steward put his hand over the phone and told Mr. Smith that his wife was calling. Mr. Smith whispered to the bartender, with obvious intent, "I'm not here"—whereupon the bartender said into the telephone, "Mr. Smith say he not here." The incident became part of Izzi's endless repertoire of humorous stories. Most were about himself, but some—like the "Mr. Smith" story—were about others. Still, Izzi almost never poked fun at others by name.

By all accounts, the marriage between Izzi and Jeanné was ideal. According to Izzi, they never had an argument during more than fifty years of marriage. Izzi joked that when Jeanné wanted to paint a room green and Izzi wanted to paint it blue, they sat down like two rational adults, talked it over...and painted the room green. (He always chuckled at the last line.)

Jeanné was frugal, which was important during their early years and became a quality much admired by her husband during their more successful years. She had many interests. She also shared Izzi's congeniality and interest in others. She enjoyed being with Izzi's mother, Rose, and welcomed Rose into their home—although Rose was so independent that she insisted on living alone until her death in 1959.

The daily lunch routine deserves at least partial credit for Izzi Wagner's success. During these daily social events, he learned about the interests and concerns of his customers—sometimes identifying an "Achilles' heel." He learned what was happening in local politics and business. He increased his ever growing circle of acquaintances, and he established important, long-lasting friendships. He learned about business practices used by those he admired, practices he often adopted for his own business. And, of course, he had an audience for his never-ending supply of anecdotes and jokes.

The information-filled lunches were, in a sense, Izzi's university education. But this particular business practice does not work for everyone. Few business leaders can match I. J. Wagner in friendliness, congeniality, and genuine interest in others. During thousands of informal gatherings, he listened more than he talked. He asked questions. He told a few jokes. He made everyone around the table feel as if Izzi Wagner cared about him or her. Because he did care. His interest was not feigned; it was real. Like his mother, Rose, when Izzi felt the urge to offer advice, it was usually brief, succinct, and to the point. In short, the postwar years were colorful years for Wagner. He learned a great deal.

But things did not always go as planned. Like most businesses, Wagner

Bag depended on a line of credit from the bank with which the company had been doing business for many years. Izzi depended on person-to-person relationships. He prized integrity, especially his own. Many of his business deals were sealed with handshakes rather than formal contracts. When the company's bank appointed a new manager and changed its policy to require formal loan committee approval for all loans in once-a-week meetings, Izzi felt his integrity was challenged. He moved his account to a different bank. That move began a friendship with the president of the new bank—a friendship that lasted many years, several partnership deals, and substantial profits for all concerned.

One of his charms was that he was never reluctant to tell stories about himself, even when they might be embarrassing. For example, during the early postwar period, he began what would eventually become monthly business trips to the East, especially New York City. On one occasion, he was with some business associates from Utah. They decided to have dinner at one of New York's more exclusive restaurants. They were astounded—first, by the prices, and second, by the number of individuals providing service to their table. They were helped by a maître d', a headwaiter, a wine steward, and a waiter. They ordered the least-expensive items on the menu, each claiming he was not hungry. Still, when the meal was over, the bill was at least triple that for any meal they had ever consumed in Utah. It severely depleted their travel funds, and there were no credit cards at that time. To compound the problem, all four of those who had served them lined up at the door with hands outstretched, expecting sizable tips. Izzi said: "We paid the bill, shook the outstretched hands, then made a beeline for the door."

On another occasion shortly after the war, Izzi visited New York. Wartime rationing was still in effect. He had used his only shoe-ration coupon to buy a pair of shoes, but the only shoes he had been able to find in his size were bright orange. When he left his hotel in New York, he felt so conspicuous in his orange shoes that he stopped at a small shoe-repair store in Queens to have the shoes dyed black. The attendant applied liquid dye, and then placed the shoes outside in the sun to dry. While Izzi was waiting for the shoes to dry, a thief came by and ran off with the shoes. Izzi tried to talk the attendant into selling him a pair of shoes not yet claimed from repair service. But the attendant did not dare sell the shoes without the owner's approval; it was Saturday, and the owner had gone home for the day. Even supersalesman Izzi could not convince the attendant to sell the shoes.

Wagner was on his way that evening to see a major league baseball game. The famous Bob Feller was scheduled to pitch for the New York Yankees.

Game time was rapidly approaching, and so Izzi walked down the street in his stocking feet, looking for a place to buy shoes. A few blocks later, he found a Florsheim shoe store, but Izzi did not have another shoe-ration coupon. He told the salesman his best stories about being a former Marine, about risking his life for the country, about desperately needing a pair of shoes in order to conduct his business and go to the ball game. Finally, the salesman said he had one pair of shoes in Izzi's size. When the salesman brought out the shoes, they were gaudy brown suede—even worse looking than the lost orange shoes. And so I. J. Wagner, from Utah, walked down the streets of New York in far-from-stylish brown suede shoes. He felt as if everyone could see he did not belong in the big city.

But the adventure was not over. He finally hailed a taxi and told the driver to take him to the baseball stadium. Instead of taking Izzi to Yankee Stadium where Bob Feller was pitching, the cab driver took Izzi to Ebbetts Field. Izzi didn't recognize the mistake until it was too late. But he could see that the stadium was already full, and so he rushed to the ticket window and asked for a ticket on the first-base line, thinking he would see a major league game, even if it did not include Bullet Bob Feller. But when he got inside, the event was not a baseball game; it was a championship boxing match. The preliminary bouts were already completed when Izzi settled into his seat to enjoy the featured fight. Much to his dismay, the fight ended with a knockout in about one and a half minutes of the first round. With thousands of fight fans, Izzi headed for the exit, only to learn that finding a taxi in the crowd added yet another challenge to the disappointing day.

For one reason or another, Izzi enjoyed gathering stories about Salt Lake City and its vices. He kept a file of newspaper clippings. One of his favorites involved the nightclub he owned before the war. It seems that one of the owners—several ownerships removed from Izzi—kept a room at a nearby hotel where he could send his best customers when they had imbibed too much and needed a place to sleep it off. He also used the hotel room to provide other rewards for his customers. For example, one night, the club owner gave the hotel room key to a prominent judge and his associate. He told the judge he would send over a prostitute later in the evening. When the two men arrived at the hotel, the judge sent his associate to get them something to eat. While the associate was gone, the prostitute arrived. Soon after her arrival, there was a knock on the door. The judge thought it was his friend returning with food. He opened the door a crack, with the intent of sending the associate away again. But it was the police following up an anonymous tip. They burst into the room to find the judge and his female visitor sans clothing. The officers did not know they were arresting a prominent judge. At the station, the judge claimed, successfully, that the woman was a masseuse he had hired to help him deal with back pain. Someone was influential enough to make sure the story was never mentioned in the newspaper. (No one explained why the masseuse was also unclothed.)

Despite such distractions, Izzi focused his attention on managing Wagner Bag Company. Following the war, burlap was difficult to obtain. Burlap was produced only in India, and the effects of World War II—coupled with India's struggle for independence from Great Britain—virtually shut off the supply. Izzi traveled extensively, looking for burlap. He bought whatever he could find, including used bags, using the skills he had acquired during the 1930s. In later years, he would travel to India many times to purchase burlap directly from growers there. When he saw how burlap was produced, he was not pleased. Workers stood in water up to their waists for hours, pulling up strands of growing jute plants. They flailed the plants to eliminate everything but the strong burlap fibers. It was hard work, and they worked twelve to fourteen hours a day for a few pennies. Most died at a young age. Izzi found the process disturbing. He knew it was futile to offer a premium price for the product, because the jute harvesters' employers would siphon off whatever extra he provided. He rationalized that without his purchases, the abused workers and their families would have no income at all, but he was not pleased with what he had seen.

During the postwar years when burlap was scarce, Wagner heard that the military had sizable quantities of burlap listed as surplus (like so many other products at that time). He knew that veterans had priority status for the purchase of war surplus materials, which meant his name would rise quickly to the top of the list when purchase opportunities arose. He traveled to military storage depots looking for surplus burlap. His search was moderately successful, and he was able to buy sufficient quantities to keep Wagner Bag operating. During his visits to surplus storage depots, he also noticed countless other items for sale. Izzi knew from experiences during the Depression years that every item had a market somewhere; the challenge was finding the right market and the right price for the item in question.

One day while looking for surplus burlap at his old military post at the Clearfield Naval Supply Depot, Izzi saw stacks and stacks of prime-quality, brand-new, virgin-wool blankets. They were blue, with "U.S. Navy" stamped prominently in white letters. He knew there was a nationwide shortage of wool blankets and a high demand for them, and so he immediately placed an order for forty thousand blankets at eight dollars each. He had neither the resources to pay for the blankets nor the warehouse space to store them, but Izzi was confident he could sell them before the military surplus agency required shipment or payment. He thought he could avoid investing in warehousing the items.

He went to New York to contact large department stores and chain outlets. His first visit was to Gimbel's Department Store. The buyer ordered five thousand blankets at roughly twelve dollars each, confident that the store could easily sell them for sixteen dollars. Izzi had similar success with other retailers. Some ordered even larger quantities. At least one retailer told Izzi he would put the blankets on the market for a competitive price in the fifteen-dollar range. Soon, Izzi had orders for all forty thousand blankets.

He had promised Gimbel's the first shipment, and so he returned to Utah to arrange for immediate transit of five thousand blankets. Once that was accomplished, he began making shipping arrangements for the remaining blankets. He was surprised to learn that the military's surplus disposal office ordered further shipments stopped, pending the resolution of some sort of legal issue. Izzi was frustrated. He had to contact all his New York buyers (except Gimbel's) to explain the situation. He felt he had disappointed his customers, and one of the greatest "sins" in the I. J. Wagner business moral code was failure to deliver on a promise.

After several weeks—and after Gimbel's had sold the first five thousand blankets—the shipping delay evaporated as quickly as it had occurred. Only later did Izzi learn that the chairman of Gimbel's Department Store was also chair of the civilian board that oversaw the disposal of war surplus materials. Obviously, Gimbel's chairman could not purchase the blankets directly; it would have been a conflict of interest. But Izzi was convinced that the chairman arranged to have the blankets "frozen" so his store could sell them at the higher price without fear of competition.

I. J. Wagner learned at least two things from the experience. First, he realized he had to have his own warehouse facilities in order to ensure that he could sell only items he had on hand. He was determined never again to disappoint his customers. Second, he realized the buying and selling of military surplus items offered real potential at the wholesale level. He was not inclined to enter the business on a retail level. He and his brother, Abe, organized a new company—American Consolidated, Inc.—for the sole purpose of dealing in surplus property. They chose the name because it implied a nationwide operation (which it was). They bought a warehouse not far from Wagner Bag Company. Abe handled the operational side of the new company, while Izzi concentrated on buying and selling. Through American

Consolidated, Izzi and Abe profitably moved a wide variety of surplus merchandise throughout the country.

The new company also offered Izzi opportunities to extend his circle of customers and friends to include merchandise buyers all across the nation. Wherever he traveled on sales trips related to the new business, he also contacted local bag and container companies. He eventually made contacts with managers from almost every bag and container company in the land. He became an active member of the bag manufacturers' association, and he joined organizations formed by those who were primary users of the bags produced by Wagner Bag—the potato growers' association, for example. The breakfast, lunch, and dinner schedule expanded to include new groups of friends in the nation's largest cities. Izzi and Jeanné traveled throughout the nation to attend meetings and conventions.

The lessons Izzi learned from Harry and Rose continued to serve him well. He knew there was a market for everything. Wagner Bag sold printed cotton bags to flour mills throughout Utah. The mills used the bags until they were no longer serviceable. Izzi bought the used bags and sold them to a laundry in Salt Lake City. The laundry bleached the bags, then cut them up for resale. Portions of bags that could not be bleached white were sold as rags and cleaning cloths. The whitened portions were made into dish towels for sale to area restaurants. The same laundry company had a plant in Ogden, forty miles north of Salt Lake. Managers at the Ogden laundry got the idea of buying used bags from flour mills in Ogden, bleaching them, and reselling them. But they didn't know what to do with bags that were damaged. Had they called their sister plant in Salt Lake, they would have learned about making dish towels and rags from torn cotton bags. Instead, the Ogden laundry called Izzi to ask if he was interested in buying damaged cotton bags. He was slightly miffed that the Ogden flour mills—some of his best customers—had cut him out of the used-bag loop, and so he agreed to buy the damaged bags from the Ogden laundry. Then he sold the materials for a profit to the laundry's parent company in Salt Lake City.

During the war, sugar companies switched from cotton bags to paper bags in order to help the war effort. Sugar was heavily rationed, but consumers with ration coupons could buy it in five-, ten-, or twenty-pound paper bags. After the war, sugar companies quickly converted back to cotton bags. One local sugar company, U&I Sugar, processed sugar from sugar beets. The company was owned by The Church of Jesus Christ of Latter-day Saints. When it came time to switch from paper to cotton bags, the company had hundreds of thousands of paper bags already printed with the U&I Sugar logo. U&I

was a good customer of Izzi's, and when he heard about the surplus paper bags, he offered to buy them for a penny each. He then turned around and sold the paper bags to the Utah State Liquor Commission for a penny and a half. The Liquor Commission was pleased to get the bags, because they were heavier than normal, and they were ideal for bagging retail liquor purchases at state-operated stores. In those days, it was illegal for Utah restaurants to sell alcoholic beverages, and so customers who wanted wine or a drink with their meals carried their own bottles in brown paper bags. The LDS Church does not approve of alcohol. One evening, a high church official who happened to be a friend of Izzi's was having dinner at the church-owned Hotel Utah. He noticed at tables around the room brown paper bags imprinted "U&I Sugar." The next day, he called Izzi to say that it did not look good for bags containing alcohol to be advertising the church-owned sugar company. Izzi immediately went to the State Liquor Commission, bought back all the paper bags with U&I imprints, and destroyed them. He knew that satisfied customers are more important, in the long run, than a few short-term dollars of profit.

Izzi Wagner believed in thinking, planning, and managing for the long term. Customers became lifelong friends, and their families became almost second families for Izzi. One of his customers and friends was Jim McNeil, who ran the Pillsbury flour operation in Ogden and later became a Pillsbury executive in Minneapolis. Izzi and Jim McNeil often played golf together and sometimes traveled together. Jim made sure Izzi became a member of the Ogden Country Club when other social groups refused to offer him membership. One day the McNeils and the Wagners were enjoying a swim at Utah's Lagoon resort. Jim's young son, J. C. McNeil, fell into the deep water. Izzi jumped in to pull him out. "Izzi saved my life," young McNeil later told friends. J. C. McNeil went on to create and head United Concerts, an organization that brings big-name entertainment to Utah and other venues. J. C. was often invited to Izzi's lunch meetings. "All through the years, Izzi has given me good advice," he said. Many other Wagner friends echo those sentiments.

In the early 1950s, Izzi and Jeanné moved from their duplex apartment into a house they bought in the Avenues section of Salt Lake City. Izzi and Abe also purchased a house on Fourth Avenue for Rose after a local furniture store bought Rose's property in Sugarhouse to use as part of a new parking area.

Abe did not marry until he was in his midforties. Until his marriage, he continued to live at home with his mother. The sale of the Sugarhouse

property was one of the first real estate transactions Izzi completed. It resulted in a handsome profit.

More important, the experience with Rose's house stimulated Izzi's interest in real estate. During the decade of the '50s, he would buy—and usually
sell—property on Salt Lake City's Main Street, on Third South, on First West,
and on Pierpont Street, as well as in Ogden and in Pocatello, Idaho. He
planned to expand the Wagner Bag plant, and so he bought as much property around the facility as he could. Surviving records show that in 1957 he
bought a building at 21 West Third South for $30,000. He would later lease
it to Skyline Office Supply for $400 a month. Records of many other pur-
chases and sales were not saved.

As Izzi moved into real estate, Wagner Bag Company continued to grow.
Izzi worried about how to protect the family-owned business in case anything happened to one of the members. In 1950, he had his lawyers draw up
a survivors' agreement. It provided that if Rose, Abe, Izzi, or Leona should
die, that person's interest would be divided among the remaining family
members. The agreement listed the total value of Wagner Bag Company as
$193,129.91. By the end of the decade, that number would increase signifi-
cantly, as evidenced by a number of events that would unfold during the
decade.

By 1952, Wagner Bag Company was the only factory of its kind between
Denver and the West Coast. The company served primarily farmers and grain
mills.

Izzi worried that Bamberger Railroad might remove the rail spur from behind the Wagner plant. (The spur branched from the line going north on First
West. It ran behind the Wagner plant east to the midpoint of what is now the
Peery Hotel.) In 1953, the Wagners negotiated an agreement with the Bamberger interests to keep the spur in operation unless Wagner Bag Company
"shall not use said spur track for a period of one year." The negotiations provided yet another connection for Izzi—this one with the Bamberger family,
which owned considerable property in downtown Salt Lake City.

In the spring of 1952, Salt Lake City experienced one of its periodic spring
floods. Spring weather turned suddenly very hot, and heavy snowpack in
nearby mountains melted faster than streams and storm sewers could handle
it. Water ran through city streets, and the city desperately needed thousands of
sandbags to channel the raging water. The same was true for other cities and
counties in Utah. The only source of the burlap bags used for sandbags was
Wagner Bag. In order to meet the heavy demand for bags, the company hired
extra employees and scheduled twenty-four-hour operations. Hundreds of

thousands of bags flowed from the little factory on Third South to flood sites around the state. They were filled with sand by volunteers and stacked to create protective walls along streambeds and sidewalks. Sandbagged streets carried water several feet deep. Wagner sold the bags to government units at a sizable discount. Yes, Wagner made a profit, but according to one newspaper account, the company was "credited as one of the 'prime factors' in the saving of millions of dollars of industrial and private properties from damage." The flood experience would be repeated again thirty years later under quite different circumstances.

Wagner Bag Company grew rapidly during the boom years of the early '50s. In 1953, the company built sizable additions to the front and west of the original location at 144 West Third South. Whenever nearby property became available, Izzi bought it, thinking it would provide for continuing expansion of the business. In 1955, he bought property surrounding the Miles Hotel (now the Peery Hotel) as far north as Pierpont Street. According to the *Deseret News,* he paid one hundred thousand dollars for it. He then turned most of it into a parking lot for his employees and employees of other nearby businesses until such time as he would need it for plant expansion.

Shortly after the purchase, property immediately west of Wagner Bag Company became available, unexpectedly. Izzi had extended the organization's resources about as far as he and Rose thought prudent. They didn't know how they could take advantage of the opportunity to expand west. Izzi mentioned his dilemma to Jeanné. She said she had sixty-five hundred dollars in a savings account that she was willing to loan to the company. Appropriately, the property she helped buy is now the location of the Jeanné Wagner Theatre in the Rose Wagner Performing Arts Center.

Across Third South from Wagner Bag Company was the Bristol Hotel. As mentioned earlier, it was a brothel operated by a woman named Kitty. Kitty and her husband, Sam Spiegel, owned the hotel. In the late 1950s, when Sam died and Kitty moved into a rest home, Izzi bought the Bristol Hotel. He also bought another small hotel east of the Bristol. For a short time, he rented rooms to minorities who were denied rooms by other hotel owners. Eventually, he razed both buildings to make room for a parking lot used by his employees and customers.

Wagner Bag Company also expanded its product line to include bags made from cotton, synthetic mesh (primarily for onions), and paper. The company manufactured potato bags, flour bags, cement bags, and other varieties made of burlap, cotton, and paper. Izzi added employees and equipment. Young women were hired to sew bags on rows of sewing machines. Many were students at local colleges and universities, looking for part-time work. Heavy equipment was purchased to handle huge rolls of burlap. Izzi bought printing presses to print the burlap, folding machines to fold it, and more sewing machines. The first piece of heavy machinery—although used—represented a large investment, and the Wagners agonized over whether it would pay for itself (it did—easily).

Actually, one of the first pieces of equipment they bought soon after the war was a used forklift to move the heavy bales of raw burlap and the equally heavy bales of finished bags. Previously, Izzi and Abe and other workers had manually maneuvered the materials, using hand trucks and wooden ramps. When Izzi bought the forklift, Rose and Abe thought he was extravagant: why buy a machine when humans could do the job, as they had always done? It took only a couple of weeks with the efficiency of the forklift for everyone to embrace the value of machines.

Machinery was difficult to find for a number of years following World War II, as demand was high. During his travels, Izzi used his many contacts to locate machinery for sale. He bought and sold used machinery the way he once bought and sold used bottles. He found a press in Louisville, Kentucky, that could print two colors on bags. He bought a cut-and-fold machine to speed up production.

When new equipment arrived at the plant, Izzi was like a child with a new toy. He insisted on learning to operate most new equipment, beginning with that first forklift. When Wagner Bag bought its first truck-trailer rig during this same period, Izzi himself drove it to Pocatello to deliver the first shipment of bags. He stopped at truck stops along the way, talked to other drivers, and learned about their interests and concerns. When he returned, he knew about how to create and maintain a fleet of trucks, information he would find useful as the company grew.

During this period, Izzi also made it a point to share his success with others. Across the street from Wagner Bag Company was J. G. McDonald's Candy Company. The candy company came on hard times and eventually went bankrupt. Izzi bought most of the candy-making equipment in order to help a neighbor and friend pay creditors. Then he advised the company to rename itself "Mrs. J. G. McDonald's Candy Company," which would make it easier to start anew. Then Izzi sold back the candy-making equipment on very good terms. He said his profit on that transaction was "slim to none."

By 1953, Wagner Bag Company occupied thirty thousand square feet of factory and office space, employed seventy persons, and had a gross annual revenue of two million dollars. The company imported a million yards of burlap each year. It had its own trucking operation, its own art department, its own printing plant, and a production line that produced fifty thousand bags a day.

Izzi took pride in the way he treated his employees. He remembered well his own struggles during the Great Depression and his mother's generosity with those who had even less than the Wagners. When employees had personal problems, it was not uncommon for Izzi to help out—sometimes openly, and sometimes with well-disguised assistance. He often provided jobs to those in need and to family members of good friends and clients. Sometimes, his attempts to help did not work as he had planned. He was especially disappointed when his generosity was turned against him.

On one occasion, an associate came to Izzi one day to say that money was missing from the company strongbox. The same report was repeated several times. Each theft involved only small amounts, but over time the thefts amounted to a meaningful sum. Izzi could not believe anyone would steal money from the company, especially an employee. One evening, he left the plant as usual, went to a social event, and then returned quietly to station himself where he could watch the office where the strongbox was kept. Izzi had given the son of one of his good customers a job on the night shift to help him out. As Izzi watched, the son sneaked into the office to steal from the strongbox. Izzi confronted him and fired him on the spot. He did not bring charges, but he said telling his friend and customer about the theft by his son was one of the hardest things he had ever done.

Izzi's sister, Leona, was married to an artist named Burnam Pearlman. Pearlman's art career wasn't going so well in California, and so the couple moved back to Utah to see if Pearlman could succeed in another line of work. Izzi hired his brother-in-law as a salesman, but his career at Wagner Bag didn't last long. Izzi said Pearlman always saw the world with an artist's eyes, and he could not make the adjustment necessary to succeed in a business routine. Izzi talked with Leona and Burnam. He encouraged them to return to California where Burnam would have a better chance to succeed as an artist...and where Leona could return to her job in a Beverly Hills jewelry store. Izzi assured Leona that she would be protected from financial disaster through her share of ownership in the family enterprises.

Izzi's good intentions created more problems when he hired the son of another loyal customer. The young man became a leader in efforts to unionize the Wagner plant. Wagner Bag Company paid employees as much—and often a little more—than competitors. Izzi resisted efforts to unionize the company, not so much because he did not like unions as because he believed unionization was a criticism of his personal values and management ability. On two occasions, unionization efforts went so far as to organize a workers' strike against Wagner Bag Company. Izzi considered the strike to be a betrayal of the trust he had extended by offering the young man a job. His anger was directed as much at the individual as it was at the union. He was determined to prove the point that his workers would not have acted had they not been misled by the young organizer. Izzi hired workers to "crash" the picket lines. He personally led them through the line. He said the union appealed to his workers not by promising higher wages but by promising an additional day off for birthdays. He was already providing more paid holidays than his competitors, and he believed one more vacation day was not justified.

Another important event that would have lifelong impact on Izzi occurred during the 1950s. One day, a young man named Roy Simmons walked through the front door of Wagner Bag Company. He was looking for burlap to use in a duck blind he was building on the Farmington Bay of Great Salt Lake. Simmons was an up-and-coming banker in Utah. He would eventually buy Zions Bank and build it into one of the major banks of western America. Beginning with that casual meeting, Roy Simmons and I. J. Wagner "hit it off" immediately. They became close friends and business partners on many real estate transactions over the years. They lunched together hundreds of times, each learning from the other. They shared ideas and dreamed dreams. Although they would complete transactions amounting to hundreds of millions, they never had a signed business-partnership contract. Their relationship was built on trust and integrity. They eventually formed Keystone Company as a holding company for their real estate activities.

Theirs was an unlikely friendship—the liberal Democrat Jewish atheist bag salesman and the conservative Republican Mormon banker. But they had much in common. Both came from the most humble of backgrounds. (Simmons was an orphaned child who experienced several different homes and foster parents before his adoptive mother divorced an abusive mate and made her way to Utah when Roy was nine years old.) Both began working at very young ages and worked long, hard hours for years before achieving success. Both dropped out of the university for economic reasons. Both became very successful in their chosen professions. Both contributed considerable time, energy, and talent toward improving the community.

The friendship grew over half a century, based on common interests, understanding, and trust. Together, Wagner and Simmons would engage in so many business transactions that the details were forgotten by both. It was not uncommon to ride with them through the city and hear Izzi say to Roy,

"Didn't we own that building once?" Roy might respond, "By golly, I think we did."

One of their first business deals came when Izzi realized that the location of a bag factory in downtown Salt Lake City was becoming less and less viable. His plan had always been to remain near the city center, but it began to look as if that might not be the best business plan. He had purchased considerable property around his building, but he realized he could never accumulate enough downtown property to accommodate the company's long-term needs. Transportation was also a growing problem. Sometimes, it took several days and considerable expense to move boxcars up onto the rail spur that ran behind Wagner Bag Company. At the same time, the city and its traffic were growing rapidly. It appeared only a matter of time before the downtown rail spur would be shut down, in which case the company would have to depend totally on truck deliveries, not a good alternative for the bulky raw materials and finished product of Wagner Bag Company.

Izzi began looking for new property on which to build an expanded factory. In the latter part of the 1950s, he found 120 acres bordering a rail yard operated by the Denver and Rio Grande Railroad. The land was on the southwest border of the city and near a new freeway then in the planning stages. It promised to solve the increasing transportation problems experienced by Wagner Bag Company. Izzi talked it over with Roy Simmons, and the two decided to see if they could purchase the property. Izzi did not have the resources to make the purchase, but the two decided they could borrow most of the money if the property was for sale at a reasonable price. At the time, it was nothing more than 120 acres of dust and weeds.

Izzi learned through his lunch meetings how and why the property came to be owned by the D&RG. Company officials hoped to entice industrial firms into locating on the property so those firms could conveniently use D&RG to transport raw materials and finished goods. Izzi approached company officials and convinced them that he would do a better job of attracting businesses to the vacant property than the railroad had done or was likely to do. He told them that if they would sell the property, he and his partner would guarantee that 75 percent of it would be used for manufacturing and warehousing—businesses that would need railroad transportation. He told them his own company, Wagner Bag, would become the anchor tenant, and provided data showing that his company was a heavy user of rail transportation.

The railroad agreed to sell the property for one thousand dollars an acre. Roy and Izzi put together the finances to buy the land, created a development plan, and began building the infrastructure. They agreed to call the development "Wagner Industrial Park." It may have been Utah's first industrial park (certainly, it was one of the first). The two partners would more than double the original acreage over the next few months, as Izzi identified other property owners and convinced them to sell. Among other things, the partners gave Salt Lake County sufficient right-of-way to build a major roadway through the development, the first major north-south connecting road in the area west of the planned freeway. In order to guarantee adequate road access, Izzi used his best salesmanship to convince county officials that the weeded acres would soon become a bustling warehouse and manufacturing center—a prediction that proved absolutely correct.

At the same time, Izzi also had to raise money and develop plans for a new Wagner Bag manufacturing plant, a facility that would require 140,000 square feet of manufacturing and warehouse space.

Even before the new Wagner Bag facility was under construction, Izzi tackled the daunting challenge of filling the remaining acres of Wagner Industrial Park. He heard at one of his lunch gatherings that General Electric (GE) was considering a warehousing operation in Salt Lake City, and so he flew to New York to meet with GE officials. He convinced them that Wagner Industrial Park would be the perfect location for the GE warehouse: close to rail lines and the interstate highway. Eventually, half a dozen vice presidents from General Electric came to Salt Lake to look at the property and close the deal. They needed five acres.

Izzi worried all night about what price to ask for the property. By the time the meeting convened the next morning, he and Roy had agreed to price it at two thousand dollars an acre—twice what they had paid for it. After the preliminaries, the GE officials asked about the price. Izzi told them it would be ten thousand dollars, thinking they were asking about the total sales price for the five acres. The vice presidents excused themselves to confer in another room. Izzi and Roy worried they might have asked too much. They needed a big name such as General Electric in the park in order to establish credibility and make the other portions easier to sell. They worried that their asking price might derail the important transaction. Eventually, the GE officials returned. Izzi and Roy waited nervously for their response. After the requisite hemming and hawing about the high price of land in Salt Lake City, the GE officials said they agreed to the purchase price, and that ten thousand dollars an acre would be acceptable. Izzi and Roy could hardly believe what they had heard, but they quickly signed the contract.

From that experience, Izzi learned a lesson he would not forget: the seller should never set the price. You may know what a piece of property is worth to you, said I. J. Wagner, but you have no idea what it may be worth to a potential buyer. In fact, he learned later that General Electric was prepared to pay considerably more for the five acres—as much as two or three times the price agreed upon.

It was a good time to buy business property in the Salt Lake area. Like most American cities, Salt Lake was growing. At the same time, the national economy was doing very well, creating inflation and forcing prices up. Whatever one might purchase was almost sure to be worth more in a few months.

The Wagner and Simmons partnership never lost money on a real estate investment, and they broke even only once. That was on the occasion they bought a corner lot near Wagner Industrial Park but inside Salt Lake City limits, thinking it would be a good future location for some sort of business—a service station, for example. They held on to the property for quite a while.

In the meantime, Zions Bank—the bank Roy Simmons headed—was growing, building branch banks in various parts of the city. The bank looked at the possibility of building a branch bank in Wagner Industrial Park, but the bank's lawyers determined that certain rules and regulations made it more advantageous to build a branch bank within city limits. The industrial park was just outside city limits. The bank looked at various properties but decided the best location would be the corner owned by Wagner and Simmons. The market price by then was considerably more than the partners had paid for the property, but when Izzi heard about the bank's desire to build at that location, he told Roy they should sell the property for exactly what they had paid for it; otherwise, it might appear to be a conflict of interest for Roy. Zions Bank got a very good deal on that particular bank location—and the partners broke even, except for a few incidental costs that they decided to absorb.

Izzi and Roy were always playing practical jokes on one another. Izzi drove by the corner described above every day on his way to work. On several occasions, he saw a man selling fruit out of the back of his pickup truck parked on the vacant lot owned by Wagner and Simmons. One morning, he stopped to ask the man if he had permission to use the lot as a business location. Izzi told the fruit salesman that he owned the lot. The salesman asked if he could pay rent. Izzi said he would not collect rent, but if the fruit vendor would give him a sack of oranges once a week, that would be sufficient. He picked up the oranges for two or three weeks, and of course he told Roy about it during one of their lunch meetings.

A few days later, Roy stopped by the vacant lot and asked the fruit vendor why he was using the lot as a business location. The vendor said the owner had given him permission. Roy put on his best act of indignation. (He had once been an amateur actor.) He told the vender that he, Roy, was the owner and that someone was putting one over on the fruit salesman. The next time Izzi stopped by for his oranges, the fruit vendor grabbed his arm through the car window, twisted it, and accused Izzi of cheating him, saying that the "real" owner had been by the day before. Izzi asked what the "real" owner looked like.

When Izzi got to his office, he called Roy and threatened to sue him, claiming that the muscular fruit vendor had broken his arm. He told Roy that at the very least he would have to pay his doctor bill. There was no broken arm and no doctor bill, but the two friends laughed about the incident for years to come.

Prior to these shenanigans, Izzi was preparing plans for the new Wagner Bag Company plant in Wagner Industrial Park. The company continued to grow and prosper. I. J. Wagner added constantly to the company's customer base, wooing clients from other suppliers by providing higher quality, superior service, and that unmatched Wagner congeniality. A few years later, Wagner told an interviewer that his business philosophy was simple: "Success is when preparation meets opportunity." Superb preparation was about to be confronted with an opportunity no one expected.

Herschel Wigrizer (Harry Wagner) (*right rear*) married "Polly" Susman (*at his right*) about 1890. The newlyweds were photographed with the Susman family in the Ukraine.

Harry Wagner (Herschel Wigrizer) and Rose Yuddin were married in Boston in 1911, where their wedding portrait was taken.

The Orpheum Theatre (now the Capitol) was one block east and one block north of the Wagner home (1917). Izzi Wagner performed as a bareback rider on the stage of the Orpheum when he was about eight years old. (Used by permission, Utah State Historical Society, all rights reserved)

The Walker Bank Building (1914) was at the center of Salt Lake's business district, only two blocks from the Wagner home. Young Izzi dreamed of being wealthy enough to own property on Main Street. He would eventually own almost a full block of Main Street property. (Used by permission, Utah State Historical Society, all rights reserved)

The Wagner family enjoyed Sunday outings in a buggy pulled by Harry's horse, Queenie. Rose and Izzi are in the backseat. Harry and Abe are in front (1915).

Abe, Izzi, and Leona Wagner model the military-look clothing that was popular in 1919.

Abe and Izzi "sparred" in 1919 wearing clothing designed to look like military uniforms in the World War I era.

Hank Milano and Izzi Wagner became friends when they were childhood neighbors (circa 1925). Their friendship would span more than eighty years.

Fruit stands were standard features around the city in the 1920s. Both Izzi and Abe worked at such establishments. Abe is second from the right (circa 1928).

Rose Yuddin Wagner and her sister Ethel Yuddin were reunited in Salt Lake City during the 1920s, after more than a decade of separation (circa 1930).

During the Great Depression, as much as one-third of the work force was unemployed. During his formative years, Izzi saw many public works projects funded by the government. Here, workers improve the roadbed for the streetcar line on South Temple and Main near Hotel Utah. (Used by permission, Utah State Historical Society, all rights reserved)

Abe Wagner is at the wheel of the family's seven-passenger Lincoln Town Car. Leona Wagner stands on the running board. The Yuddin sisters are in the foreground— Rose Yuddin Wagner, Ethel Yuddin, and Mary Yuddin Karras (1932).

Izzi Wagner and his dog, Shep, are at the rear of Wagner Bag Company with the Lincoln Town Car. The old Salt Lake High School is in the background (1932).

In about 1934, Izzi Wagner (*left*) and his life-long friend Hank Milano visited the famous Brown Derby restaurant on Wilshire Boulevard in Los Angeles.

Izzi Wagner dated Marjorie Brown for several years. More than once he thought seriously about proposing to her (1938).

In 1938, I. J. Wagner posed at a Los Angeles photo studio. The somber pose was designed to impress movie casting agents.

In 1938, Izzi Wagner and his Plymouth coupe could often be found at Black Rock Beach, west of Salt Lake City.

Izzi Wagner struck his best Hollywood pose for another of the photos intended for his movie portfolio (1938).

Wagner's Steaks and Chops was located in the Proctor Hotel at 1413 West Ninth Street in Los Angeles. Izzi bought the restaurant in 1934. His partner, Charles Zender, is behind the counter with an unnamed waitress.

In 1934, nineteen-year-old Izzi Wagner bought a load of used brick and hired an out-of-work mason to add about twelve feet to the front of the Wagner house as an office for Wagner Bag Company. Izzi himself painted the sign above the door.

The Wagners added a second addition to the front of the building in 1939, bringing the front door to the sidewalk. Other additions were constructed earlier on the east and west sides of the building.

Shortly after he returned to civilian life in 1945, I. J. Wagner remodeled the Wagner Bag Company to unify the working area and add more space for manufacturing. He expanded to the east and added a second, more visible, sign.

In 1959, Wagner Bag Company was still located at 144 West Third South, the same address as the adobe house in which I. J. Wagner was born. The location is now the site of the Rose Wagner Performing Arts Center.

Jeanné Doré (Rasmussen) traveled the vaudeville circuit for a decade prior to the time she met I. J. Wagner. Her show-business portfolio included this portrait, taken in the mid-1930s. Izzi Wagner and Jeanné were married in 1942.

One of Jeanné Doré's most popular numbers was the Mexican hat dance. She designed and made her own costumes (1937).

In April 1942, Private I. J. Wagner arranged a weekend pass from Marine boot camp so he could be with Jeanné. They went to the Latin Quarter in San Diego.

Private I. J. Wagner was able to visit Salt Lake at least once during boot camp, as evidenced by the sharpshooter medals on his dress uniform during this Salt Lake City visit with his mother, Rose, in 1942.

After several weeks of being virtually pinned down on the beach at Guadalcanal, I. J. Wagner's headquarters company was able to erect an operations tent. Izzi sent this photo to Jeanné with this note on the back: "Darling: This picture was taken on February 10th, 1943 on Guadalcanal, Solomon Is. You might have it enlarged to an 8x10 and give a copy to mother. /s/ I. J. Wagner. Left to right, 1st row: Major F. P. Henderson, Lt. Col. Jessie Cook, Capt. Richard Johnson; 2nd row: PFC Andreozzi, PFC Bray, Corp. Cane, 1st Sgt. Shuman, Pvt. Berry, Corp. I. J. Wagner."

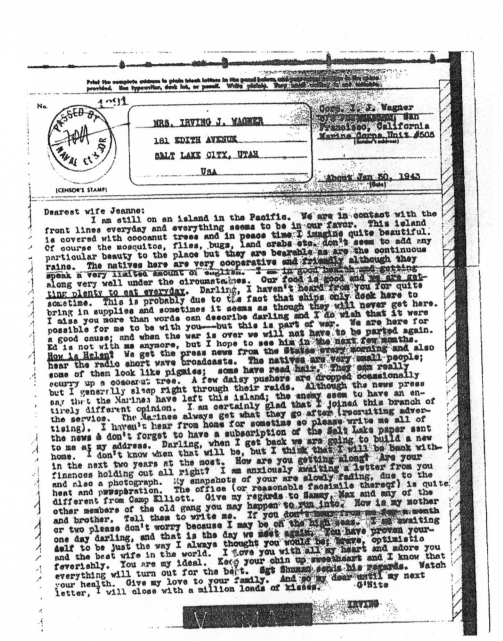

No. 1091

MRS. IRVING J. WAGNER

181 EDITH AVENUE

SALT LAKE CITY, UTAH

USA

(CENSOR'S STAMP)

Corp. J. J. Wagner
c/o Postmaster, San
Francisco, California
Marine Corps Unit #505

About Jan 30, 1943

Dearest wife Jeanne:

I am still on an island in the Pacific. We are in contact with the front lines everyday and everything seems to be in our favor. This island is covered with coocanut trees and in peace time I imagine quite beautiful. Of course the mosquitos, flies, bugs, land crabs etc. don't seem to add any particular beauty to the place but they are bearable as are the continuous rains. The natives here are very cooperative and friendly although they speak a very limited amount of english. I am in good health and getting along very well under the circumstances. Our food is good and we are getting plenty to eat everyday. Darling, I haven't heard from you for quite sometime. This is probably due to the fact that ships only dock here to bring in supplies and sometimes it seems as though they will never get here. I miss you more than words can describe darling and I do wish that it were possible for me to be with you——but this is part of war. We are here for a good cause; and when the war is over we will not have to be parted again. Ed is not with me anymore, but I hope to see him in the next few months. How is Helen? We get the press news from the States every morning and also hear the radio short wave broadcasts. The natives are very small people; some of them look like pigmies; some have read hair. They can really scurry up a coocanut tree. A few daisy pushers are dropped occasionally but I generally sleep right through their raids. Although the news press say that the Marines have left this island; the enemy seem to have an entirely different opinion. I am certainly glad that I joined this branch of the service. The Marines always get what they go after (recruiting advertising). I haven't hear from home for sometime so please write me all of the news & don't forget to have a subscription of the Salt Lake paper sent to me at my address. Darling, when I get back we are going to build a new home. I don't know when that will be, but I think that I will be back within the next two years at the most. How are you getting along? Are your finances holding out all right? I am anxiously awaiting a letter from you and also a photograph. My snapshots of your are slowly fading, due to the heat and pewsparation. The office (or reasonable facsimile thereof) is quite different from Camp Elliott. Give my regards to Sammy, Max and any of the other members of the old gang you may happen to run into. How is my mother and brother. Tell them to write me. If you don't hear from me for a month or two please don't worry because I may be on the high seas. I am awaiting one day darling, and that is the day we meet again. You have proven yourself to be just the way I always thought you would be, brave, optimistic and the best wife in the world. I love you with all my heart and adore you feverishly. You are my ideal. Keep your chin up sweetheart and I know that everything will turn out for the best. Sgt Shuman sends his regards. Watch your health. Give my love to your family. And so my dear until my next letter, I will close with a million loads of kisses.

G'Nite

IRVING

Izzi sent this v-mail to Jeanné in January 1943. Some of the words were code words the two agreed upon before he left. For example, any use of the name "Helen" was code for "Guadalcanal." It was common practice for military personnel to use code with family and friends in order to circumvent military censorship. (Note the censor's stamp at upper left.)

In 1945, Izzi Wagner created and trademarked a cartoon logo for the company. He called it "Wagbag," and it was used on trucks, letterhead, and other materials.

I. J. Wagner's mother, Rose Wagner, loved music. In her later years, she taught herself to play the piano (about 1950).

In about 1955, I. J. and Jeanné Wagner moved into a house in the Avenues section of Salt Lake City.

In the 1950s, bags were sewn by hand at Wagner Bag Company. Young women attending local colleges and universities were often hired by the company.

In about 1955, the Wagner family came together at Izzi and Jeanné's new house. *Left to right:* Abe Wagner, Rose Wagner, Leona Wagner Pearlman, Burnam Pearlman, Jeanné Rasmussen Wagner, and I. J. Wagner.

By 1958, Wagner Bag had installed much heavy machinery to produce many varieties of bags. Izzi Wagner took pride in the company's ability to fill small orders for local growers.

Rose Wagner provided the foundation for Wagner Bag Company's success. When she died in 1959, she knew her efforts had resulted in a secure future for her family.

Utah governor George Dewey Clyde (*center*) welcomed St. Regis
Paper Company vice president Peter Sloan at the grand opening of
the new Wagner Bag Company plant in 1960. As usual, Izzi Wagner found something to laugh about.

Guests at the banquet celebrating the opening of the new Wagner Bag
Company plant in 1960 included Salt Lake City mayor J. Bracken
Lee and Mrs. Lee (*center*), Salt Lake Chamber of Commerce presi-
dent Gus Backman (*far right*), and Izzi Wagner (*next to Backman*).

During the 1960 open house of the new Wagner Bag Company plant, visitors received a thorough tour of the complex bag-making process.

Izzi Wagner's office at the new Wagner Bag Company plant was large and well appointed. He had the circular desk custom made, modeled after a desk he had seen in another executive's office in Los Angeles (1963).

In 1964, I. J. Wagner (*front row, bow tie*) spearheaded a campaign to create parking space behind businesses on Main Street and Third South. He organized local business leaders to accomplish the task. Others in the photo include television news anchor Doug Mitchell (*far left*), Mayor J. Bracken Lee (*second from left*), bookstore owner Sam Weller (*fourth from right, rear*), Lou Callister Sr. (*behind Izzi's left shoulder*), Henry Pullman (*far right*), Chamber of Commerce president Gus Backman (*second from right, rear*), and others.

The Wagner home offered unobstructed views of Salt Lake Valley from inside the house and from the garden terrace at the rear. A few years later, Izzi and Jeanné would change the circular drive to make room for a garden room and a second two-car garage. They also covered a portion of the terrace to provide shade for outdoor gatherings.

Izzi and Jeanné stood on the terrace at the rear of the home in 1968.

During the 1970s, Izzi Wagner introduced his wife, Jeanné, to Marjorie Brown, one of his women friends from before 1940. The two became good friends. Ms. Brown lived in California, and Izzi stayed in touch with her for many years. The Great Dane, Kodo, became part of the Wagner household. Kodo was often seen riding with Izzi or Jeanné in one of their convertibles, his head well above the windshield.

Utah governor Calvin L. Rampton prepares to sign the repeal of the state's inventory tax in 1979. *Standing, left to right:* Chris Johnson, Senator Warren Pugh, Rick Warner, Vern Brazell, I. J. Wagner, and William Cockayne.

I. J. Wagner considered as his friends many general authorities of The Church of Jesus Christ of Latter-day Saints. He served on the Hotel Utah board of directors with several LDS Church presidents, including Spencer W. Kimball (*left*).

Izzi Wagner spent considerable time on golf courses, including this course in Hawaii, during the annual Wagner vacations (1983). He was a good golfer, and he had several holes in one to his credit.

Jeanné Wagner prepares for an evening out in about 1987. She is standing in the living room of the Wagner house.

Jeanné Wagner learned to design and make her own clothes during her years in show business. She continued to design her clothes throughout her life, partly because her petite size made it difficult for her to find clothing she liked that fitted.

I. J. Wagner (*center*) associated with some of the most influential men and women in Utah, including Thomas S. Monson of the First Presidency of The Church of Jesus Christ of Latter-day Saints (*left*) and Earl J. Holding of Sinclair Oil, Little America Hotel, and other business operations (*right*).

I. J. Wagner (*left*) and Roy Simmons (*right*) were friends and partners for more than fifty years. Jeanné Wagner smiles her approval for another of their many handshake deals.

Dee Smith (*left*), founder of the Smith's Food King grocery chain, was one of Izzi Wagner's close friends. He was also an important customer of Wagner Bag. Bill Hazelton (*right*) was an executive of St. Regis Paper Company. The Smiths, the Hazeltons, and the Wagners were on their way to an unspecified destination in a St. Regis corporate jet (about 1980).

Dick Van Winkle (*left*) and Izzi Wagner (*right*) were classmates at West High School in 1930. Both went on to become community leaders. Salt Lake County's Van Winkle Expressway is named after the banker and transportation leader (about 1975).

Impresario Jim McNeil Jr. was the son of I. J. Wagner's longtime
friend and customer James McNeil Sr. with the Pillsbury Company
(1996).

When Jeanné Wagner died in 1993, Izzi placed a double tombstone in
Salt Lake City's Congregation B'Nai Israel Cemetery. The tombstone
reads, "All our dreams came true."

For more than fifty years, Roy Simmons (*left*) and I. J. Wagner (*right*) were close friends, handshake partners, and community leaders. Roy's wife, Elizabeth "Tibby" Simmons, added her own valuable input to the friendship (1996).

At age eighty-one, Izzi Wagner still played golf regularly. The 1996 Arthritis Foundation tournament team was (*left to right*) attorney Charles Bennett, police chief Ruben Ortega, Izzi Wagner, LDS Church apostle Robert Hales, and clothing entrepreneur Mac Christensen.

When legendary television producer Fred W. Friendly came to
Utah to record a series of televised discussions about the U. S.
Constitution, I. J. Wagner was one of the panelists (about 1985).

I. J. Wagner and his sister-in-law, Kay Schott, greeted Lech Walesa, former president of Poland, when he visited Salt Lake City in 1998.

I. J. Wagner (*left*) greets Israeli prime minister Shimon Peres in 1998. Irene Tannenbaum looked on. Izzi and Jeanné Wagner visited Israel on at least two occasions.

Saundra Peterson, Kay Schott, and I. J. Wagner break ground for the Rose Wagner Performing Arts Center in 1999. Shovels entered the ground at the exact spot where once stood the adobe house in which Izzi Wagner was born. Across the street behind them was the former Boston Hotel, managed for many years by Izzi's aunt Ethel Yuddin.

Izzi Wagner memorialized his mother, wife, and sister and the place where he was born when he provided funding for Salt Lake County's Rose Wagner Performing Arts Center.

Photos of I. J. and Jeanné Wagner are prominently featured in the front hallway of the Jewish Community Center. Izzi used the center's exercise room at least three or four times a week until shortly before his death.

6

An Offer No One Could Refuse

In 1958, IZZI WAS WORKING HARD on plans for a new and expanded Wagner Bag manufacturing plant. He had already done some planning for expansion on the Third South site, where he had purchased a considerable amount of property near the existing building. However, the creation of Wagner Industrial Park eliminated the downtown option. Planning was no longer restricted by the shape of the property and the need to keep the plant operating during construction. He could now plan a building from the ground up to meet his own specifications. He had already visited every other bag manufacturing plant in the nation; he knew their strengths and their shortcomings. He was determined to have the most efficient and up-to-date plant in the world. He also wanted Wagner Bag Company to be a showcase for the new industrial park. It would be the catalyst for industrial development in what was then a barren landscape located far from what had traditionally been the industrial center of Salt Lake Valley. In Izzi's mind, Wagner Bag Company would set the standards for others who would locate in the park.

I. J. Wagner put in motion the necessary activities to design and construct a 140,000-square-foot building that would combine administrative offices, manufacturing, warehousing, and shipping. The new facility would be almost five times the size of the existing plant on Third South, and it would employ about twice as many workers. The cost of the new plant would be at least a million and a half dollars, and so another challenge facing him was to secure financing.

At the same time, Izzi Wagner and Roy Simmons made plans for development of Wagner Industrial Park. They were determined that whatever happened at the new park would be of the highest quality. They established strict zoning requirements on the property. Every building had to have a brick or stone front, with the same treatment running at least 24 feet on each side of the building. Setbacks were established at 50 or 35 feet, depending on whether buildings were on the main street or side streets. Paved parking and landscaping were required. Only light manufacturing and warehousing were permitted. No smoke, dust, or "packing house" odors were allowed. As a result of these strict covenants, property values in Wagner Park increased faster than values at any other industrial area in the state. (According to the University of Utah Bureau of Economic and Business Research, the land value was eight thousand dollars an acre in 1959, but it had become sixty thousand dollars an acre by 1977.)

More than a decade later, Izzi summarized his feelings about Wagner Industrial Park in a newspaper interview: "We have provided through the Park thousands of jobs for local residents. It is all the result of good planning. I believe in strong zoning codes and strong enforcement.... Necessity never makes a good bargain. We planned to put the land to the best and highest use for the long pull. As a result, everyone has benefitted."

While he was deeply involved with planning his new facility and developing Wagner Industrial Park, Izzi received a call from the president of St. Regis Paper Company, a major supplier of paper and paper products. The St. Regis president said he would like to meet with Izzi in New York, because he had a business proposition to discuss. St. Regis was one of the largest companies in the paper industry, with seventy-one plants, twenty-five thousand employees, and more than three million acres of timber land. The company's sales in 1959 would approach five hundred million dollars.

In New York, St. Regis officials told Izzi that a large bag company in Texas, Lone Star Bag and Bagging Company, was in financial trouble. Izzi knew the company well because he had been doing business with the Houston company. Wagner Bag was not yet ready to manufacture paper bags in huge quantities, and so Izzi had located a manufacturer in Texas who could meet his needs. Lone Star manufactured a few burlap and cotton bags, but the emphasis was on paper bags. According to St. Regis officials, the Texas company had ordered large quantities of paper from St. Regis and was now unable to pay the bills. St. Regis did not want to force the company into bankruptcy, because the company not only was a major paper buyer but also served many customers who also bought products from St. Regis, and St.

Regis wanted to protect its customer list. Paper company officials decided the best course of action would be for St. Regis to purchase the Texas company.

The problem was, the officials explained, that St. Regis already owned a number of firms involved in the manufacture of paper products. Company officers knew that federal government regulators were looking into the vertical integration practices of the giant company. It was quite apparent that a St. Regis purchase of the Texas company would not please government regulators unless the Texas company moved more aggressively into the manufacture of burlap and other textile bags, thus de-emphasizing paper products. Officials explained to Izzi that in order to avoid government attention, they had devised a complex strategy involving Wagner Bag. They suggested to Izzi that Lone Star purchase Wagner in order to expand Lone Star's capacity in burlap- and cloth-bag manufacturing. At the same time, Wagner Bag's growing activity in the paper-bag business would be a natural "fit" for the Texas company's operation, the St. Regis officials explained. (They did not tell Izzi something he already knew—that Wagner Bag was marketing its products so successfully that the small Utah company was cutting deeply into the customer base of St. Regis firms. In fact, St. Regis had come to know about Wagner Bag as a result of an internal investigation to identify the "little guy in Utah" who was taking so much business away from them. Izzi told friends later that St. Regis had problems because they didn't know much about customer relations. "They throw all kinds of money at it," he said, "but they never apply the personal touch.")

St. Regis further sweetened the proposal by letting Izzi know that the company would merge Wagner Bag Company into the St. Regis operation after an appropriate delay designed to satisfy government regulators. The Wagner company would be able to keep its name. Izzi listened to the unexpected proposal in his usual noncommittal fashion. He told them he was planning a new and modern plant in Salt Lake, and that he was looking forward to managing the expanded Utah operation, and so he needed to think it over. He also suggested that with his knowledge and experience he might be able to correct the problems at the Texas firm so that the purchase might not be necessary.

St. Regis officials listened with interest to every suggestion offered by Wagner. But he could not change their minds. Apparently, they wanted very badly to conclude a transaction. Izzi knew from their comments that he would have considerable leverage as negotiations proceeded. As usual, he intuitively understood more about the company's need than company officials were willing to tell him. And as usual, Izzi remained totally noncommittal throughout the discussion.

For some time, Izzi had watched changes taking place in the bag business—dramatic changes. Some of his customers were already switching from bags to large trucks with stainless steel hampers. Instead of filling individual bags with flour, they "blew" the flour into the trucks, then unloaded it the same way at the large bakeries and food manufacturing plants springing up around the nation. The produce business was headed in the same direction. Increasingly, potatoes were shipped by the truckload rather than in bags. Izzi wondered if the bag business as he knew it could survive much longer. He was also aware that giant companies such as St. Regis were consolidating bag manufacturing into larger and larger operations. All of these considerations made the St. Regis proposal an offer difficult to refuse.

However, Izzi knew better than to accept the offer too quickly. He told St. Regis officials he would have to discuss it with other owners of Wagner Bag Company (his mother, brother, and sister). He told them he also wanted to run it by a few key employees in order to defuse any negative reactions. Izzi's flight back to Salt Lake City that day seemed to take an inordinate amount of time. His mind was racing. By the time he arrived home, he had already formed his plans for Wagner Bag Company's relationship with St. Regis—and for his own role in that relationship.

The Wagner family met to discuss the offer. Rose had reduced her involvement with the company; she spent about half of each year in Los Angeles with Leona at her apartment. Abe had never been heavily involved with operations at the bag company; his concerns focused on ancillary businesses he and Izzi had established. Izzi told them the St. Regis offer was an opportunity they would not likely see again. He explained to Leona and Abe that their share of the sale would put them in very comfortable positions for the rest of their lives. Of course, Jeanné played an important part in the discussion. She, too, saw it as a marvelous opportunity. It did not take long for the family to agree that they should pursue the offer from St. Regis, so long as the Wagner Bag division would remain in Salt Lake City. They were concerned about the welfare of their employees and what they thought of as a significant contributor to the local economy.

Negotiations with St. Regis Paper continued for several weeks. When the deal was finalized, St. Regis officials knew they were doing business with a shrewd partner. First, St. Regis agreed to pay construction costs for the new plant in Salt Lake City—a plant already under way. They agreed to pay the going rate for land on which the 140,000-square-foot operation would be

located—land owned by Wagner and Roy Simmons. Second, the Salt Lake
City division would be called "Wagner Bag Company, a Division of St. Regis
Paper," and I. J. Wagner would continue managing the plant as long as he
wanted. Third, Izzi would become a paid consultant for improving operations at the Lone Star Bag and Bagging Company. Fourth, he would also be
a troubleshooter for other St. Regis operations around the world. Fifth, he
would have sales responsibility for the entire western United States. Sixth,
when the actual merger took place, Wagner and his family partners would
receive a large sum of cash, St. Regis Paper Company stock, and other com-
pensation based on each individual's position within Wagner Bag Company.
Seventh, for the purpose of calculating retirement and other benefits, Wagner
would be considered an employee of St. Regis with longevity going back to
when he first took over management of Wagner Bag Company in 1932. And
eighth, he would become a member of the St. Regis management group, with
input into company practices and operations.

The good deal proposed by St. Regis officials had become an even better deal, thanks to the business savvy I. J. Wagner learned through years of
trading bottles, bags, government surplus, and real estate. He knew, almost
by instinct, that the St. Regis proposal to an obscure Utah company signaled
an interest in the transaction that went far beyond surface appearances. The
giant company needed Wagner Bag, but it also recognized an opportunity for
growth that could not be achieved in any other way. It was obvious that going head-to-head in competition with Wagner Bag Company would not have
been a sound business decision, since Izzi "owned" most of the bag business
in western America.

The company agreed to the stipulations Izzi presented, and in a compli-
cated transaction, Wagner Bag Company because a subsidiary of St. Regis
Paper Company. First, in August 1958 Lone Star Bag and Bagging bought
83.33 percent of Wagner Bag Company for three hundred thousand dollars.
That purchase did not include property, equipment, or inventory. Then St.
Regis bought the remaining 16.67 percent in a stock-exchange deal. The final
merger of St. Regis and Wagner Bag was completed in April 1960, providing
the time lapse St. Regis needed to satisfy regulators. The Wagners have never
divulged the full sale price or the terms. Suffice it to say that Izzi's promise
to family members that the transaction would make them "comfortable"
for the rest of their lives was no exaggeration. Ironically, Wagner Bag would
survive longer than St. Regis Paper. The merger mania of the last half of the
twentieth century resulted in several ownership and name changes for St.
Regis, but the benefits Izzi negotiated for himself and his company continued

in force through every corporate change. Izzi often told friends, "Selling to St. Regis was one of the smartest things I ever did."

The new plant had its official opening on April 7, 1960. It could produce 300,000 textile bags a day, plus 450,000 multiwall paper bags. Several executives from St. Regis were on hand for the opening and the banquet that night at Hotel Utah. Guest speakers included Utah governor George Dewey Clyde and Salt Lake City mayor J. Bracken Lee. The master of ceremonies was Salt Lake Area Chamber of Commerce president Gus Backman. Izzi, Abe, and Leona Wagner were honored.

For the next forty years, I. J. Wagner traveled to New York almost every month to attend management meetings, usually accompanied by Jeanné. St. Regis put them up at the company suite in the Waldorf-Astoria Hotel and provided tickets to Broadway shows or other events Izzi and Jeanné wanted to attend. Izzi criticized the company for such extravagances as the suite at the Waldorf, but nevertheless he took advantage of such benefits. He was openly critical about some of the excesses he saw in St. Regis operations, including allowing one vice president to use the corporate airplane for weekend trips to his condominium in Florida. He said if he had done business the way St. Regis did, Wagner Bag would never have survived.

Shortly before the merger was completed, Rose Wagner died. She was visiting Leona in southern California when she suffered a stroke. Leona rushed her mother to the hospital, but she passed away five days later in the early morning hours of March 26, 1959. They arranged to transfer Rose's body to Salt Lake for funeral services and burial next to her husband, Harry Wagner, and her sister Ethel Yuddin in the Congregation Montefiore Cemetery.

The loss of Rose Wagner was difficult for Izzi, but her death was not unexpected (she had told her family that she knew it wouldn't be long until she would "be with my sister"). Izzi lost his mother, but he also lost a valued adviser, counselor, and friend. He remembered much of what she had taught him, and he vowed that he would find a way to memorialize her. From that point forward, Izzi prominently displayed in his office a portrait of Rose, as well as a large photograph of his father. When visitors were in his office, he would sometimes call attention to the portrait of Rose and relate a story about her. One of his favorites was: "My mother could never say 'sacks.' She always said 'sechs.' When people asked her about the business, she would say, 'We're in the sechs business.' I told her, 'Ma, don't say we're in the sechs business; tell them we're in the bag business.'"

After about three years, I. J. Wagner grew uncomfortable about running the Salt Lake City plant for St. Regis. He did not like certain conditions imposed on him by New York, especially those involving relationships with employees. He enjoyed congenial relationships with employees, and when he learned an employee was in trouble, he often helped out, anonymously. The absentee managers in New York frowned on such things.

The relationship between I. J. Wagner and St. Regis officials was not always an easy one. Izzi was not reluctant to express his views, even when they disagreed with company policy. One Salt Lake City executive tells a story about receiving a call from a high official at St. Regis. The caller asked if the executive could come to New York to discuss important business. St. Regis would provide a first-class airplane ticket plus other benefits. When the Utah executive arrived in New York, he was taken to dinner at an exclusive restaurant. Eventually, St. Regis officials steered the conversation to a discussion about Izzi Wagner. They wanted to know what they could do about Izzi, since he insisted on questioning company policies and disagreeing with company actions. They did not want to lose his effectiveness in the sales area, but they were not happy with some of his day-to-day management policies at the Utah plant. After a lengthy discussion that continued the following day, the Utah executive suggested that St. Regis give Izzi a title and a downtown office. That way, he could continue to influence sales, and he could also represent the company in a wide variety of community activities.

St. Regis officials thought the suggestion made good sense. They gave Izzi the title "director of sales" for the western states. Then they offered to provide a very comfortable office and a secretary in any downtown building of his choice. Izzi selected a corner office in the new Kennecott Building in the heart of Salt Lake City at Main and South Temple Streets. He maintained an office in that same building for more than forty years—even after his formal association with the paper company ended. (The building was later named Gateway Tower East, and it recently became the Zions Bank Building.)

Izzi recognized what was happening, and so he resigned from his responsibilities as plant manager, but he continued his association with St. Regis until the mandatory retirement age of seventy-five. He had resigned from his position as director of sales for the western states about ten years earlier, but he and Jeanné continued to attend monthly management meetings and annual management "retreats" until 1990.

During the time Izzi served as western-area sales manager, his responsibility was not necessarily to make sales or take orders, directly, but to pave the way for St. Regis sales reps. His "work" consisted mostly of building and maintaining good relationships with major customers—a job Izzi Wagner could do better than most. He had on his desk a cartoon given to him by St.

Regis officials when he retired. The cartoon shows two executives talking. Behind them is a map of the United States titled "Sales Territories." The eastern area is divided into small territories, each carrying the last name of an individual. But the entire western half of the United States is labeled "Wagner." One executive says to the other, "We've got a problem. Wagner quit." And even though St. Regis was swallowed by larger conglomerates, I. J. Wagner received a monthly check from the St. Regis Paper Company pension fund.

During this entire period, Wagner's status and influence in his home state continued to increase. In 1964, Izzi took one of his many trips to New York. On the way home, he changed planes in Denver. In those days, Utah's secretary of state was next in line should something happen to the governor. When he boarded the plane in Denver, Izzi learned that Utah governor George D. Clyde was also on the flight. After about five minutes in the air, the cabin filled with smoke, and the flight attendant announced that the plane had to return to Denver for repairs. Naturally, passengers were worried about their safety. Izzi leaned across the aisle toward Governor Clyde, and he said in a loud voice, "If [Secretary of State] Lamont Toronto doesn't become governor of Utah in the next five minutes, he'll never make it!" Everyone laughed. Izzi's comment broke the tension. The airplane landed, was repaired, and safely made the trip to Salt Lake City.

Utah is the only place in the world where a Jew is a gentile. That's because members of The Church of Jesus Christ of Latter-day Saints sometimes label those who are not members of the LDS Church "gentiles." (Izzi often joked after closing a deal with one of his many LDS friends, "I gentiled him down.")

One advantage to being a highly visible Jewish gentile in Utah—and a Democrat in the predominantly Republican state—is that business, government, and other entities consciously try to ensure diversity on governing boards, committees, and advisory organizations. Thus, I. J. Wagner was often at the top of the list when it came time to add new members on influential boards or committees. And it did not take long for word to get around that when Izzi Wagner agreed to serve on a board, he not only came to the meetings but also provided meaningful leadership. He took such assignments seriously.

Many opportunities came as the result of the friendships he had cultivated. During the 1960s and '70s, Izzi's longtime friend Roy Simmons increased his banking interests to include ownership, first, of Lockhart Savings and, later, Zions Bank. Naturally, Simmons asked his friend Izzi Wagner to join both the Lockhart Savings and the Zions Bank boards of directors. Wagner served on the Zions Bank board for almost forty years, taking emeritus status in 2003.

Utah native Sam Skaggs built a nationwide chain of drugstores and supermarkets that he eventually named American Stores Corporation (recently purchased by Albertson's). When Skaggs took his company public, he asked his friend I. J. Wagner to serve on the board of directors. Izzi served on the board until an ugly management conflict caused Skaggs to sell his billion-dollar interest in the company. Izzi resigned in deference to his old friend, but American Stores had paid its directors handsomely, and Wagner continued to receive pension payments from the company.

Wagner Bag did business with many national food-processing companies, providing bags for flour, wheat, sugar, and other key components of processed food. Izzi was asked to serve on the board of directors of General Host Corporation, headquartered in New York City. He also served on the boards of Certified Warehouse and Transfer Company, Keystone Insurance and Investment Company, the Main Parking Mall, Spenco Medical Products, and others.

As mentioned earlier, he was an active member of industry associations—from the American Bag Association to the National Wheat Growers Association. His involvement provided opportunities to strengthen existing business ties or generate new business contacts. He joined the Utah Manufacturers Association (UMA) in the early days of Wagner Bag Company, and he became president of UMA in 1968.

He was also involved with several volunteer community service organizations, serving on boards and making donations. He had a special interest in the Arthritis Foundation because Jeanné suffered from that disease. He became chair of the Utah Arthritis Foundation.

This list of associations is far from complete. But the point is that each of these "involvements" expanded I. J. Wagner's circle of friends, acquaintances, associates, and business partners. These activities also increased his already significant involvement in the community.

In addition, Izzi's business connections increased his contacts with officials of The Church of Jesus Christ of Latter-day Saints. In those days, it was the practice of major business and service organizations in Utah to include on their boards representatives from the highest councils of the LDS Church. This practice was characteristic of local business organizations, but it also spread to national corporations with major operations in Utah and the West. There were good reasons to include church officials on governing boards. First, the Mormon Church is a lay church, and since many church leaders came from business backgrounds, their input was valuable. Second, in Utah many business customers are members of the LDS Church; it made sense to seek informed input about what those customers may or may not consider appropriate. Third, companies gained a certain degree of credibility from having church officials on their boards. (This practice of placing church leaders on business boards was discontinued in 1996, when the LDS Church decided to limit commercial activities by church officials, citing increased workloads required by the growing worldwide church.)

Since Wagner served on several boards with LDS Church officials, he developed friendships with many of them. For example, he counted as friends every president of the Mormon Church from 1945 on. Through these connections, Izzi was asked to serve on the board of directors of Hotel Utah Corporation, a hospitality company owned and operated by the LDS Church from the hotel's opening in 1911 until Hotel Utah was shut down in 1987. (The historic building was upgraded to meet seismic codes and converted into the Joseph Smith Memorial Building, a church building used primarily for activities that interface with both members and nonmembers.)

By tradition, the president of the church always served as chairman of the board for Hotel Utah Corporation. One day after a board meeting, the church president walked out of the meeting with Izzi and said, "Brother Wagner, when are we going to convince you to become a member of the church?" Izzi said, jokingly, "If you would reduce tithing from 10 percent to 6 percent, I might consider it." The church president said, with a smile, "I'll think about it. We might be better off getting 6 percent from you than getting 10 percent from all the rest." (Obviously, it was not the first time the church leader had heard that particular comment from someone not a member of the Mormon Church.)

Wagner developed a great appreciation for members of the LDS Church, especially church officials. He did not agree with their religious philosophy, but he considered them sincere, ethical, value-oriented individuals. He especially admired the value placed on family—a priority similar to the importance of family during his own upbringing. He also remembered that during the Great Depression, a church-owned bank was the only bank willing to help the Wagners deal with what then seemed an insurmountable debt after Harry Wagner died. After World War II, the same bank made it possible for Izzi and Abe to start American Consolidated Corporation. The fiasco with the surplus blankets convinced them they needed a loan to secure a warehouse and fill it with surplus materials. Izzi worked out an arrangement whereby the bank owned the surplus materials in the warehouse until they were sold. The bank received all payments from buyers until the original cost of the surplus items was recovered. In that fashion, the bank claimed collateral that constantly turned over, rather than showing on its books yet another building in a market overburdened with business properties.

Many of Wagner's close friends were Mormons—some active, some not so active in their faith. He enjoyed talking with them about religion, and he did not hide his agnosticism (or atheism, depending on the audience). But neither did he question their religious beliefs. His philosophy was that when religion helps provide an individual with high ethical, operational, motivational, and interpersonal beliefs, it is worthwhile—so long as the beliefs translate into action.

The "action" part of the equation did not always take place in Izzi Wagner's Utah. As mentioned earlier, he was a joiner, a social being, an individual who worked hard at building a large circle of friends. But when his social-business instincts led him to seek membership in certain organizations, he was sometimes rejected because of his Jewish heritage. He had no trouble joining the Ogden Country Club, where many of his customers were members, but he found the doors closed at some of Salt Lake City's most prestigious organizations. When friends volunteered to sponsor him, he often discouraged them, citing club policies prohibiting membership of Jews, African Americans, other minorities, and, often, women.

He was especially annoyed by such policies at the Fort Douglas Country Club, Alta Club, and Salt Lake Country Club. As mentioned earlier, he eventually bought the Fort Douglas Club social facility and gave it to the Salt Lake Jewish Community Center. He also paid for major remodeling of the building and grounds to make it a complete fitness center, with two swimming pools, a gymnasium, a well-equipped exercise facility, and meeting rooms. Located adjacent to the University of Utah campus, the facility is now named the I. J. and Jeanné Wagner Jewish Community Center. Izzi took great pride in watching children from all ethnic backgrounds play together in the facility he provided. His eyes twinkled when he saw children having fun. "Twenty years from now," he said, "no one will recognize my name...but children will still be laughing at the Jewish Community Center."

Even after the prestigious Alta Club eventually dropped its restrictions against women, Jews, and other ethnic groups, Izzi refused to join. (The Alta Club was created during the late 1800s by Salt Lake City businessmen who were not members of The Church of Jesus Christ of Latter-day Saints. It was a private club where members and guests could buy a drink, gamble, socialize, and pretend they were not in Utah. The distinction largely vanished during the latter half of the twentieth century, but some still regarded the Alta Club as a symbol of anti-Mormonism, another reason Izzi did not want to join.)

Izzi had several friends who were members of the Salt Lake Country Club. He knew that at least two members of the club were Jewish. They had joined during the Depression when economic pressures and a desperate need for new members forced the club to "work around" its anti-Jewish policy. During the late 1950s, two of Izzi's friends said they wanted to sponsor him for membership at the country club. Both were Mormons. Both were very prominent community leaders. Izzi explained to them that club policies would never allow it, that he would be rejected quietly by the admissions committee. The two men told Izzi—and club officials—that if such a thing happened, they would resign from the club, and they would go to the press to explain their reason for resigning. It was a "threat" the country club directors could not ignore. The barrier was broken. Club policies were changed. And Izzi Wagner was an active member of the Salt Lake Country Club for fifty years. He had lunch at the club with friends almost every week, and he continued to play golf into his eighty-ninth year.

During this period of Utah's (and the nation's) history, many deals came along that were "too good to refuse." Few recognized such opportunities at the time, and fewer still had the emotional strength to chance the risks involved. One deal gone bad could easily bankrupt even those as successful as I. J. Wagner and his partners had become.

He always had partners. Some observers might think that he simply wanted to share the risk. Perhaps. But the desire for partnership was probably driven more by congeniality than by fear or greed. Izzi Wagner liked to share his good fortune with his friends—whether it was lunch or a business deal. He often claimed that he sought partners because he didn't have enough money himself to complete the deal. But that, clearly, was rarely the case. Many of his partners had fewer resources than he did, and most of them had fewer contacts and more aversion to risk. Izzi would find a deal and then find a partner. In many cases, he had to do a sales job on the prospective partner in order to convince him or her to share in the potential profit. He never made a deal that did not produce a profit, but some partners were reluctant to believe his past performance guaranteed future success.

One "deal" Izzi liked to talk about was the building he and Roy Simmons bought and sold twice—each time for a sizable profit. The Clift Building is a multistory structure on the northwest corner of Third South and Main Streets in downtown Salt Lake. It was constructed in the 1920s (in fact, it was a doctor in the Clift Building who set the broken arm of young Izzi Wagner when he fell off his bike many years earlier). There was a cigar store in the ground-floor corner of the building, a Western Union Telegraph Office on the Third South side, and the Rialto Theatre on the Main Street side.

During the boom years of the 1950s, the building was purchased by American Oil Company to be used as corporate headquarters. The building name was changed to the AMOCO Building. Some years later, American Oil decided to move its headquarters to another city. The company advertised in the *Wall Street Journal* to sell its Salt Lake City building for $1.25 million (figures used here are not precise, but they are close enough to be realistic). Izzi saw the ad. He noticed that it continued to appear for several weeks, indicating that the building was not easy to sell to a national audience. He suggested to Roy Simmons that they make an offer of $800,000. Roy agreed. Izzi made the offer, and he was turned down abruptly. Company officials virtually laughed at him. Izzi explained to those officials that the building would soon be almost empty, and that whoever purchases it would be faced with the task of securing new business tenants at a time when building-occupancy rates in Salt Lake were already dangerously low. He also noted that the building did not provide parking for tenants or customers. Then Izzi withdrew from negotiations. But he continued to watch the advertisement in the *Wall Street Journal*.

After several months, the same AMOCO official who had summarily re-jected the offer called Izzi to ask if the offer still stood. Izzi said he wasn't sure, that he would have to talk to his partner. After a few days of strategic delay, he called the AMOCO official to say that the original price offer was okay, but the down payment and interest rates would have to be adjusted so he and his partner could better use their resources to attract tenants. AMOCO accepted the revised offer.

Izzi and Roy set about filling the largely vacated building, which they did by establishing certain tenant restrictions, securing nearby parking facilities, and providing reasonable amenities. As soon as the offices were leased, the partners put the building up for sale—this time for $1.5 million. They found a local buyer who was attracted by the high occupancy level. Unfortunately, after a few years of making payments to Keystone Investments—the com-pany created by Izzi and Roy to handle real estate transactions—the buyer declared bankruptcy as a result of other investments that went sour; he could no longer make payments on the mortgage. Izzi and Roy found themselves owning the Clift Building once again.

After a few months, Izzi received a call from the representative of a buyer in California. She said her client was interested in buying business property in Salt Lake City. She wanted to know if the Clift Building was for sale, and, if so, for how much. Izzi said he would have to talk to his partner, but he asked the prospective buyer to make an offer so he would have some actual numbers to take to his partner. A few days later, the California realtor called to say that the best her client could offer for the building was $2.5 million. Izzi said once again that he would have to talk to his partner, and that he would call the realtor back within the week. He immediately called Roy Simmons and said. "Roy, we have an offer of two and a half million for the Clift Building. I think we should sell it. What do you think?" Obviously, it was another offer they could not refuse.

And so they sold the building for the second time. The California buyer was a little naive about real estate values in Utah, and even though monthly payments have been "adjusted" a couple of times in reaction to changing market conditions, regular payments continued to arrive on schedule until the final payment was received late in 2005.

Over the years, Izzi Wagner and his various partners bought and sold property in many locations, mostly in the downtown area where Wagner spent his boyhood. At various times, Izzi and his partners owned every building on the west side of Salt Lake's Main Street between Second and Third South Streets—with the exception of the Continental Bank Building on the southwest corner of Main and Second South (now the Monaco Hotel). Each building has a story—and a partner—of its own, from the Chinese restaurant immediately north of the Clift Building to the Pullman Wholesale Tailor Building immediately south of the Continental Bank (the Pullman Building was razed in about 2001).

When Izzi looked at those buildings during his later years—many of them vacant—he shook his head and said, "I sure was lucky. When I was growing up, I thought owning a building on Main Street was the most important sign of success anyone could have. I owned all those buildings and made a profit on them. Now, so many are vacant. I was lucky." But Wagner's "luck" usually meant being prepared, finding a good opportunity, then making "an offer no one could refuse."

7

Friend, Partner, Deal-maker

DURING THE 1960S AND '70s, Izzi continued to oversee St. Regis Paper Company sales in the western United States, and he settled into a very comfortable office on the ninth floor of the new Kennecott Building, located on the corner of Main Street and South Temple. He had the office appointed to suit his taste, including his large custom-made, crescent-shaped desk and other amenities suitable for a corporate executive of a large international corporation.

He also continued to be a troubleshooter for the company, correcting problems at various St. Regis plants throughout the world—from Belgium to the Hawaiian Islands. As a result of their business visits to Hawaii, Izzi and Jeanné fell in love with the islands. For the next twenty-five years, they took time annually to vacation on Maui. They enjoyed lounging on the beach and playing golf. Unlike many of their friends, they did not buy vacation property on the islands—or anywhere else, for that matter. They preferred the amenities and the flexibility of fine hotels.

Suddenly, the boy from the little adobe house on west Third South found himself independently wealthy—at least relative to his own upbringing and relative to most Utah citizens. He was never as wealthy as some thought, but he was comfortably well off.

Izzi and Jeanné began planning their dream home. They had lived in tiny apartments, duplexes, and a small house. At one point early in their marriage, Izzi had to sell his saxophone, and Jeanné had to sell her clarinet in order to make rent payments. (Izzi refused to sell his violin; it would later occupy a position on the mantelpiece in their house.) After a couple of decades in frugal living accommodations, Izzi and Jeanné dreamed of a spacious home where they could live in comfort and entertain guests. They were in a position to design and build a house specifically for their tastes. They had been unable to have children, and so their plans did not include the multiple bedrooms and other facilities a growing family might need.

They wanted to locate in Salt Lake's Avenues area, near downtown and Izzi's office. They spent weekends looking for suitable property on which to build. They found what they considered an ideal building lot near downtown, bordering a park and City Creek Canyon. Izzi offered six thousand dollars for the property, a sizable price for a building lot in those days. The owner accepted his offer. The couple knew the single lot would not be big enough for the type of house they were planning, and so they contacted the owner of the lot next door. He told them it was not for sale; he planned to build a small multiunit apartment building on the property in order to provide him and his family rental income for years to come. Izzi made a generous offer and asked the owner to think it over. The answer was still negative. Izzi reasoned with the owner. "Look," he said, "my property is no good to me without your lot, and your property would be much more valuable to you if you also owned my lot. Either accept my offer or buy my property. It will allow you to more than double your potential investment income."

As usual, Izzi was correct, and his sales points were sound. The man bought Izzi's lot for a little more than Izzi had paid for it. But the man's family either could not obtain financing or was never willing to take the risk involved in building rental units. Eventually, someone else came along, bought both lots, and built a small apartment building. "The owner did us a great favor by not selling to us," Izzi said later, "because we had to begin looking again, and the property we found is a much better location than that first site."

Izzi and Jeanné found a building lot high on the Avenues with an unmatched view of the entire Salt Lake Valley. They bought not one or two lots, but three building lots to permanently protect their view. The price for the lots was eight thousand dollars each. By the turn of the century, the same lots, if vacant, would have been worth at least a quarter of a million each.

Jeanné was in charge of designing and decorating. Izzi made sure everything was "first class" and structurally solid. He knew something about sound building practices after planning several structures for his business and after having spent several years on the city building board. The Wagner building lots featured a steep falloff to the rear of the house, and so substantial cement footings and steel columns were required. Izzi's construction standards were so high that none of the cement shifted or cracked after more than forty years, despite the building's location on a steep hillside. Jeanné selected Italian marble for many of the floors, and she specified equally luxurious amenities for other applications.

When it came time to furnish the master bedroom, Jeanné and Izzi decided they wanted a round bed (they had seen one in the movies). Local furniture stores did not stock round beds, but Jeanné found a dealer who was willing to order one. Finding a headboard and bedding were equally difficult challenges, but Jeanné was her usual determined and resourceful self in tracking down the necessary items.

The house was a showplace, but when compared to twenty-first-century standards, the cost of the Wagner luxury home was not unreasonable—considerably less than a million dollars, including the property. Jeanné was always frugal, but she and Izzi splurged on their new home. Still, she made sure every dollar was well spent. She told Izzi the marble floors would be especially beautiful, would wear well, and would never have to be replaced. She was right. Other extravagances were not as easily rationalized. Jeanné found an elaborate gold and silver table base on Rodeo Drive in Los Angeles. Izzi had a large beveled glass top made to fit on the base. It served as their dining room table, where they could host as many as sixteen guests for a sit-down meal. Wireless remote control had not yet been invented, so Izzi had technicians install an elaborate wall-mounted control panel near the bed, with wires running to the television, the music system, the lights, and the power-operated window draperies. With the push of a button, they could open the drapes and see from their round bed the downtown neighborhood where Izzi grew up. Because they were on the side of a steep hill, nothing could obstruct the view.

The Wagners moved into their dream home in 1966. They liked to entertain, and most of Utah's "movers and shakers" visited the Wagner home at one time or another, along with many who were neither "movers" nor "shakers," but just friends.

During the early years of the new century, the house was almost exactly the way it was when originally built. It featured a large marbled entry hallway leading to a huge sunken living room with a panoramic view of the Salt Lake Valley. The large formal dining room was nearby. A paneled den off the hallway had a wet bar. Glasses were monogrammed IJW, the initials for both Irving Jerome Wagner and Ilene Jeanné Wagner. A wall of bookshelves contained Izzi's library, an eclectic collection of mostly nonfiction volumes. The bookshelves were discreetly hidden behind sliding wall panels. (Izzi had a habit of waking at around two in the morning, reading for an hour or two, and then going back to sleep until five thirty or six when his workday began.) The den had a state-of-the-art (for the 1960s) music system, with a turntable for records and an eight-track player for the latest audiotapes. The system cost $2,174.50, according to sales receipts. The den also included a spinet player piano so guests could gather around and sing popular songs of the 1930s, '40s, and '50s. Both Izzi and Jeanné loved to perform, and both had performance-quality voices.

Outside at the rear of the house, a landscaped entertainment area, supported by steel columns, hung over the open lot below. Deer, quail, and other animals frequently migrated through the yard. Izzi made sure the birds had plenty to eat. Guests could wander around the small, elevated garden, or stand at the railing to view the entire valley—from the Point of the Mountain on the south to Antelope Island in the Great Salt Lake on the north. (During his later years, Izzi sometimes slept on the patio on a chaise lounge, where he could enjoy the sights and sounds of the city he loved.) A few years later, Izzi and Jeanné added a hot tub in their garden room and a second two-car garage, but those are basically the only changes they made.

The house, while large in square footage, had only two bedrooms. The basement—with its very high ceilings—was unfinished. Izzi fancied that someday it would become his office and an entertainment center, but he never acted on those plans, preferring to keep his office downtown, where he could interact daily with his many business friends. The only way to get to the basement was from the outside or via a narrow circular stairway accessed through what appeared to be a closet door in a hallway off the kitchen.

When not entertaining or relaxing at home, Izzi and Jeanné attended all kinds of fund-raising banquets and social events. They were regulars at the Salt Lake Country Club, and Jeanné loved to dream up outrageous costumes for the annual Halloween party. Izzi went along with whatever his wife suggested in the way of costumes, wigs, and masks. They tried to disguise themselves, but it's difficult to be fooled by a Count Dracula who is only five feet, six inches tall. Jeanné played bridge regularly at the country club, and Izzi sometimes played gin rummy with friends at the club during the evening. Card-game chatter provided another source of information about opportunities in the community. He filed casual tidbits of information in his mind like an accountant storing data in a computer. He could always access his mental "file" when he needed it.

When they were home alone, the Wagners liked to read or watch television—especially the news and movies. Saturdays were reserved for lunch at the country club and, often during the summer, golf. They frequently joined together in mixed foursomes. Jeanné played golf every week on "Ladies Day," and Izzi had a regular golf group each week. On Sundays, they went to the country club or other venue for brunch. Then they rode around town while Izzi looked for potential properties to buy. On Sunday afternoons, they usually went to a movie. On some Sundays, they would take in two movies. When their tastes differed—as it often did with movies—they flipped a coin to decide. Izzi sometimes slept through the movies Jeanné selected, but he never argued against her selections.

Both Izzi and Jeanné liked to travel. Izzi's connection with St. Regis Paper Company required him to travel to New York almost every month. Whenever he traveled on company business, Izzi insisted that Jeanné be included at company expense. The company permanently rented a luxury suite at the Waldorf-Astoria Hotel for visiting executives. Izzi and Jeanné stayed at the company's Waldorf suite and became well acquainted with the hotel and its staff. Izzi may have thought the hotel suite was an unnecessary company expense, but he used it nevertheless. (He once said—with obvious disapproval—that the hotel suite reminded him of a Jack Lemmon movie called *The Apartment*.) Both Izzi and Jeanné loved show business, and so every trip to New York included at least one visit to Broadway or some other performance venue in the city. Once each year, St. Regis managers met in more exotic climes—Bermuda, Mexico, Hawaii, and others. The Wagners were eager tourists. They enjoyed the beach, the pool, deep-sea fishing, or whatever activity was most popular at their various destinations. And, of course, both continually "networked" with everyone from fellow executives to fishing-boat guides.

Izzi made friends wherever he went. On one flight east, he sat next to an executive from a large corporation in Baltimore. Of course, Izzi told jokes and made conversation. When the Baltimore executive returned to his office, he wrote to Izzi, "Boy, oh boy, have I had fun with your 'Port vs Sherry' joke. Frankly, Izzi, it's the best I have heard ever.... I cannot remember when I have had better company during a flight. I can only look forward to an 'encore' one of these days."

Izzi's consulting work also took him to St. Regis operations in foreign nations, such as Belgium and the British Isles. Over the years, he went often to India to buy burlap and to Taiwan to buy millions of plastic bags for his grocery store clients. Jeanné almost always went along.

They tried on more than one occasion to visit Latvia to see where Rose Wagner was born, but the Russian government would not allow it. They did go to the Soviet Union, but had to be content with visits to Moscow and Leningrad. (Later, as Soviet travel restrictions eased, they were finally able to visit Riga, Latvia, but they were unable to make the short journey to the small town where Rose Yuddin Wagner was born. When Latvia finally acquired its independence from the old Soviet Union, Izzi tried to muster the energy for a return journey, but he could never quite make it happen.) They went to Israel and made connections with some of Izzi's relatives there. They visited most European nations and the nations of the Far East. They toured the islands of the South Seas, and they took the long flight to Australia and New Zealand (Izzi said his first visit to New Zealand was on a "cruise ship," courtesy of Uncle Sam, during the war). The two continents they did not visit were Africa and South America—not because they could not or did not want to, but because at the time those destinations were neither popular nor easy to access.

As one might expect from the gregarious Wagners, on a few of their journeys they went with friends—one or two other couples who shared their interest and curiosity. Organized tour groups and ocean cruises were not at all common in those days, and so the travelers had to make their own arrangements. Jeanné became adept at finding transportation and lodging in faraway places.

Izzi played golf often—in Salt Lake, Ogden, Hawaii, Bermuda, and various resorts around the world. He became very good at it, and others enjoyed playing with him. (In 1983, when he was sixty-eight, a local newspaper reported that I. J. Wagner had a hole in one on hole number 6 at the Salt Lake Country Club.) He frequently included his brother, Abe, in his foursomes. Abe was probably a better athlete than Izzi, and he took athletics more seriously. Earlier, Abe had made sure that the Wagner Company sponsored softball teams and bought tickets to local sporting events, from University of Utah football games to Salt Lake City's minor league baseball games. Neither Izzi nor Abe ever went to such events alone; they always included clients or other business associates. Abe also liked to play the horses. He was much more successful at it than their father had been.

Some of the business ventures in which Izzi was involved also included Abe. For instance, six or seven years after they sold Wagner Bag to St. Regis, Izzi and Abe pooled $25,000 to start a new company called Wagner Corporation. The company handled packaging supplies, and sales soon reached into the multimillion-dollar range. A mailed promotion piece listed more than fifty types of products handled by the company. The mailing piece included a minuscule toy plastic gun with five plastic bullets and the legend: "We aim to shoot down your packaging problems." The company listed Abe Wagner as president, Hank Milano as vice president and general manager, and I. J. Wagner as secretary-treasurer. Wagner Corporation operated from a warehouse building on Second West between First and Second South Streets. In 1973, the board of directors (Abe, Hank, and Izzi) authorized I. J. Wagner to find new warehouse facilities "at a cost not to exceed $250,000." Izzi found a new company home on west Second South.

Izzi said many of his friends in the packaging business told him that the two brothers could not succeed in the highly competitive packaging market. But they succeeded even beyond their own expectations. Izzi said, "Our competitors focused on each individual sale to make sure it was profitable. We didn't look at what we earned on every order; we looked at the bottom line at year's end. We concentrated on providing 1932 service, just as we had learned to do at Wagner Bag."

At the same time, Izzi continued to perform well for St. Regis Paper Company, earning frequent accolades from the company. He kept track of major customer accounts, especially those in the western United States, and he maintained close relationships with key representatives of St. Regis clients. When the company had a production or sales problem at one of its many manufacturing facilities around the world, I. J. Wagner would soon appear on the scene to share his expertise and work his charm on facility managers. He frequently offered his input regarding company policies and operations at corporation meetings, by telephone, or through the mail. On at least one occasion, Izzi wrote a long letter about a company vice president who "has made some very derogatory remarks concerning people of Jewish origin.... Personally, I am thoroughly disgusted with this type of talk and it is to the point where I sometimes wonder whether my efforts and concern with St. Regis Paper Company should continue, especially when I must work with a man with his kind of morals." He closed the letter with: "I know this will receive the urgent attention of those responsible for corporate policy, and a solution to protect the company's reputation will be found." Primarily as a result of Izzi's letter, the vice president in question was fired.

At the same time, Izzi continued to be a "deal-maker," buying and selling commercial properties in the Salt Lake area and, sometimes, in Ogden and Pocatello.

For each of these transactions, he invariably found a partner. In many cases, the partner was his old friend Roy Simmons, who had become president, chief executive officer, and chairman of Zions Bancorporation, one of the largest banking concerns in western America. As mentioned earlier, the two never had a formal contract for their partnership; everything they did was based on mutual respect and friendship. They created Keystone Corporation as a vehicle for some of their investment activities.

In all of Izzi's property deals, he never once went through the process of "due diligence" analysis. He made his own intuitive assessment of a property's value. Rather than make an offer, he usually allowed the owner to set the price. If it fell within his predetermined parameters, he moved forward. If not, he withdrew. In fact, Izzi rarely accepted a first offer. He wanted the seller to worry a little and perhaps lower the price. That was another reason for having partners. Izzi could always say he wanted to talk it over with his partner. It gave the seller one more thing to think about. (Giving the buyer or seller time to worry was a hard-and-fast practice for Izzi. During the Utah Winter Olympics in 2002, an Olympic pin trader came to Izzi to inquire about setting up a small tent in the corner of a parking lot Izzi owned. The tent would be used to sell and trade pins. It was attached to a small pickup truck. Together, the tent and the truck would take up three parking spaces. The trader asked Izzi how much he would ask to rent the space for three weeks. Izzi said he had never had such a request, and so he didn't know. He asked the trader how much the space was worth to him. Izzi would have accepted an offer of $150, the monthly fee for three parking spaces. The trader said he couldn't pay a dime more than $700. Izzi said he would think it over. He agreed to meet with the trader the next day. Of course, the next day he closed the deal—cash in advance.)

Sometimes, Izzi's partners were individuals who had access to the money needed to complete a transaction. Sometimes, they were major tenants of a commercial building Izzi wanted to buy. His strategy was always to make sure buildings he owned were filled, and if he could guarantee continued tenancy by forming a partnership, he thought it worth the effort. Sometimes, Izzi's partners were friends Izzi wanted to help out by sharing a sound business opportunity. In such cases, the partner's investment was usually minimal, while the return was substantial. Izzi Wagner helped make a number of individuals wealthy.

A few of these partnerships were unsatisfactory and short-lived—not in the sense that they lost money, but in the sense that the partners did not share Izzi's values. In one case, a partner refused to make even minimal improvements on a commercial property. When windows broke, they were patched with tape or plywood. When a roof leaked, the partner said, "Buy them some buckets; buckets are cheap." That was the end of that partnership...and the end of a friendship.

In another case, Izzi was playing cards with a partner at the man's office one evening. Izzi had taken on this partner because he was a major tenant in one of the Main Street buildings Izzi bought. He liked to become partners with a tenant, because that meant the tenant would remain in the building. As the two partners were playing cards, an employee knocked and then entered the office, sheepishly, to ask for a five-cent hourly raise in pay. Izzi's partner—known to gamble away thousands at a sitting in Las Vegas—scowled at the employee and shouted, "Get out of here. You're fired!" Following that display, Izzi sold his interest in the building and severed his relationship with that particular partner.

Izzi did not easily tolerate those who would not take care of their employees or their property. He thought Salt Lake City—his city—should set an example for quality business operations. He drew a distinction between first-class office space and what he called "junk buildings"—those that had been allowed to deteriorate so that tenants could occupy only the ground floor. He said junk buildings should be refurbished or razed, and he charged that "the only thing wrong with a lot of [Salt Lake City] buildings is the people that own them."

During a summer evening in 1969, Izzi was playing cards with friends at the University Club. One participant, an attorney, mentioned that he was working with a Denver firm to market an entire block of property not far from Salt Lake's city center. The block had been used as the repair and operations center for the city's bus and streetcar system. The old "car barns" had been largely vacant for several years. The property had changed hands several times over recent years, but the transit company was out of business and the Denver owners wanted to dispose of the property. Three or four rows of railroad tracks ran through the long redbrick buildings that filled the ten-acre site. It was in a run-down state, but the buildings encompassed two hundred thousand square feet of potential retail space. Izzi knew it well, because he had ridden the streetcars as a youngster and the trolley buses as a teen. He asked how much the owner wanted for the property. When he heard the price, he was pleasantly surprised. He told the attorney he and his partners would be interested. At the time, Izzi did not have any partners for the venture, but he knew he could find friends who shared his assessment of the opportunity.

The next day, Izzi met separately with a couple of friends and asked them to join him as partners on the venture. One of them was an old friend of Izzi's who had once been an influential state senator and had recently retired as head of the Utah Highway Department; he was trying to establish himself as a property developer. He had limited resources, but Izzi liked him and

wanted to do him a favor. The other partner was a young developer with big
ideas whom Izzi had met through his lunchtime gatherings. Literally within
hours of hearing about the opportunity, Izzi and his partners had an offer on
the table. Exact figures are hard to come by, but it was less than half a million for the entire block. The partners offered one hundred thousand dollars
as a down payment, with the remainder to follow after the site was entirely
vacated, a process that would take two years. During that two-year period,
Izzi and his partners would receive no rent, and the transit company would
continue to take care of any property taxes that might come due. The offer
was soon accepted, and Salt Lake's "Trolley Square" was born. Izzi guided
the early development. He made sure adequate parking was provided, and he
insisted that movie theaters play an important role in the development. He
removed unsightly power lines from overhead poles and placed them underground. He made sure to preserve the old water tower as a visible landmark.
And he suggested inclusion of an eclectic group of shops and restaurants.
He and his associates found an old streetcar, paid one hundred dollars for it,
brought it into the square, made it a flower shop, and named it Desire after
the famous play and movie Izzi and Jeanné remembered. Many of the ideas
he brought to Trolley Square he had seen in his travels to San Francisco,
Denver, and New Orleans. After a few years, Izzi sold out to his partners.
He made a handsome profit on the venture, and his partners did even better.
Trolley Square was one of the first boutique malls in Utah, and it continues to
be a vibrant retail, restaurant, and entertainment venue.

Sometime later, the Internal Revenue Service (IRS) challenged Izzi on the
Trolley Square property. The IRS said that if Izzi owned the property for
those first two years, he must have received rent of some kind. The IRS took
Izzi to court, and the local court sided with the government. Izzi appealed to
the district court in Denver. The Denver court threw out the judgment based
on the facts of the case. It was the only time I. J. Wagner was ever questioned
about his tax returns. He believed in paying a fair tax and called his tax payments "a good investment." Still, the experience with the IRS was not a pleasant one for Izzi. He did not like to be involved with lawyers, even though
he had once intended to become one. He claimed that the total amount he
spent on attorneys during his long business career was sixty-seven hundred
dollars. When he was ready to complete his first real estate transaction, he
paid an attorney a few hundred dollars to draw up a four-page agreement.
He used the same agreement for every other transaction in which he was involved, changing names, dates, and property descriptions. He thought much

of what is included in modern contracts—running twenty pages or more—is unnecessary.

Izzi's focus on property acquisition was almost always in the downtown area, near where he was born and grew up. On the southwest corner of Main and Third South Streets was a building constructed in the early part of the twentieth century as Walker's Department Store. In the early days, the building had a penthouse apartment on the roof where some of the Walker family lived and held extravagant parties. The building later became the Darling Building, named for the department store that replaced Walker's. Then it became the main Salt Lake City store for Sears, Roebuck and Company. During the 1950s, Sears moved a few blocks south. The old Walker building housed a variety of tenants for the next few years, including a tiny cigar store at the corner. (Izzi told a story about a man who double parked, ran into the cigar store, and said, "Quick, can you give me two tens for a five? I'm double parked." The frazzled clerk handed the man two tens for his five. By the time the clerk realized his mistake, the customer was long gone.)

When Sears moved, Izzi and Roy Simmons bought the building, including in the partnership a prominent attorney by the name of Lou Callister Sr., a good friend to both Izzi and Roy. Izzi and another partner already owned the small building immediately west on Third South, and Izzi was convinced that the corner location would soon attract a developer. He heard that the J. C. Penney Company was planning to establish regional offices in Salt Lake City, and he thought Main at Third South would be the ideal location. Roy Simmons agreed, and the three partners made an offer through Keystone Investment Company. The offer was accepted, and Keystone became the new owner of the building. Izzi convinced another friend and partner of his, Henry Pullman, to place a retail outlet, Pullman Wholesale Tailors, on the ground floor.

In the meantime, J. C. Penney Company was talking to officials at Zions Securities Corporation, the real estate arm of The Church of Jesus Christ of Latter-day Saints. Penney management did not want to buy a building. Instead, they wanted to lease most of a new building built to their specifications. Both parties thought the Third South location would be ideal.

Zions Securities approached Izzi and Roy Simmons about buying the building. They also talked to Simmons about the possibility of placing a branch of Zions Bank on the street floor and other Zions Bank offices in the building. Izzi and his two partners talked it over. They were not in the development business, and so they did not want to tear down the building and replace it with a new structure, even though it may have been quite profitable. And since both Izzi and Roy were on the board of Zions Bank (Roy was chairman), they decided it would be a conflict of interest if they made a large profit from the sale of a building where Zions Bank might locate some of its operations. Callister agreed. They decided to sell the building basically for what it had cost them, plus whatever expenses they had incurred. Zions Securities bought the old Darling/Sears building, tore it down, and built a modern eight-million-dollar office building in its place—the J. C. Penney Building. Much of the building is now occupied by various departments of Zions Bank, although J. C. Penney still leases a number of offices.

Izzi found a block of buildings not far from his childhood home on west Second South Street. The buildings were not in good shape, but the owner had passed away, and his family wanted to get rid of the burdensome problems associated with rentals and property maintenance. The arrangement Izzi worked out required a down payment of one hundred thousand dollars. Izzi and Roy were somewhat overextended at the time, and they had trouble raising the money, but they were finally able to close the deal. When they took over the buildings and the ownership company, they learned, to their surprise, that the company had almost one hundred thousand dollars in the bank. That left them with unexpected cash, which they immediately invested in building improvements. They named the refurbished structures Westgate Center, and since they were able to offer lease rates somewhat lower than comparable office space, much of the building was soon rented. The partners then sold it for a profit.

As mentioned, Izzi preferred properties with existing tenants and, where possible, long-term leases. In 1964, he bought a small building on the east side of Main Street between First and Second South Streets. It was called the Singer Building because it had been occupied for many years by the local outlet of Singer Sewing Machine Company. Singer continued to lease the building for several years after Izzi bought it. He was hoping to buy adjacent buildings, as he had done a block south, but the project did not work out. He sold the Singer building for a profit shortly before the sewing machine company vacated the space.

The downtown building that housed the Greyhound Bus depot caught his fancy. It was built sometime in the 1950s or '60s specifically to house the bus depot, and it was located only a block and half from Main Street on South Temple. At one of his lunch or dinner meetings, Izzi heard that Greyhound was in the process of selling off much of its real estate in order to raise cash. The bus company was switching from ownership of buildings to leasing them. Once again, Izzi teamed up with a partner to buy the bus depot through Keystone Company. Izzi's first partner later sold his share of the building to Roy Simmons.

For some time, Zions Securities Corporation had been buying property on the block bordered by West Temple, North Temple, South Temple, and Second West Streets—the block where the Greyhound Bus terminal was located. Zions Securities built a large but short-lived motel on the north part of the block, but the Mormon Church had other plans for the important block immediately west of Temple Square. It would soon become the site of a church museum and a family history center. Zions Securities became interested in owning the entire ten-acre block, as well as the block immediately west. Officials approached Izzi and Roy about buying the bus-depot property. The offer they made was based on current market values. It was substantially greater than Keystone had paid for the property. Izzi and Roy talked it over at lunch. They decided they did not want to profit excessively from the church, and so they agreed to sell the property for less than market value. They made the offer to church officials and sealed the deal with a handshake—the way Izzi did most of his business.

Some would question whether such dealings were wise. But both Izzi and Roy Simmons had ethical standards higher than many in the business world. Roy was born in Oregon, where his birth mother put him up for adoption. After several unfortunate experiences, he was adopted by a woman who would move to Salt Lake City when Roy was still a child. His early life in Utah was difficult, to say the least. He began working before his teen years, and he worked long and hard to establish himself as a capable businessman. Over the years, he held a number of lay positions in the Mormon Church, and he felt his church membership had resulted in many blessings.

While Izzi was certainly not an orphan, he grew up in circumstances similar to Roy's. His family was poor. He began working as a child and achieved success by working long, hard hours over many years. He always loved and appreciated the city in which he was born and raised, even though he sometimes confronted discrimination because he was Jewish. And he never forgot that life-saving six-thousand-dollar loan made to his mother by the "Mormon bank" after his father died. Izzi did not have any ties to the LDS Church—or any other church, for that matter—but he appreciated what church members, including Roy Simmons, did for him, and he respected church leaders.

He gave advice freely—especially business advice—but he was never bothered when others failed to act on his advice, even when it became obvious that his advice had been correct. It was not in his character to say, "I told you so." He was more likely to offer yet another suggestion. Friends considered him an adviser, counselor, and mentor. Louis H. Callister Jr., the son of Izzi's longtime friend Lou Callister Sr. and one of Utah's most respected attorneys, said the "understanding, wisdom, and vision which he so freely shared were invaluable to me."

Izzi's advice was often coupled with a joke, or a one-liner, or even a pointed jab, but friends soon learned to distinguish seriousness from flippancy. It was a technique he used throughout his sales career: always make them laugh before you ask for the order.

No chronicle of I. J. Wagner's business dealings can be complete. He did not even remember many of his business transactions, because his satisfaction came from the deal, not from the memories. He did not keep records for long, because he saw no point in it. And most of those with whom he dealt are no longer alive. Late in life, Izzi's whole being still ached to "make a deal." He often drove through the downtown area, and those who rode with him would hear him comment about properties that were tempting...or not tempting, as the case may have been. He saw opportunities in run-down buildings, or vacant lots, or properties with well-established tenants. He expressed sadness about the empty buildings on Main Street, the empty sidewalks, and the "For Lease" signs.

Izzi believed not just in making money but in making friends...and in keeping friends. Stories abound of his generosity to friends who needed help, employees who found themselves in trouble, or acquaintances looking for opportunities. For some, he used his influence to secure seats on powerful and remunerative boards of directors. For others, he helped find jobs or business contacts. And for a few, he encouraged political activity, backed by campaign contributions. He joked about those running for office, "Anyone can be mayor. All you have to do is get enough votes." But he genuinely understood and appreciated the importance of electing qualified individuals.

One community leader told about the important role Izzi Wagner played in her political life. She served on a community improvement board with Izzi. He would call once in a while and say, "This is Mr. Hackensack calling. Would you like to go for pie?" Izzi would pick her up in his Rolls-Royce, and they would go to a well-known café for pie and coffee. Of course, Izzi would tell a few jokes—most of which she had heard before—then get down to business, which might be discussing an issue being considered by the board on which they served. At one of the meetings, Izzi asked if she would be interested in running for a city council seat being vacated by the current council member. The answer to Izzi's question was an unqualified no. But

Izzi brought up the subject again and again. One day, he asked her to do him a big favor. He asked her to borrow the city council manual from the retiring member and "just look it over." She did as he asked. She borrowed the manual. Others noticed. The act of borrowing the manual spawned a rumor. By the end of the day, everyone at city hall had heard that she was running for the position. Izzi knew that if *he* borrowed the manual and gave it to the prospective candidate, no one would think twice about it. But if the prospective candidate borrowed the manual, observers would draw the inevitable conclusion. Soon, the rumor was so widespread that the prospective candidate felt she had little choice but to announce her candidacy. Izzi provided seed money for her campaign, and she won. "It was one of the best experiences of my life," she said, "and it's all Izzi's fault." It was vintage Izzi Wagner. His personal rewards came from "making deals"—whether in real estate, politics, or finding a new job for someone he met over morning coffee.

8

The Gadfly

—◆—

In may 1978, *Utah Holiday* magazine published a lengthy article titled "Probing the Power Structure." The article named nineteen individuals who had the most "power and influence" in Salt Lake City. Each of the power brokers was given a nickname by the magazine. I. J. Wagner was on the list. His sobriquet was "The Gadfly." The article said, in part:

> Wagner is listed on his Kennecott [Building] office door as a corporate sales representative for St. Regis, his job when he isn't gadflying about town trying to rid Salt Lake City of its garish commercial signs (which he has partially accomplished), its old railroad tracks on 2nd West (which he is in the process of doing), and its downtown billboards (which he is trying to do).
>
> Wagner, a man who does his homework well and has a weakness for practical jokes, has a vision of Salt Lake as a slumless metropolis with tree-lined boulevards and sidewalk cafes.... "He just wears you down with his persistence," says Gov. Calvin Rampton.

The article listed Wagner's primary areas of influence as government, politics, business and finance, and civic affairs and education.

His position with St. Regis gave him the freedom to do what he wanted to do when he wanted to do it. His office location at the center of the city made it easy for him to continue, as well as expand, his regular daily meetings with men and women of influence—including almost all of those named in the *Utah Holiday* article. He had breakfast or coffee every day either at

140

the Hotel Utah, just across the street from his office, or at Lamb's Cafe, two blocks south. He lunched with friends at a select list of restaurants, ranging from out-of-the-way small eateries on the west side to what passed for Salt Lake's finest. He liked to introduce his friends to newly opened restaurants, hoping to help those restaurants establish themselves.

When opportunities presented themselves, Izzi and Jeanné went to the theater, symphony, or ballet, or opera. They both loved show business, and they looked forward to Broadway offerings at the Capitol Theatre, downtown, and Kingsbury Hall or Pioneer Memorial Theatre at the University of Utah. They rarely went alone, and they almost always took theatergoing friends to dinner before the performance.

Izzi was not above dozing off during some performances. He said he learned to sleep under any conditions, including the nonstop bombing on Guadalcanal. One night, early in their courtship, Izzi and Jeanné were at a performance in the old Wilkes Theatre on State Street (later the Lyric Theatre and later still the Promised Valley Playhouse). He recalled that Reginald Denny was the lead actor in the live performance. Izzi dozed off, but at one point the script called for Denny to shout, "Look out!" The loud stage command awakened Izzi. He bolted upright. He was standing conspicuously in the center of the theater. He stopped the show for a few moments. Everyone stared at Izzi. A few giggled. Jeanné pulled at his sleeve and whispered, "Sit down." Izzi tried to disappear in his seat.

At the time of the theater incident, Izzi had plenty of reason to doze off. It was in the early 1940s, when his workday began at six thirty at Wagner Bag Company and ended after one in the morning at the Chi Chi Club. Squeezed into the long workdays were administrative duties; breakfast, lunch, and dinner meetings; visits with customers from Ogden to Provo; daily physical labor of one kind or another around the plant; changing into a tuxedo in order to greet clients at the Chi Chi Club; and, of course, almost nightly dating—first with the city's most beautiful young women and then exclusively with Jeanné.

While his daily schedule became less crowded in later years, he and Jeanné continued to crowd a variety of activities into their lives. For Izzi, those activities sometimes included elaborate practical jokes. One day, a wealthy friend of Izzi's named Sam Skaggs told Izzi he was planning to sell his limousine in order to buy a new one. Izzi immediately offered to buy Skaggs's limousine, not knowing exactly what he would do with it but confident he could dream up a whimsical use or two. On more than one occasion, Izzi put on a chauffeur's hat, drove Jeanné to the Capitol Theatre or some other performance venue, ceremoniously opened the rear door of the lengthy limousine to let Jeanné exit, and then went to a nearby parking lot to leave the car and the chauffeur's hat before joining her at the performance.

He often told a story about the day he put his friend Roy Simmons in the backseat of the limousine, donned the chauffeur's hat, and drove to a local drive-in restaurant. The carhop arrived and prepared to take their order. Izzi asked the price of a hamburger. The carhop said, "Twenty-five cents" (or something similar). Millionaire Wagner turned and said a few words to millionaire Simmons in the rear seat of the limousine. Izzi then turned back to the carhop and said, "The boss thinks that's too much. He says they have hamburgers down the street at five for a dollar." Izzi thanked the carhop and drove away. (He soon tired of the limousine jokes and sold the car to a local mortuary—at a profit, of course.)

Izzi was a longtime member of the Salt Lake Rotary Club (he finally dropped his membership in 2003). Rotary met weekly in the ballroom at Hotel Utah until the hotel closed; then the club moved to the nearby Marriott Hotel. Izzi's purpose in attending Rotary meetings was not to hear the speakers, many of whom he had already heard and questioned during his lunch-time gatherings. Instead, his primary reason for attending was to spend the hour chatting with old friends and making new friends—always asking questions and learning about business, politics, or happenings around town. In recognition of significant contributions to local and international Rotary Foundations, I. J. Wagner was named a Richard L. Evans Fellow and a Paul Harris Fellow, both in 1984.

He was also a longtime member of the Utah Manufacturers Association, and he became president of that organization in 1968. At the time, the UMA was a very powerful organization in Utah, with influence throughout the state and, especially, at the state legislature. Izzi used his UMA position to promote efforts designed to entice Utah citizens to buy Utah products, and he argued that the state should spend at least as much money and effort to support Utah businesses as it did to attract new business organizations. He and his friends also successfully lobbied to eliminate the state's inventory tax. Izzi knew many of the lawmakers personally, and he knew those individuals who had influence with Utah lawmakers. His many appearances at the UMA podium as master of ceremonies or speaker were salted with jokes and one-liners from his endless repertoire. One of his favorite lines was: "I had 'em in the aisles; they were heading for the door." In 1975, the UMA named I. J. Wagner "Business Executive of the Year."

He joined the Salt Lake Area Chamber of Commerce, and was appointed to that organization's board of governors in 1976. He was a longtime member of the Salt Lake Country Club, a life member of the Japanese-American Civic League, and a life member of the Second Marine Division Association. In 1969, the United States Information Agency selected I. J. Wagner to be a member of the committee responsible for planning the nation's participation in the 1970 World's Fair at Osaka, Japan. Committee members were selected because they had "made outstanding contributions to furthering friendship with the Japanese people."

He joined the University Club and became a trustee there during the time the club planned and constructed a twenty-four-story building on South Temple Street. He and Jeanné attended monthly meetings of the Bonneville Knife and Fork Club, where Izzi was elected to the board of directors in 1969. He was often asked to serve as program chairman. His show-business connections allowed him to bring in such speakers as Jack Benny, George Jessel, and David Niven. (Izzi and Jeanné hosted Niven for a couple of days, and the actor invited them to visit him at his villa in Spain. The invitation letter from Niven was one of the few memorabilia Izzi kept over the years. He regretted that he and Jeanné did not follow through on Niven's offer.)

The couple often took visitors for dinner to the city's private clubs, where their guests could order wine or other beverages not available at that time in most Utah dining places. Izzi was a member of the board of directors of the New Yorker, a private club noted for elegant dining.

Another of Salt Lake City's elite private clubs was the Petroleum Club. Izzi was named to the club's board of governors shortly after it opened. In 1982, a *Deseret News* columnist by the name of Clifton Jolley wrote about having lunch with Izzi:

> Lunch at the Petroleum Club, one of Salt Lake City's newest private clubs. Lunch at the Petroleum Club, because someone else is picking up the tab. I. J. Wagner, one of Salt Lake City's movers and shakers. If you work in a downtown Salt Lake City office building, chances are that Wagner owned it once....
>
> Conversation with Izzi Wagner is pretty much a matter of listening. He has a lot to say, a lot of opinions. But since his opinions have had more power in shaping Salt Lake City business and politics than have the opinions of the rest of us, one does not mind listening and learning the ins and outs of what it means to be successful in this town.
>
> "You know what runs this city? [Izzi asks]. Money. People will tell you a lot of other things; they'll point to 47 East South Temple [headquarters

of the LDS Church], but power from money is what makes the decisions in this town. As far as the other is concerned—the Church—it's done more good for Salt Lake than any other influence. But money turns the wheels."

Izzi should know. He's made a little money himself. And he has influence. His conversation is full of references to the people you and I only read about, to the dinners he has had with them, the lunches....

We finish eating. Izzi picks up the tab, $21, plus tip.

The Salt Lake City Police Department named Izzi an "Honorary Colonel." The Honorary Colonels' organization was a group of "movers and shakers" created to help improve the image of city law enforcement. In 1969, Izzi was officially named a "Special Deputy Sheriff." He always carried a sheriff's badge in his wallet. Izzi served as president of the Honorary Colonels' group in 1980. That same year, he joined the board of directors of the Utah Arthritis Foundation, partly because Jeanné suffered from the disease as a result of many years of professional dancing. (She would later have one of her knees replaced with an artificial implant.)

State, county, and city government called upon I. J. Wagner to add his wisdom and expertise to many volunteer citizen boards, including the city's Downtown Development Committee (1965–1972), Utah Committee for the Freeport Amendment (1964), Salt Lake City Planning Commission (1963–1975), Salt Lake County Development and Promotional Board (1966), Citizens' Review Board on Salary and Revenue Problems (chairman, 1967), Chamber of Commerce Civic Pride Committee (chairman, 1975–1979), Chamber of Commerce Board of Governors (1985–1991), Salt Lake City Corporation Citizens Advisory Committee on Wages and Salaries (1966–1975; chairman, 1970–1971), Downtown Planning Committee (1972–1976), Utah Blue Ribbon Committee on Revenue and Taxation (1981–1982), Pioneer Trail State Park Advisory Board (1974–1993), Salt Lake Planning and Zoning Commission (1963–1969 and 1977–1989), Salt Lake City Board of Adjustment (1983–1995), National Alliance of Business Advisory Board (1980–1986), Salt Lake International Airport Authority, Crime Solvers Steering Committee, Salt Lake County Promotion Board (chairman, 1966–1968), Salt Lake County Convention Bureau Advisory Board (1983–1989), Para-Med Foundation, and the Utah Industrial Relations Council. Izzi's service on these and other boards was anything but perfunctory. He cared little about being a figurehead or a member in name only. He agreed to serve only when he felt he could contribute something meaningful to the group and its function.

During his travels, he learned about cities that had removed billboards and overhanging marque signs from downtown areas. He determined to accomplish the same thing in downtown Salt Lake City, and he used his position on the Salt Lake Planning and Zoning Commission to accomplish that goal. Much to the consternation of billboard companies and electric sign companies, Izzi lined up powerful friends and was able to convince the city council to pass an ordinance banning overhead signs in the downtown area, effective May 1, 1973. The affected area was from North Temple to Fourth South and from West Temple to Second East. The battle was intense. Many of Izzi's business friends objected to removing their own cantilevered signs that hung over city sidewalks. They said signs were part of doing business, and that at least one of the electric signs had been there since 1919. Izzi countered that there were no signs on Park Avenue in New York City or in Beverly Hills. He said there were so many electric signs on Main Street that any one of them, individually, had little impact. Critics called the move everything from thought control to communism to excessive government interference. But Izzi won the battle. He also won the battle to restrict billboards in the city. Today, few can remember the obtrusive jungle of signs and billboards that once characterized Salt Lake's Main Street and State Street. Izzi sent out a photographer to take slide photos of the obtrusive signs so he could use them at a commission meeting. Today, downtown Salt Lake City is much more friendly and attractive, thanks to the efforts of I. J. Wagner.

Even so, representatives of the billboard industry still considered Izzi "the enemy" after four decades. They had a point. Izzi disliked billboards, especially in and around the city. In 1997, the Salt Lake County Commission considered easing billboard restrictions. Izzi made some phone calls and talked about the issue at his regular mealtime meetings with powerful friends. A political cartoon appeared in the *Salt Lake Tribune* showing billboard advertisements atop the state capitol building and on the walls surrounding Temple Square. The balloon caption above the capitol said: "Geez—those billboard people are certainly persuasive." Apparently, they were not as persuasive as I. J. Wagner. The move to ease restrictions was defeated, and the *Tribune* cartoonist sent the signed original to Izzi.

In July 1977, one of the major sign companies sued the Salt Lake City Commission, the Salt Lake Airport Authority, and I. J. Wagner over a technicality in the city's sign ordinance. Three days later, the judge ordered that all claims against I. J. Wagner "are hereby dismissed with prejudice."

Wagner's objection to intrusive advertising was not limited to billboards and overhead signs. In 1970, an advertising firm offered to donate benches at city bus stops if the city would allow advertising messages on the benches.

According to a report in the *Salt Lake Tribune* on May 4, 1970, Izzi objected strongly: "I think it's degrading and has no aesthetic value whatsoever. Someone's just trying to make some money at the expense of the city. Violently opposed is the mildest phrase I can think of. We're trying to eliminate eyesores, and these guys come up with a plan for 1,000 more. If we're going to allow this, the city ought to go further and lease out each square of the sidewalk for an ad."

He loved the city of his birth, and he was always trying to improve it. Jeanné once said of her husband:

> He loves Utah. This state has been good to Izzi. Sure, he has worked hard for his success. But there had to be a climate of opportunity in order to reap the benefits of hard work. This, Utah supplied. He wants so badly to improve that climate so that others will have the same chances he has had. Everywhere we travel, when he sees something beautiful or that suggests growth, he equates it in terms of how it could help Utah. On Sunday, his favorite pastime is loading me in the car and driving around the city to see new houses, buildings or schools. He is sincerely interested in the growth of Salt Lake City.

Izzi also wanted outsiders to visit and enjoy the friendliness of Utah citizens and the scenic beauty of the state. His membership on the Salt Lake County Convention Bureau Advisory Board—and his experience as a long-time convention attendee in other cities—strengthened his belief that the city and county should do much more to attract visitors. Tourism's economic impact on the state was, and is, significant. Izzi and other members of the advisory board grew impatient with the way county and city governments went about attracting convention business. They felt a government-run convention bureau could never be aggressive enough to serve the need. The board successfully pushed bonding as a means to finance the Salt Palace Convention Center, and then convinced county officials to create a semi-independent, private agency to operate the convention center and attract convention business to the area. Decades later, the success of both the convention facility and the semi-independent Salt Lake County Convention and Visitors Bureau exceeds any expectations those early framers of the idea might have had.

Later, when the Salt Palace Convention Center was planning to expand across Second West Street, Izzi campaigned vigorously to keep the street open by running the roadway under the new addition. He argued that Second West was one of few north-south streets remaining west of Main Street and that it would take truck and delivery traffic off busy West Temple Street and the Third West thoroughfare. At a city commission meeting, Izzi said, "The closure idea is a foolish proposal. Here we're spending hundreds of thousands of dollars to remove the railroad tracks, have a tree-lined boulevard entrance to our city, and to close the street so the Salt Palace can have a free parking lot is ridiculous." Powerful voices argued against his position, claiming that keeping the road open was unnecessary and would cost too much. Izzi used his many connections, including his position on the Salt Lake Planning and Zoning Commission, to win the battle, even though it cost him a few friends. His victory has proved fruitful for both the Salt Palace Convention Center and downtown traffic, especially in recent years after Main Street was closed north of South Temple. And the street will certainly provide a vital link to the education center planned by the LDS Church for city blocks immediately north of the underpass.

It was also during this period that Izzi succeeded in having the railroad tracks removed from Second West Street. For three-quarters of a century, the Denver and Rio Grande Railroad had tracks running along the middle of what is now Second West Street. Numerous spurs served businesses east and west of the street, including the original Wagner Bag Company and, later, Wagner Corporation, one block north. In 1974, Izzi began a campaign to have the unsightly tracks removed in order to improve the appearance of the downtown area. To set an example, he paid to have the tracks removed from his own business location, a move he said would cost Wagner Corporation three thousand dollars a year in added trucking costs. A March 10, 1976, story in the *Salt Lake Tribune* quoted Izzi about removal of the tracks: "It's worth it. We are talking about millions for a Center for the Arts, and here we have a conductor conducting the symphony with railroad cars being switched in the background" (he was referring to nearby Symphony Hall, the city's bicentennial project).

Many of the business owners in Izzi's old neighborhood disagreed with him. They argued that railroad service was vital to their operations. The controversy continued for two years, in and out of city council meetings, but Izzi's viewpoint prevailed. In 1976, the city refused to renew the D&RG franchise, citing poor maintenance as a primary reason. On February 4, 1977, the final locomotive moved along the tracks on Second West, pushing an empty boxcar unloaded earlier at Sweet Candy Company on Second West between Second and Third South Streets.

Izzi was also instrumental in adding more parking spaces in the downtown area. He strongly believed that no business can survive without adequate parking nearby. When he owned buildings on Main Street, he convinced other property owners to join in a successful effort to create more parking behind the Main Street buildings. Years later, he would turn some of the land he owned on Third South into a parking lot to serve establishments in that area, even though the return on his investment would have been much greater had he sold the property to a developer. In 1967, he urged the city to buy the run-down property on the east side of West Temple Street between Second and Third South Streets to build a parking facility for twenty-five hundred cars. He argued that it would be needed when the Salt Palace Convention Center was finished, half a block away. Before the city could act on his proposal, the Sheraton Hotel chain bought the property to build a new hotel.

At a 1970 meeting of the Downtown Development Committee, Izzi argued that landlords (including himself) should pay the costs of beautification. "The landlord has to be protected," he said, "and the success of the landlord depends on the success of the tenant. So the landlord has to make the commitment to pay for the improvement." Izzi also urged city leaders to add five thousand more parking spaces downtown, as recommended by an earlier study. Others at the meeting strongly disagreed, but Izzi's position eventually won approval of the city commission (only a small portion of the five thousand spaces were added, but the commission eventually toughened requirements for parking provisions with new buildings).

Izzi traveled extensively by air, and he knew firsthand about problems at the Salt Lake City Airport. For many years, the airport had a citizen advisory board with little power. The airport was considered a city department and was under the supervisory control of a single city council member. In 1976, a new mayor, Ted Wilson, was elected. One of his campaign promises was to "take the politics out of the airport." He created an Airport Authority Board, naming I. J. Wagner as one of the original members. What Izzi learned from membership on the board was even more shocking than he had imagined. He knew the airport was inefficient, but he did not expect to find the corruption and mismanagement the board uncovered. Facility maintenance crews were poorly supervised and marginally productive. Airport officials (city officials too) accepted hundreds of thousands of dollars worth of free travel and other kickbacks from airlines, suppliers, and concessionaires. Planning for continued growth was grossly inadequate. Izzi and his friends on the Airport Authority Board took control. They insisted that the then-current airport manager be released, and they changed operating policies and procedures at every level. The board searched for and named a new airport manager who would report directly to the board. No longer could he or she go around the board to seek favor with the mayor and city council. The changes marked the beginning of a new era for air transportation in Salt Lake City.

Within a few months of his appointment to the Airport Authority Board—and after accomplishing a great deal—Izzi resigned so that he could accept what he considered a more important position on the Planning and Zoning Commission, his second appointment to that body. (Izzi lost the position in 1975 because he did not support Mayor Conrad Harrison in his bid for re-election.) In all, Izzi served eighteen years on the commission, and it provided his most influential political role in city affairs.

In the late 1960s, Izzi helped organize the Help Utah Grow Committee for the purpose of stimulating economic growth. The committee's primary goal was to eliminate the state inventory tax, which required businesses to pay tax on product inventories on hand at the end of each year. The committee argued that the tax forced businesses to deplete their inventories in December, creating scarcities of some consumer goods. It was also an expensive tax to administer, and it hit some businesses much harder than others. With the committee's help, a bill to gradually eliminate the inventory tax was enacted into law by the 1969 Utah state legislature. Repeal of the tax opened the way for attracting more businesses in the warehousing and transportation industries.

Not all of I. J. Wagner's campaigns were successful. In 1974, the city and state were embroiled in a continuing battle over so-called land-use planning—little more than a broader application of zoning regulations such as those used in every Utah city of any size. Opponents of planning included many among Utah's conservative majority, plus a very active and vocal John Birch Society. On October 27, 1974, I. J. Wagner wrote a "Viewpoint" in the *Salt Lake Tribune*:

> The need in this state for the Utah Land Use Act is so obvious and so compelling that any opposition to it has to be self-serving or shortsighted.
>
> If the Utah public buys the far-out arguments of the realtors and Birchers against this act, the public is short-changing itself. What the citizens should remember is that this measure is designed to protect their homes and property from uncontrolled industrial and recreational sprawl....
>
> Let's determine the best use of our own land and plan for the future through the mechanism of the Utah Land-Use Act. Then we won't have to worry about these fast-buck operators who sell a mountainside for homes, then walk out and leave all the problems behind.

Despite Izzi's efforts, the act failed to pass. It was one of the few times he went public instead of working behind the scenes to secure support from opinion leaders first, then let those individuals appeal to the general public.

On May 27, 1983, spring floods once again struck Salt Lake City and other Utah communities. Sudden late-spring high temperatures melted the heavy snow in nearby mountains. Water from raging canyon streams—especially the stream in City Creek Canyon—overwhelmed existing underground channels and began flowing down key city streets, such as State Street and Thirteenth South Street. The situation was even worse than the 1952 floods. Salt Lake City and other cities in the state needed thousands of sandbags. Officials called on Izzi Wagner. He rounded up all the burlap bags he could find, and he arranged for Wagner Bag Company (now a division of St. Regis Paper) to maximize production of the bags. Still, it was not enough. Izzi called friends all over the country to arrange shipments of bags from Chicago, Dallas, and the West Coast. He found a sizable supply in California, where they were preparing for a spring harvest, and he dispatched Wagner Bag Company trucks to pick them up. But he soon realized that getting the trucks to California and back would take too long. The water level on State Street and elsewhere was rising at a frightening rate. Besides, Donner Pass over the Sierra Nevada was in terrible shape from heavy snows; trucks would undoubtedly be delayed.

Izzi called Utah's governor to ask if the state's giant National Guard transport airplanes might be called into service. The governor said he didn't think it would be possible because the National Guard had to operate within very strict guidelines. But the governor agreed to call the commanding officer to see what might be done. Izzi called the Utah National Guard commander before the governor had a chance to make contact. Izzi knew the commanding officer very well. He used his best sales effort to convince the general that since he had to fly the airplanes a certain number of hours each month anyway, he might as well fly them to California, load up with burlap bags, and fly them back to Utah. Izzi said he would arrange to have the bags delivered to whichever California airport the general designated. It was a very unusual request, and not an easy sell. But Izzi succeeded in convincing the general that the National Guard could play a vital role in handling the floodwaters. The general said he would have to talk to the governor. Izzi knew how that conversation would come out, and so he began making phone calls to California. Within hours, a National Guard transport was in the air, and within a few more hours, thousands of burlap bags were unloaded at the Salt Lake Airport, ready to be filled with sand by volunteers. Volunteers appeared by the hundreds. Thousands of sandbags were filled and placed at strategic points. Volunteers made a sandbag river on State Street two or three feet deep. City crews built pedestrian bridges and automobile bridges over the sandbag river. One man claimed to have caught a thirteen-inch trout on State Street. Another paddled a canoe along the street. Thousands came to take photographs. Water ran down the streets-turned-to-rivers for two weeks. As was the case after the 1952 floods, I. J. Wagner was honored for his service to the community.

Wagner also found time for many business activities. He was president of Keystone Company, the real estate investment company he created with Roy Simmons. He was chairman of the board of Wagner Corporation—an operation separate from Wagner Bag Company—until 1993, when the company was disbanded. (Wagner Corporation was an umbrella operation for a number of activities involving Izzi's brother, Abe; his sister, Leona; and his lifelong friend Hank Milano.) He was a partner in West Temple Properties, A. Keyser Company, Armco Realty Company, Wagner Investment Company, North Main Properties, Trolley Square, Roper Investment Company, Wagner Industrial Park, 326 LC, and other business groups that came and went over the course of forty years.

He served on the boards of directors of AMS Industries (Connecticut), Cudahy Company (Connecticut; 1972), Jewel Food Stores (Illinois), Lockhart Capital Corporation (Utah; 1962–1969), Hotel Utah Company (1974–1984), Skaggs Companies (Utah; 1967–1975), Osco Drugs (Illinois), Spenco Medical Products (Utah), Yellowstone Park Company (Wyoming; 1969–1975), and Certified Warehouse and Transfer (Utah), among others. He was on the board of directors and the audit committee of American Stores, the giant national company created by his friend Sam Skaggs, from the time it was created in 1975 until it was sold to Albertson's in 1998, at which time Izzi was given emeritus status. During the 1970s, Izzi served on the Advisory Board of KCPX Television.

When the Hotel Utah closed in 1987, Izzi summed up his feelings about the hotel in an interview with the *Wall Street Journal:* "I feel very, very sorry that it has to close. My first high school dates were there, and that's where I met my wife. The loss is a sentimental loss for all of us.... They [the LDS Church] have been trying to make it viable and have lost hundreds of thousands of dollars.... I think they ought to be allowed to do what they think proper."

The board on which he served the longest was Zions Bancorporation, a large western banking operation created by Roy Simmons. Izzi served on the board of Zions Savings and Loan Association from 1965 to 1969, when he was named to the board of the parent company, Zions Bancorporation, where he served until 2003. At that time, he requested and received emeritus status on the board. He was on the executive committee and the audit committee for many of those years. During his tenure on the board, Izzi watched Zions Bancorporation grow from an institution with about $140 million in assets and a few branch offices in Salt Lake City to a $27 billion corporation with eight thousand employees and more than four hundred offices in eight states. With regard to Wagner's thirty-eight years of service, Zions Bancorporation chairman and CEO Harris Simmons said, "Along the way, we have benefitted greatly from his common-sense approach to business, his advocacy on the company's behalf and, not least of all, from his wonderful sense of humor. We are grateful to Izzi for his leadership and service."

Izzi's service on these many boards was not simply perfunctory; he was an active participant. In 1988, Izzi helped to arrange for branches of Zions Bank to be established in grocery stores operated by a longtime friend and customer Dee Smith. Board chairman Roy Simmons wrote to thank Izzi for the idea, and in typical repartee between the two longtime partners, Roy included this tongue-in-cheek paragraph: "I especially like the fact that you agreed to guarantee any losses that we sustain [through the grocery store branches]. I realize that you have probably put a cap on that of $10 per store, but whatever, it was a great idea and we do appreciate it. Thanks a lot! I also appreciate the many other worthwhile suggestions that you have made. Best wishes."

I. J. Wagner received many awards and honors over the years. He did not bother to record most of them or to retain the certificates, wall plaques, medals, and trophies given him. During his later years, only a few of the most recent awards hung on his office wall or resided on his crowded desk. In 1965, the American Public Works Association named him an "associate member" in recognition of work he had done with that organization. In 1977, St. Regis Paper Company honored him for "forty-five years loyal and conscientious service," obviously considering the years he spent building Wagner Bag Company as part of his service to St. Regis Paper. West High School named I. J. Wagner "Alumnus of the Year" in 1993, citing his longtime support of the West High Alumni Scholarship Fund. When he received the award, he told the student assembly, in typical Wagner fashion, that he did not deserve such honors, that they should be reserved for individuals such as Jonas Salk who "do so much for so many people." The Utah Arthritis Foundation honored him with the organization's "Man of the Year" award in 1996. In 1986, the

Utah chapter of the American Planning Association gave I. J. Wagner an award for "outstanding achievement in planning" for his work to eliminate overhanging signs and billboards in downtown Salt Lake City.

In addition to his multiple activities on the local level, Izzi continued to be fully involved with St. Regis Paper Company. He kept track of major customer accounts, especially those in the western United States, and he maintained close relationships with key representatives of St. Regis clients. When the company had a production or sales problem at one of its many manufacturing facilities around the world, I. J. Wagner would soon appear on the scene.

His wisdom and experience were valued, as was his endless sense of humor. He was frequently asked to speak at gatherings of local and national business leaders. In June 1984, the Utah law firm of Greene, Callister, and Nebeker asked Izzi to speak at a firm meeting. His speech included these comments:

When Lou Callister advised me that I had volunteered to speak here today, it was more of a compliment than you realize. It is somewhat of an anachronism to have me here thinking you will learn something from me, as I am probably the only one here without a college degree.

Having been involved in various large corporations, I have observed that practically every business operates in the same way. They ask what does the customer or client expect from a business? What do I expect from a lawyer or a paper company? We all expect the same thing. We expect service, we expect courtesy, we expect honesty and integrity. The experience of being a member of some of these large companies has been invaluable. I have learned that experience is the history of all of my past mistakes, and I am probably the most experienced person in this room.

I hope when I was asked to appear here today that you did not think you were getting a typical executive, because that is what I am not. In today's business world, I guess I would be described as unorthodox. I answer my own telephone, and I have had the same secretary for fourteen years. I have never had a speech written for me in my life, so everything I tell you here today was prepared by my own efforts....

It is important to me to enjoy what I am doing. I always investigated my complaint letters or my complaint calls. Answering complaints or hearing about complaints is the best mirror of your business. By handling them myself, I feel I am staying in touch with what is going on.

A few of my friends made more money the day they were born than I have made in my entire life. The rich have heirs, and the poor only have children. I started at the bottom and sold newspapers when I was only seven years old. I was nine years old before I could read one. I was able to be fairly successful because I was fortunate in always choosing the right boss. Generally, the right boss was myself.

Izzi's speech continued in the same vein for about twenty minutes. It was filled with one-liners, jokes, and good advice. It was vintage Izzi Wagner, as were all of his speeches. When he was given awards, his acceptance speeches were exceptionally short. On one occasion he quoted Jack Benny: "I don't deserve this award. But I don't deserve the arthritis I have either. Thank you."

The activities above are far from complete, but they give some idea of how widely involved Izzi was during the last half of the twentieth century. At the same time, he and Jeanné found time to travel and carry on an active social life. They were fascinated by show business and its mystique. They saw almost every Broadway show produced over the last half of the twentieth century. Most of the great stars of the day—singers, musicians, dancers, and comedians—performed in Las Vegas. Izzi had friends in Las Vegas, and the Wagners rarely had to pay for a room, even though Izzi was far from being one of the "high rollers" feted by Las Vegas establishments. He did not gamble, citing the lesson learned when his father lost the "family fortune" to gambling . . . and noting that the odds always favor the house. "I learned early in life," he said, "that there are three places where you get nothing for your money—traffic court, divorce court, and gambling casinos." When Rose was alive, Izzi and Jeanné sometimes took her along with them to Las Vegas, because she also admired the celebrities of the time. On several occasions, Izzi arranged for major stars to come to their table and say hello to Rose.

Izzi's sister, Leona, worked for a jeweler in Santa Monica, an elite suburb of Los Angeles. Many movie stars bought jewelry at the store. When Izzi and Jeanné were visiting Los Angeles, Leona would sometimes call and say, "If you come to the store at two this afternoon, you might see Cary Grant" (or Clark Gable or whoever had an appointment that day). Izzi and Jeanné would go to the store and wait for the named celebrity to appear. Sometimes they were introduced, but they did not collect autographs or try to approach celebrities without an invitation to do so. It was enough for Izzi and Jeanné simply to be able to tell friends in Salt Lake that they had seen Mickey Rooney, Humphrey Bogart, or whichever star might have come into the store.

In 1972, Izzi and Jeanné flew to Los Angeles on a combination business and pleasure trip. It was their thirtieth wedding anniversary. Izzi arranged

ahead of time to buy a new Rolls-Royce Silver Shadow as an anniversary gift
for Jeanné. (Thirty years later, he still remembered the exact price of the automobile—somewhere in the neighborhood of twenty-five thousand dollars,
a hefty price for a car in those days.) He concocted a pretext for the two of
them to walk along the street where the Rolls-Royce dealership was located,
asking her to go shopping with him or to lunch or some such thing. As they
strolled past the dealership, he called attention to the Rolls-Royce in the
showroom window and asked Jeanné, "How would you like a car like that?"
She laughed, but he insisted they go in to take a closer look. Jeanné loved the
car, but her frugality caused her to dismiss the idea. When the salesman came
over, Izzi told him it was their thirtieth anniversary, and he would like to buy
the car as a gift for his wife. The salesman acted surprised. He suggested they
take it for a drive while he completed the paperwork. There was a Frank
Sinatra tape in the eight-track tape player; Sinatra was a Wagner favorite.
When they returned to the dealership, Izzi signed the necessary papers, and
they prepared to leave. Izzi noticed, however, that the gas gauge was almost
on empty and that the Sinatra tape was gone. He said to the salesman, "When
I'm paying this kind of money, couldn't you at least put gas in the car and
throw in the tape?" The salesman responded, "If you don't want the car, you
don't have to take it." Izzi drove away, heading for the nearest gas station. He
drove the Rolls-Royce for thirty years; the dealership did not survive as long.
During his final years, Izzi had four cars: the Rolls-Royce, a 1993 Cadillac
Allante convertible he also bought for Jeanné, a 1979 Mercedes-Benz 450 SL
two-passenger coupe-roadster convertible, and a 1993 Jeep Grand Cherokee.
None of his cars had traveled more than fifty thousand miles. He also owned
and maintained a 1994 Ford Mustang GT, which he loaned permanently to
Jeanné's sister.

Jeanné's brother Dr. Grant Lister Rasmussen became a well-known sci-
entist at the National Institutes of Health. In 1988, he was honored by the
American Otological Society for his pioneering work in neural anatomy and
the physiology of hearing. He identified what is now called "Rasmussen's
bundle," a collection of nerves vital to processing sound. He was also honored
for his "ability to motivate medical students." Izzi and Jeanné went to Washington, D.C., to attend the award ceremony, another indication of Izzi's high
regard for the Rasmussen family. Grant Rasmussen died in 1989.

During his "gadfly" years, Izzi and his friend Roy Simmons continued to
pursue real estate ventures, some of which were mentioned earlier. Izzi had a
fondness for real estate in the neighborhood where he grew up. It was almost
as if he had to prove to himself, over and over again, that the little Jewish

kid from the adobe house on west Third South had made a success of his life. He bought and sold properties on both sides of Third South, between West Temple and Main Streets. One property on the south side of the street was leased to an office supply store. Property he owned on the north side of the street included a popular restaurant. Across the street from what had once been the adobe house where he was born, he bought two small hotels. During his early years, they had been bordellos. When he was about twelve, Izzi had his first "real" job at Falconbello Grocery on the ground floor of one of the hotels. His duties included stocking shelves and cleaning up at the end of the day.

He bought the buildings and land east of the Wagner Bag Company at the site of the old adobe house. He planned to expand the company, and so he bought business buildings and parking lots between Wagner Bag and the Miles Hotel (now the Peery Hotel). As mentioned earlier, the planned expansion did not occur because of developments at Wagner Industrial Park. However, in anticipation of Wagner Bag expansion, he had also purchased land north of the Miles Hotel where a service station and parking lot were situated.

For years, he patronized the service station, operated by one of his Japanese friends. And when the son of the original operator closed the station and moved to a location near the country club, Izzi continued to buy gasoline, service, and repairs from the son. On one occasion, Izzi and Jeanné drove the Rolls-Royce into the station on West Temple and Pierpont Streets to fill up after an evening at the theater. It was dark and only minutes away from closing time. As the attendant was filling the car with gasoline, Izzi noticed a suspicious character inside the station. Izzi paid the attendant—all transactions were in cash in those days before credit cards—but he and Jeanné did not leave. He watched to see if the suspicious individual left. When he did not, Izzi took the pistol he always carried in the glove box, put it in his coat pocket, and walked into the station, pretending to look through some of the candies for sale on the counter. He remained in the station—with the pistol in his pocket—until the stranger left. Then he told the attendant about his suspicions. The attendant agreed that the man had acted strangely. He said he was sure that if Izzi had not come into the station, he would have been robbed.

Izzi had a gun in his car because his friends in the police department advised him that he might be a target for robbers. After all, they told him, you ride around in expensive cars, and your name appears often in the newspaper as one of the city's wealthiest individuals. Izzi also kept a gun under his bed in case robbers should invade his house. But the gun did not do much good when the possibility turned to reality. One night, Izzi and Jeanné were asleep (sans night clothes, as usual) when two robbers entered the house. The robbers quietly came into the bedroom. One held a gun to Izzi's head. Izzi's own gun was only inches away, but he dared not move toward it. The robbers forced the couple to tell where Jeanné's jewelry was located and how to get into the locked cabinet. Then they tied up the two rudely awakened and unclothed Wagners with duct tape before filling a bag with jewelry. It took Izzi almost two hours to squirm out of the duct tape and call police.

Police eventually caught the robbers. They were tried and sent to prison. Izzi's friends at the police department also identified the pawn shop where the robbers had fenced the jewelry. However, Izzi was unable to prosecute the pawn shop owner, even though he was convinced the man had orchestrated the robbery. The robbers sold the stolen jewelry to the pawn shop owner for about nine hundred dollars; it was worth more than fifty thousand dollars. The insurance company paid for the jewelry, but Jeanné replaced only a few of the items, those with the most sentimental value. From that point on, they kept valuable jewelry and other items in their safe deposit box at the bank. When Jeanné was inclined to wear jewelry, she either took it from the safe deposit box for the evening or wore inexpensive imitation stones. Izzi never wore jewelry himself, except a gold watch given him by St. Regis Paper when he retired. He installed an elaborate security system at his home to guard against future robberies. As with most robbery victims, his distress over the incident was caused more by the violation of privacy than by the loss of valuables. Years later, he worried when the thieves were released from prison. He had been tenacious in making sure they were caught and convicted, and he feared they might retaliate, but no incidents occurred.

Izzi and Roy Simmons continued to buy and sell property through Keystone Company. As usual, Izzi did not bother with "due diligence," legal investigations, or other procedures considered necessary these days. He looked at a property, decided if it had potential, and made an offer. As mentioned previously, he spent little on attorney fees. He hired accountants to handle his business and personal accounts, and he gave them firm instructions never to cause him any problems with customers, clients, partners, or the government. He said he did not mind paying taxes, so long as they were fair. In fact, he said he looked favorably on his tax bill every year because it indicated how well he had done during the year. Rose Wagner told her children that paying taxes in the United States was a privilege. She told them having money and paying taxes was better than having no money and paying no taxes.

At one point during this period, a friend of both I. J. Wagner and Roy Simmons approached Roy with an opportunity. Her husband had died, and in his estate was majority ownership of the property on which the Salt Lake Marriott Hotel was (and is) located. The Marriott paid an annual lease fee to the landowners. The other co-owners were anxious to sell because they were more interested in current cash value than future income. However, the widow cared more about steady income. She could not afford to buy out her partners, and so she asked Roy Simmons if he would be interested in buying what amounted to almost half of the property. Roy talked it over with Izzi, and they agreed to help their friend by purchasing equal shares. Hotels were not doing well at that particular time, and so Izzi negotiated a new agreement with the Marriott Company that tied lease fees to income. Under the new agreement, Marriott would pay the landowners a small percentage of room rentals, thus tying the annual lease expense to hotel revenue. In return, the Marriott Company was responsible for everything from taxes to property improvements. Izzi knew the property was directly across the street from the new Salt Palace Convention Center. His service on the Convention and Visitors Bureau Advisory Board convinced him that the convention business had a bright future in Utah. The Marriott property looked like a solid investment. What neither Izzi nor Roy could have imagined was that inflation and demand would significantly increase hotel room rates and, thus, income for the three partners. The original purchase price was repaid in a very short time. And in 2001, they signed a fifty-year extension of the lease, promising a long-term, steady income for the partners and their heirs.

Obviously, "the gadfly" was a busy man during the 1970s and 1980s. His frenetic pace would continue well into the '90s. But in 1993, a tragic event dramatically changed his focus and his life.

9

Time to Give Back

———•◦•———

ON A BRIGHT SATURDAY morning in early May 1993, Izzi and Jeanné put down the top on their new Cadillac Allante convertible. They drove to a favorite coffee house near the city's Liberty Park. The coffee house offered a blend that Jeanné especially favored. As they were enjoying coffee and a pastry, Jeanné complained about not feeling well. Neither Izzi nor Jeanné hesitated to visit doctors at the least sign of discomfort or concern. As a result, both were in good health. Izzi had undergone heart bypass surgery a few years earlier, and Jeanné had a successful knee replacement, but neither had experienced significant medical problems since their surgeries. Both had quit smoking years earlier. They exercised regularly. Izzi took his blood pressure almost every day to make sure it stayed within the range advised by his doctor. And Jeanné carefully monitored her diet. She had experienced a few minor heart incidents, but her cardiologist felt her heart was strong and healthy.

At the coffee house, Jeanné's discomfort increased. It soon became more pain than discomfort. Izzi immediately drove Jeanné to the emergency room of LDS Hospital, located not far from their home. Doctors soon determined that one of the arteries near her heart was almost completely blocked. They asked Izzi for permission to perform angioplasty—a procedure to open the artery using a balloonlike device—and then insert a metal stent in order to keep it open. He agreed, and medical personnel moved Jeanné to the operating area of the cardiac care unit. While she was in the operating room, Izzi contacted their regular physician and urged him to come to the hospital. The operation was a success. The family doctor made certain Jeanné was receiving the best care possible. Izzi stayed with Jeanné at the hospital Saturday night and all day Sunday. Everything seemed to be going well. Her electronic heart monitor showed some distress associated with the new object residing in her circulatory system, but it was nothing out of the ordinary. On Sunday evening, Jeanné urged Izzi to go home and get some rest. She assured him she would be okay. Reluctantly, he went home for the night. He fell asleep easily. In the early morning hours, he was awakened by a telephone call from the resident physician. The doctor explained that Jeanné's heart had stopped beating; they were not sure why. Ilene Jeanné Rasmussen Wagner died on Monday, May 3, 1993. The cause of death listed on the death certificate was "acute myocardial infarction." Izzi was devastated. Ten years later, when friends asked how his life was going, he would say sadly, "My life ended in 1993."

On their shared tombstone, he had stonecutters carve beneath a Star of David and the large capital letters WAGNER, "All our dreams came true." Beneath "Ilene Jeanné" and the date of her death is "Wonderful Wife & Sister." Beneath "I. J. 'Izzi'" was a blank for the date of his death, followed by two words: "Devoted Husband." The granite marker also shows their wedding date: "Married Aug. 13, 1942." The tombstone does not include birth dates. As mentioned earlier, Jeanné was several years older than Izzi. She was always sensitive about it. She had not told Izzi the truth about her age when they were dating. In fact, Izzi did not know Jeanné's year of birth until they applied for passports many years after their marriage. Only then did she confess that she had lied about her age because she was afraid that if he knew the truth he might be less interested in marrying her. Izzi omitted their birth dates from the tombstone because he knew Jeanné would have preferred not to show the difference in their ages.

Izzi was determined that Jeanné—and eventually himself—should be buried in the same cemetery where his mother and father were buried, Congregation Montefiore Cemetery in Salt Lake City's Avenues area. However, when he applied for burial plots in the cemetery, Orthodox Jews rejected the application. The reason for their decision was that Jeanné was not Jewish. The rejection did not sit well with Izzi. It reminded him of rejections he had experienced for simply being Jewish. He saw little difference between being rejected for being Jewish and being rejected for not being Jewish; he thought such distinctions were foolish. Izzi cared little about religion, but he cared a great deal about family. He wanted to be buried near his mother, who had meant so much to him, and his father, whom he came to admire and respect.

Instead, he chose to be near the woman he loved for more than fifty years. He selected a site for Jeanné and himself at the non–Orthodox Jewish burial ground, Congregation B'Nai Israel Cemetery, located a few yards away from the Orthodox cemetery.

Izzi told friends their marriage was "as close to perfect as it is possible for a marriage to be." In more than fifty years of marriage, the couple never had an argument, according to Izzi. They shared interests, and when the interests of one were not fully shared by the other, the differences were minor. For example, when Izzi wanted to see an action movie, Jeanné went along without complaint, even though she did not always enjoy such movies. And when Jeanné wanted to see a romantic movie, Izzi went with her without hesitation (he often dozed off during slow-moving scenes). In his business association with St. Regis Paper, Izzi insisted that whenever the company required him to travel, Jeanné should be included. At social events and other activities in and around Salt Lake City, one rarely saw Izzi without Jeanné. She always laughed at his jokes—even those she had heard many times before—and she often added her own wit and congeniality to his irrepressible friendliness. Jeanné played golf with friends at the Salt Lake Country Club on "Ladies Day," and Izzi played with business and political associates on Saturdays. They also played often as a couple in mixed foursomes. Such outings were filled with chatter, laughter, and congenial banter. Interfamily relationships did not create challenges either. Izzi had great admiration and respect for Jeanné's Mormon family, and they accepted him without reservation. Jeanné and Rose were not simply daughter-in-law and mother-in-law; they were also best of friends.

In a 1977 television interview at their home, Jeanné told about her four-dollar wedding ring. Izzi asked who paid for it, and Jeanné said she did. They laughed. During the interview, Izzi did a song-and-dance impersonation of Jimmy Durante, complete with cane and false nose. Then he and Jeanné danced together, looking like two young lovers. The interviewer observed that it looked as if they were still deeply in love and that they had a good marriage. "I think we have," said Jeanné. Izzi interrupted to say, "She thinks we have; I know we have."

And so it was not surprising that the loss of Jeanné left a deep void in Izzi's world. Jeanné's death not only changed Izzi's life but also changed his perspective on life itself. He always understood that life is limited, but Jeanné's death forced him to confront the reality that life's limitations are unpredictable. He had no more control over his own mortality than he did over Jeanné's.

Izzi reacted by making sure his own affairs were in order. He convinced his brother, Abe, and his lifelong friend Hank Milano that they should sell Wagner Corporation, the packaging supplies company they had founded many years earlier. The selling price was $1.5 million. He had an attorney friend draw up power-of-attorney and special-power-of-attorney documents—one to take care of his financial affairs, and the other dealing with injury, illness, and end-of-life issues. He also revised his will, directing the purchase of insurance annuities for family members and a longtime secretary and dividing the remainder of his estate among four of his favorite charitable causes (these documents would be changed several times during the years ahead). Then he set about giving away most of his fortune.

One of Izzi's favorite stories was about the two men at a funeral looking at the casket of a departed friend. One man says to the other, "I guess Maurice was pretty well off. How much did he leave?" And the other man replies, "All of it." Izzi decided he didn't want to leave "all of it." The Wagners had no children and few living relatives. It was time, he thought, to give something back to the community he loved. It was time to make sure that whatever he had accumulated would be used in ways that reflected the interests of himself, Jeanné, and other departed family members—especially his mother, Rose.

I. J. Wagner never had as much money as most people thought he did. Certainly, he was wealthy, compared to most. But compared to many of those with whom he associated throughout his life, his personal fortune was less than spectacular. In a 1973 newspaper story by Robert Woody of the *Salt Lake Tribune,* Izzi had said honestly, "My financial reputation far exceeds my net worth." The article was titled "4 Millionaires Tell How." Izzi's response to a question about how he had achieved his fortune was, "I learn from other people. Associations are important—whether doctor, dentist or broker. You learn from their experiences."

Another of Izzi's favorite stories was about the Jewish gentleman who was struck by a car while crossing the street. A passerby rushed to help, covered the injured man with his overcoat, took off his jacket, and rolled it up to serve as a pillow. The helpful passerby asked the fallen man, "Are you comfortable?" And the injured pedestrian fought through pain to proclaim, "I make a good living."

Izzi Wagner was "comfortable." But when Jeanné died, he became especially conscious of his good fortune. The statement on their tombstone that "All our dreams came true" was deliberately stated in the past tense. It implied that few dreams were left, that the sum total of major accomplishments was in the past, and that the most meaningful dreams need a partner with whom to share them. His dreams had been many—and they had been largely fulfilled. The poor Jewish kid from west Third South had owned property on Main Street…had become a power broker in the community…had been a mover and a shaker…had become a friend and associate to the city's most important individuals…had helped improve relations among the city's diverse religious groups…had traded the old adobe house across from the bordello on west Third South for a house of steel and marble on a hill overlooking the city…had traded that first twenty-five-dollar Pontiac for four luxury cars…and through shrewd business deals had accumulated significant wealth. "All my inventory is in cash," he said with a smile, "and I can't afford to deplete my inventory."

He attributed much of his success to good fortune, timing, and "luck," but he knew thousands of people with backgrounds similar to his own were not so beneficently smiled upon by good fortune, that good fortune is worth little unless wisdom acts upon it. And timing may have been important in many of his business deals, but knowing the time is right means little unless it prompts swift, decisive, and often risky action. Much of I. J. Wagner's success came from his own vision, his own wisdom, his own willingness to take risk.

In typical Wagner fashion, Izzi dismissed his success with a self-deprecating quip. "The secret," he said with a smile, "is to do business with those dumber than I am…and it's becoming harder and harder to find them." He also said, "I quit the university after two weeks because I decided it was easier to hire college graduates than to be one."

Despite all of his success, he never considered himself to be anything other than an ordinary individual. On his office door and on the checks he signed he may have been "I. J. Wagner," but in every other setting—and to everyone he knew, from the most to the least—he was always "Izzi." He was the Izzi who sneaked out of the house at night to go swimming in the pool at Pioneer Park. He was the Izzi who was Black Bart after the five-cent cowboy movies. He was the Izzi who was reprimanded for asking questions at Hebrew school—and never went back. He was the Izzi who picked up old beer bottles and used burlap bags in order to recycle and resell them. He was the Izzi who thought anyone who owned property on Main Street must be rich. He was the Izzi who waited patiently on a chair in a Los Angeles jewelry store to get a glimpse of Clark Gable. He was the Izzi who loved his wife partly because she made her own clothes. He was the Izzi who played practical jokes on friends and bought books filled with jokes to increase his repertoire. He was the Izzi who responded with a quick wit and a well-remembered story. He was the Izzi who made friends easily and recalled names readily. In other words, Izzi Wagner was totally at peace with what he had been, what he was, and what he would become.

That explains, in part, why he decided to give something back to the community that had "given" him so much. He learned about giving from his mother, Rose. She always gave to those in need, even when the Wagner family had barely enough to survive. The wandering hobos of the Depression era could always find a piece of bread and a bowl of soup at the little adobe house on Third South, together with the dignity of a few hours' work if they wanted it. And Rose did not judge her neighbors. When the prostitutes in nearby bordellos needed help, they came to Rose. Her circle of friends included minorities of every kind, and while she was dedicated to her own Jewish religion, she genuinely respected those with different beliefs. She attended synagogue with some of the most successful men and women in the city. She hoped, but did not demand, that her children would follow her own religious beliefs. Neither did she pass judgment on them when they chose not to follow her example of commitment to Judaism. She loved music, dance, theater, and the arts, without reservation or false arbitration. She enjoyed equally a popular song sung by Al Jolson and an opera aria sung by Lauritz Melchior.

Following the example set by Rose, Izzi was always generous to those in need. Most of his gifts were given quietly, sometimes anonymously, to individuals he knew—an old friend come upon hard times, an employee with a problem, a neighbor confronting unexpected illness. He supported arts organizations, education, and a select few health-related groups such as the Arthritis Foundation. He rarely responded to mail requests or even personal organizational appeals, because he was inundated with such things and he did not want to encourage additional requests by mail, phone calls, or personal visits. He chose his charitable causes the same way he chose his business ventures—by experience and instinct. He believed strongly that private contributions cannot solve the nation's health care challenges and that government should play a much larger funding role in medical research, prevention, and treatment for major diseases. He also believed government—which means society as a whole—should do a better job of caring for the homeless, the poor, and those who are handicapped. He saw no reason for anyone to suffer through hunger or homelessness in a nation as affluent as the United States. But his philosophical position did not serve as a personal excuse to avoid helping those in need.

Stories about Izzi's generosity come from many sources. The record does not show how much he gave, but it does show that the image he tried to convey about being tightfisted was far from the truth. In 1989, Gordon B.

Hinckley, president of The Church of Jesus Christ of Latter-day Saints, wrote to thank him for a contribution to the BYU Jerusalem Center: "Over the years you have been a great friend of the Church. We appreciate all you do to assist us and particularly at this time this wonderful gift."

In 1999, Salt Lake City police chief Ruben Ortega wrote to thank Izzi for his help in hosting the International Association of Chiefs of Police Conference in Salt Lake: "Your financial support especially lessened the stress of worrying how I was going to financially pull this off."

Utah Symphony Orchestra Maestro Maurice Abravanel wrote to thank Izzi for his help in hosting a social event following the first concert of the 1971 season: "It was very generous of you to donate it, but then you are a wonderfully generous man."

In 1972, Utah governor Calvin Rampton wrote to thank him for his help during the election campaign: "I would like to personally thank you for your generosity in providing space for the campaign headquarters. It was an excellent location."

In 1977, Salt Lake City mayor Ted Wilson wrote: "Your unselfishness in contributing to your city is to be appreciated and honored. Also, I deeply thank you for all you do for me."

When a doctor friend went on a service mission for the LDS Church in 1998, Izzi kept in touch through correspondence. Izzi also sent the doctor a gift he thought the missionary might appreciate. The doctor wrote: "It was good to get your letter of Jan. 19th and to learn that we would be getting the Deseret News. We have received three weeks of papers and have greatly enjoyed reading the things about home."

One restaurant in town never charged Izzi for a meal because he once rescued the business for the current owner's father. The always-free meals embarrassed Izzi, and he did not go to that particular restaurant as often as he might have liked, simply to avoid the owner's appreciative generosity.

Izzi was a strong believer in the United Nations. When UN visitors came to Salt Lake, officials often called on Izzi to host them. One such visitor wrote of "how grateful Ambassador Bishara and I are for all you added to the pleasure and interest of our visit to Salt Lake City.... I know now how fortunate we were to have you as our guide and companion. We felt we were in the hands of one who not only loves the city but has keys to open any door there.... For all this, we are indebted to you—as we are for your thoughtfulness in sending us each a generous fruit basket and taking us to the airport. Sincerely, Roger Enloe, President, U.N. We Believe."

Friends and former partners confess: "I owe a lot to Izzi." In addition to direct monetary help, he introduced friends to opportunities, arranged meetings that led to valuable board appointments, and offered counsel freely. One of his friends spent time in the hospital but never received a bill. He suspects Izzi had something to do with it.

"Everyone has problems," Izzi said. "I can't help them all." But it's surprising to learn how many he did help. He gave jobs to those who were down and out—an old Marine buddy, a childhood friend with a drinking problem, struggling relatives, children of friends and clients. Sometimes, as reported earlier, his generosity was not repaid.

No matter who or what may have disappointed him, Izzi's faith in the goodness of human beings never wavered. Neither did his love for and commitment to the city and state. Nevertheless, on one or two occasions, both his faith and his commitment were tested.

When the mayor of Salt Lake City found herself in serious financial trouble due to some business dealings she had engaged in long before she became mayor, she turned to friends for help, including I. J. Wagner. She first asked for ten thousand dollars, together with help in raising funds from others. Izzi declined both requests. The mayor returned personally to repeat her request. This time, Izzi gave her a small contribution, listed in a local newspaper article as one thousand dollars. He told her he would not solicit money for her. He later came to regret making the gift—not because he didn't think it was the right thing to do, but because it put him in the spotlight, caused him to be brought to court to explain why he had helped rescue the mayor from her financial problems, and forced him to hire an attorney. During the deposition process, the prosecutor implied that Izzi must have received something for his contribution. He probed Izzi's memory, and almost certainly was surprised when Izzi remembered every meeting he had ever had with the mayor, where he had gone with the mayor and her husband to dinner, the menu, how much it had cost, and endless other details. (He remembered because it was his habit to keep track of such things on the pocket calendar he always carried.) He even remembered giving the mayor's husband several two-dollar bills—not the exact date of the gift, but the month. When the attorney asked why Izzi had given them the money, Izzi said, "Just because I felt sorry for them." When the attorney accused him of making the payment in return for the mayor nominating him for powerful committee assignments, Izzi named all the city boards and committees he had served on—in detail. He explained that not a single one of his appointments had come from the mayor in question. He said, after questioning, that he had never sold any property to the city, county, or state, and that he had never asked for rezoning of any property he owned. When asked if he would declare the gift as a deduction on his income tax return, Izzi said, "Absolutely not." And when the attorney finally asked Izzi about his reason for giving the money, he said, "I was concerned about the image of the office for Salt Lake. That was my entire reason for giving it to her." The experience was not pleasant for Wagner. He felt his reputation had been tarnished and his motives had been misinterpreted.

The record shows that Izzi Wagner sincerely cared about others. He preferred the telephone to writing letters, and so the written record is limited. He used the phone to keep in touch with literally hundreds of friends around the world—a distant relative in Israel, a former gin rummy partner living in New York, a girlfriend from high school down on her luck in California, the widow of a longtime customer and friend. Izzi kept in touch, offered encouragement, watched over them. One of his friends said that when her husband died, Izzi called every week for months just to cheer her up and make sure her attitude was positive.

He helped a friend buy a car when hers was totaled in an accident. He helped send his secretary on a cruise when she needed a break from family problems. When friends mentioned their own health problems, Izzi would call one of his doctors to make an appointment for the friend. No matter how fully scheduled they may have been, doctors made room for Izzi's friends. In at least one instance, Izzi's intervention may have saved a life.

A building janitor asked Izzi to a family birthday party. To the janitor's surprise and great pleasure, Izzi went to the party, and while he could not speak much Spanish, he had a good time. He offered counsel to a waitress at the sandwich shop where he often went for tea and a donut. When she married, Izzi went to the wedding, and the bride sent him a large wedding-day portrait. He invited struggling young friends to lunch at Granato's, where he introduced them to senators, judges, mayors, and other luminaries. At such meetings, Izzi leveled the playing field so that everyone felt equally important. He took women friends to dinners, plays, concerts, and other events. Some had survived difficult challenges in their lives. Izzi helped them regain their dignity and self-respect. These were not isolated incidents. They reflected his pattern of living, his commitment to generosity.

Another factor that influenced Izzi's philanthropy was his belief that having one's name on a building has little meaning. He was fond of pointing out downtown buildings and saying, "That's the McIntyre Building. Do you know who McIntyre was? Does anyone alive today know who McIntyre was?" He went on to say that buildings don't last much longer than the human beings for which they are named. They wear out, become outmoded, and are replaced by newer, bigger structures. The only thing that survives, Izzi said, is the function of the building—assuming that the function has long-term value. All these factors entered into Izzi's contemplation about how best to "give something back" to the community.

He made a significant contribution to the University Hospital during construction of that facility. The hospital named a room after him, but he had no idea where the room was located. He also contributed half a million dollars to LDS Hospital, but when they wanted to put his name on a portion of the geriatric-care unit, he insisted that it be named instead to honor his friend Roy Simmons. In 1989, the Friends of LDS Hospital and the Deseret Foundation gave Izzi and Roy the Gold Caduceus Award, the organization's "most prestigious award." Izzi also gave a major contribution to Holy Cross Hospital (now Salt Lake Regional Medical Center), and he served on the hospital's capital-campaign steering committee.

Over the years, he made several contributions to health and education projects of The Church of Jesus Christ of Latter-day Saints, including a sizable gift to the Brigham Young University Jerusalem Center, for which he received a personal thank-you from his friend Robert Hales, then presiding bishop of the church. It included this handwritten message: "Thanks for your many considerations of good-faith and kind words in personal and community affairs. Your friend, Bob."

As mentioned earlier, he made several contributions to the Utah Arthritis Foundation, and he was active on the foundation's board for many years. In 1996, the Arthritis Foundation named I. J. Wagner "Man of the Year" at its annual black-tie dinner gala "in recognition of his dedication to community service and improving the lives of people with arthritis." The gala raised more than seventy-five thousand dollars for research, training, education, and patient services. The chair of the foundation's board of directors wrote: "No one in the history of the Foundation has ever been more deserving of this honor. The only problem was it took such a long time to get you to agree to do it." A member of the board wrote: "Many have told me that is the best honorary dinner of any kind they have ever attended. Best of all, it is the most successful dinner gala, financially, we have ever had. Thanks to you and the many contacts and friends you have. I can't tell you how glad I am that you finally agreed to be the recipient."

Izzi's longtime friend Sam Skaggs did not attend the Arthritis Foundation gala, but he sent a large contribution, together with a letter that said, in part: "Izzy [*sic*] is not only a trusted business associate but a loyal friend. He is one of those rare individuals wherein his hand shake is as good as his word.

I have always been honored to be counted among his friends. Please extend my sincere best wishes to Izzy on this occasion to honor him for his quiet service to this most worthwhile charity and for his contributions to the betterment of our community and state."

Izzi wanted to somehow memorialize his wife, his mother, and his sister. He had no idea how to go about achieving that goal. But one day in 1994, he was walking through his old neighborhood on Third South (as he often did). A building he had once owned on the site of the old adobe house had recently been purchased and renovated by Salt Lake County to serve as studios and a rehearsal hall for a local dance company, Repertory Dance Theatre (RDT). The company had been evicted from space in the Salt Palace Convention Center while that facility was being rebuilt. Through a large window, Izzi could see the dancers rehearsing. They reminded him of Jeanné, and he stopped to watch. He came back the next day . . and the next. Watching the dancers soon turned into a regular ritual for Izzi.

After a few days, the dancers became a little nervous about the gentleman in tennis shoes and a baseball cap who stopped to watch through the window while they practiced their dance routines. Eventually, Linda Smith, artistic director of RDT, stepped outside, introduced herself, and offered Izzi a seat if he wanted to come inside. He declined, but he told her about the adobe house once located on the same site, about Wagner Bag Company, and about Jeanné. Izzi's reminiscences led Linda to share her dream about a permanent home for RDT and other small performing arts groups in the county. Later, she mentioned the conversation to county officials, many of whom already knew I. J. Wagner.

That casual meeting was the beginning of what would eventually become the Rose Wagner Center for the Performing Arts, located exactly where the Wagner family's first home had been at 144 West Third South. Inside the center would be the Jeanné Wagner Theatre, (a five-hundred-seat performance venue) and the Leona Wagner Black Box Theatre (a smaller, more intimate, all-purpose facility). The Rose Wagner Center would also include rehearsal rooms and office space for several arts groups. Almost eighty performing groups would schedule performances in the facility during its first year. But when Izzi talked to Linda Smith in 1994, the opening was only a dream, still several years down the road.

County officials and arts organizations had been looking for some time toward a smaller performance venue to augment existing auditoriums. Two-thousand-seat auditoriums at Abravanel Hall and the Capitol Theatre were excellent facilities, but small groups could neither fill the seats nor pay the rent. Officials knew these smaller groups would be much more comfort-able—and successful—in a theater with five to seven hundred seats. Inter-ested groups had already looked at several possible locations. They had even formed an association with the primary purpose of identifying a location and raising money. The county had purchased two properties on Third South, but plans were relatively unfocused and unambitious. Fund-raising was not going well. That is, until Izzi Wagner stopped to reminisce and watch RDT rehearsals.

At first, he wasn't sure a theater-type project reflected the memory of his mother. She was a businesswoman, not a performer. Then he remembered how much she loved music, theater, dance…and how much the perform-ing arts meant to her. As a child in Latvia, music had been one of the few pleasures in her life. In Boston, she expended considerable effort to attend Sunday concerts in the park. Later, she saved pennies in order to take Izzi and his siblings to concerts, plays, and vaudeville performances. She insisted that her children take music lessons. And in later years, she always preferred live performances to movies or television. Of course, Izzi had changed his name to Irving Jerome Wagner partly because he knew his mother admired Irving Berlin and Jerome Kern, two famous Jewish American songwriters. Rose Wagner believed in the performing arts; they added beauty and meaning to life. "She loved music and all the arts," Izzi said. "We were poor, but every extra cent went to violin lessons for me and piano lessons for my sister." He added, "She would have liked watching the performances in the building we will name for her, just as my wife would have liked watching today's per-formers. The arts meant much to my mother and my wife."

Besides, Izzi reasoned, business is short-term, whereas the arts have stay-ing power. Much of the bag business—where Rose had such success—was already a thing of the past, replaced by bulk movement of wheat, flour, pota-toes, and other commodities. But the performing arts survive every economic downturn and technological advance, he reasoned. A performing arts center would be a community asset for many years to come.

Izzi's first contribution came in 1995. It was a half-million dollars to be used for planning and site preparation. By the end of 1996, total contribu-tions from all sources reached almost three million dollars. Much of it was from Wagner family members. In 1998, Izzi gave another block of his Zions Bancorporation stock. He also bought a piece of property adjacent to the county-owned properties and gave it to the project. He became involved in the planning process and in design decisions. The original plan called for building the structure in phases as donated money became available. Izzi said he didn't have time to wait for such things; he wanted the project completed as soon as possible. The architectural drawings showed cinder-block facing. Izzi said it looked temporary and cheap; he wanted stone facing and offered to pay for it.

It is difficult to determine exactly how much I. J. Wagner and the various entities he controlled contributed to the Rose Wagner Performing Arts Center. Izzi's brother, Abe, was certainly involved. And others added contributions also—sometimes because Izzi asked for contributions, and sometimes because contributors respected the Wagner family and wanted to honor family members. Izzi remembered his own gift as being in the neighborhood of seven million dollars. In any case, it was the major portion of the total cost of the project. In addition, he owned the parking lot across the street, which was and is vital to the success of the Rose Wagner Center. He believed that no enterprise can succeed without provision for adequate parking. And as indicated earlier, he made certain that the parking lot he owned would continue to provide parking for the Rose Wagner Center in perpetuity. He also insisted that the company operating the parking lot provide a full-time attendant to welcome visitors and collect parking money. His was probably the only parking lot in town with an attendant. It gave Izzi pleasure to provide one more job.

As the facility took shape, and as tenants began to occupy space, Shirley Ririe, co–artistic director of the Ririe-Woodbury Dance Company, wrote:

> The entrance of Izzi Wagner on the scene was the magic potion that made everything come together. I often pinch myself to see if all of this is true. The environment is so aesthetic. Every day as I walk up from my office I gaze at the mountains through that spectacular window wall of a view, or I glance at the black marley [a type of dance floor] on the floor or the bird's eye maple on the walls, and say to myself, "You have finally arrived." The ambiance is so uplifting. I have been to three gala parties in the lobby and the Rose Room, and each time the elegance cannot be surpassed.

Later, Shirley Ririe wrote to Izzi, "This is such a great present to us, to have a beautiful place to work and perform. We feel very fortunate. All our East and West Coast friends are mighty jealous. In the arts you always talk about having an angel. You are our angel. You made miraculous events happen and our city and our artists will pay homage throughout the next century and longer."

The first phase of the center, the Leona Wagner Black Box Theatre, opened in 1997. Repertory Dance Theatre presented the first event on the Leona Wagner Stage, a production titled *The Essence of Rose* created especially for the opening. Izzi donated funds to pay for videotaping the performance.

A newspaper report about the dance performance stimulated a letter to the editor by Mack Donald Sullivan:

> An article, 'The Essence of Rose' (*Tribune*, Jan. 26) brought back wonderful memories of my youth....
>
> My buddies and I lived in apartments in the downtown Salt Lake City area, and we found a surefire way to raise money. On Saturday mornings, three or four of us would take a red wagon and cover all of the Salt Lake downtown alleys and between and behind stores, hotels, restaurants, etc., gathering refundable beer and whiskey bottles discarded from the Friday night binges.
>
> We took our bottles to an adobe house on 100 West and 300 South (Wagner Bag Co.), where a cheerful-natured little short lady would count our bottles with much teasing and banter in her accented English. When she discovered we were using our money to go to the Isis Theater to see Tom Mix, Hoot Gibson or Jack Steel, we were forever known as "the cowboys."
>
> When Mrs. Wagner learned that on our way to the movies we'd stop at Keeley's Restaurant and Candy Store for a bag of "scrapple," a mixture of candy discards from their Ogden factory, she then called us "the candy cowboys."
>
> These are my pleasant memories of friendly, cheerful, patient, little Mrs. Wagner.

Izzi was obviously pleased with the facility. In 1999, five days before the formal opening of the second phase, which included the Jeanné Wagner Theatre, the *Salt Lake Tribune* reported:

> One of Utah's most jovial business tycoons, I. J. "Izzi" Wagner, steps into the center of the newly finished theater that bears his mother's name [*sic*] and breaks into his best Al Jolson impersonation.
>
> "Mammy, how I love ya, how I love ya, my dear old Mammy. I'd walk a thousand miles for one of your smiles, my dear old Mammyyyyy," he improvises, arms outstretched, hands waving.
>
> "Sounds pretty good, huh?" he says. "The acoustics, I mean. It's going to sound great in here."

On March 31, 1999, I. J. Wagner's eighty-sixth birthday, the Rose Wagner Performing Arts Center held a grand-opening gala. The event began with a performance by the Utah Symphony Orchestra of *Fanfare for the Common Man,* a reference to Izzi Wagner's commitment to openness and diversity. The Utah Symphony was followed by performances from the arts groups to be housed in the facility. A children's dance group dressed in burlap performed a "bag dance." The culmination of the evening was the presentation to Izzi of a birthday cake with the words "Happy Birthday Izzy" [*sic*]—a cake large enough to feed the assembled crowd, a cake bedecked with frosting formed into red and white roses.

I. J. Wagner made brief remarks:

Thank you. I am not the one who should be honored here today. The honors should go to Rose Wagner, my mother, and Jeanné Wagner, my wife. They deserve the credit for this celebration.

My mother and father came to Utah almost by accident nearly a century ago. They had about sixty cents between them. This great nation and this friendly city gave them the opportunities they needed. They supplied the wisdom and the hard work to begin a small business. They sold bottles and rags before finding an opportunity in the packaging industry.

We lived in a two-room walk-up apartment where the Rose Wagner Performing Arts Center is located. Later, my father bought a house only a few steps away.

When my father died, I was only sixteen. My mother and I had to take over operation of the Wagner Bag Company. It was the time of the Great Depression, and the business was deeply in debt. My mother schooled me in the ways of business and taught me to deal honestly with customers and employees. She loved the arts and taught me to appreciate music and dance. It is only fitting that this complex should bear her name.

About the time we got the Wagner Bag Company on solid footing, along came World War II. I joined the marines. But on the day before I shipped out, I married Jeanné. She was a beautiful dancer with roots in Utah. She waited patiently for me while I went from island to island in the Pacific.

She taught me to understand the sacrifices it takes to be a dancer…or an artist of any kind. We traveled all over the world, and we met hundreds of dancers, actors, singers, and other artists. She was graceful and beautiful until the day she died. It is only fitting that the dance theatre here should bear her name.

My successes—whatever they might be—were due largely to the powerful influences of Rose Wagner and Jeanné Wagner. Regardless of my
eventual status in life, I would have revered and honored them. But I'm
pleased to be able to share their memory with the community through this
facility.

I hope the Rose Wagner Performing Arts Center and the Jeanné Wagner Theatre bring half as much happiness to others as those two brought
to me.

Thank you, again.

Those who knew Rose Wagner are confident she would be pleased with the
Rose Wagner Performing Arts Center. And being involved with the facility
gave Izzi many opportunities to tell Rose Wagner's story—growing up in
Latvia, coming to a strange land, arriving in Salt Lake City with no resources,
building a business, losing a husband at an early age, becoming the sage
matriarch of a successful family. Through Izzi's telling, the story of Rose Yuddin Wagner became a permanent printed record in newspapers, magazines,
and other media. The memory of Rose, Jeanné, and Leona will not fade for
many decades thanks to I. J. Wagner and the Rose Wagner Performing Arts
Center. Appropriately, the center is generally referred to as "The Rose." It is
probably the most frequently used performance venue in the city. In 2003,
the center presented 390 events—more than one a day.

Next, Izzi turned his attention to another of his great interests: children.
Watching Izzi around children was one of life's great delights. His eyes brightened, his smile widened, his enthusiasm blossomed. He reached out to touch
a child's hand, and it appeared as if he was reaching back across the decades
to once again "touch" his own magical childhood.

In a strange juxtaposition of coincidence, none of Harry and Rose Wagner's children produced children themselves. Abe married late in life, and he
and his young wife adopted two daughters, but the Wagner-Yuddin genetic
strain ended with Abe, Izzi, and Leona.

Izzi dreamed of giving back some of his own life experience to children
he would never know. The James L. White Jewish Community Center on
east 1700 South in Salt Lake City was woefully short on space. The center
offered limited recreational and educational programs to children and adults
from all backgrounds. It had become a fairly popular gathering place for
children during the summer, on weekends, and after school. But the facility
had no swimming pool and very little space for basketball, volleyball, and
other activities. The Jewish community had constructed a new synagogue a

mile south of the White Center, and plans were under development to construct a new school adjacent to the synagogue. The school would augment the White Center to provide additional educational opportunities for children and adults. It would also have a swimming pool and other recreational facilities. But the lot on which the synagogue was located could accommodate only limited facilities. The only way to build the education center was to sacrifice much of the available parking area. The facilities committee sought additional land for parking in an adjacent city park, but area residents and city officials rejected the request, citing covenants made when the land was donated to the city for the purpose of creating a children's park.

At about this same time, representatives of the Jewish Community Center approached I. J. Wagner, seeking advice and financial help for the proposed new education center. Izzi looked at the plans and told his friends on the committee that the space was too small, that there was insufficient room for parking, and that the crowded facility would be obsolete within a few years. He offered to help fund architectural studies, but his instincts told him the project was not viable, and he did not hesitate to express his concerns.

Izzi's response spurred the facilities committee to look for other solutions to their problem. As one member of the group wrote, "How can we accept a gift…from a self made man…and not take his advice on what to do with it? Seems foolish." The group's attention turned to another piece of property, this one also located about a mile from the James White Jewish Community Center in the other direction, north.

The Fort Douglas Country Club was situated at the northeast corner of the University of Utah campus. It had once been an officers club, adjacent to a beautiful eighteen-hole golf course created by the army during the 1930s and '40s. When the military turned over Fort Douglas land to the university in the 1950s, '60s, and '70s, the spectacular officers club was sold to a local group that named it the Fort Douglas Country Club. Club members made improvements to the swimming pool and added several outdoor tennis courts. The golf course was not part of the land purchase, but use of the course was included as part of the arrangement. As the years went by, the university needed more and more of the golf course land for campus expansion. Soon, the golf course was down to nine holes…and the nine holes became shorter and shorter.

At the same time, members of the Fort Douglas Country Club acquired a new golf course called Hidden Valley in the southeast quadrant of Salt Lake Valley. The Fort Douglas building became the social center, while the distant golf course was a primary attraction for recreation. It was an untenable situation for Fort Douglas–Hidden Valley Country Club members, and so they set about raising money to abandon the Fort Douglas site and build a social facility at the golf course location.

In the late 1990s, the Fort Douglas Country Club building and property came onto the market. The asking price was three million dollars. But parts of the building were more than fifty years old. It presented structural challenges, and it did not meet government requirements for access or safety. Many organizations—including the University of Utah—wanted the building and its 4.86 acres, but none could raise the funds necessary to buy the property and finance improvements necessary to make the building functional, safe, and accessible to handicapped individuals.

It didn't take Izzi Wagner long to see the potential of the Fort Douglas Country Club building. He offered the Jewish Community Center a million dollars to match another million from a national foundation, with a third million to be raised locally. On September 5, 1997, the Salt Lake Jewish Community Center purchased the Fort Douglas Country Club.

The project was not without opposition from a few area residents, who feared it would generate too much traffic...and a few members of the Jewish community who considered the project too ambitious. Izzi did not totally disregard the assumption that his interest was stimulated, in part, by the fact that he was once rejected for membership in the Fort Douglas Country Club because of his Jewish heritage. However, the primary driving force behind his commitment to the project was his well-tested instinct about location, potential, and space—especially space for parking. He envisioned the majestic setting of the club as a place where all segments of the community would be welcome, and where children could experience the diversity he had experienced in his youth—without the prejudice and discrimination he remembered.

He also insisted that the project not be simply a remodeling of the old building but a completely new structure built around the attractive stone structure and designed to reflect the new functions of the facility. The focus was to be on family activities—swimming, basketball, tennis, physical fitness, educational opportunities, and so on. There would be room for small social events, but food service would come from outside. The only food available on-site would be hamburgers, hot dogs, and a few other basics necessary to sustain children and adults engaged in recreational pursuits. In a letter to the president of the Salt Lake Jewish Community Center, Izzi wrote, "It is my desire that the project be completed with all deliberate speed and that the quality of materials and design be first rate."

Izzi emphasized again and again that his participation was contingent on keeping membership open to everyone, regardless of race, religion, or belief system. The only membership limitation was to be the number of individuals the facility could comfortably handle. The old building was on the National Register, and so much of the outside appearance had to be preserved. This necessity turned out to be a benefit, because the architectural beauty of the structure added dignity to the development.

Architects improved the Olympic-size outdoor pool to make it more family-friendly. They added a new wing to house administrative offices, classrooms, gymnasium, indoor pool, exercise room, open meeting space/atrium, and other facilities. They increased the number of tennis courts and made it possible to enclose most of them in "bubble" covers during winter months. The result is one of the most complete and modern recreational centers in the city. The atrium has a climbing wall, and the exercise room contains all types of mechanical training devices, from treadmills to stationary bicycles and weight-lifting platforms. Thanks to Izzi's insistence on high quality, it is, without question, the most beautiful facility of its type in the state. And it is located in one of the most scenic spots in the city, with a spectacular view of the entire Salt Lake Valley.

The I. J. and Jeanné Wagner Jewish Community Center was officially dedicated on October 14, 2001. In a few weeks, all available memberships were sold (for a very reasonable price). In response to continuing requests, Izzi asked managers to open a few more memberships…which was done. The center operates about eighteen hours a day, and it is always buzzing with activity. Professional men and women come in during the early morning hours to work out before going to their offices. Both children and adults use the facilities during the day. Classes and other activities run until ten o'clock. Izzi Wagner was there three or four afternoons a week, working out on a treadmill or stationary bicycle. Of course, there was a special parking place near the front door marked "Reserved for I. J. Wagner."

He enjoyed taking visitors to the center, buying them kosher hot dogs, and showing off the well-used facilities. During the summer months, he drew special satisfaction from pointing to children of all races playing together in the outdoor swimming pool while parents sat in nearby chairs cementing friendships.

On a wall near the entrance of the center are framed photos of Izzi and Jeanné. Between the photos is a commemorative plaque that includes these words: "[I. J. Wagner] hopes children of all backgrounds will grow up in an atmosphere of tolerance and acceptance, free from hatred and bigotry."

But Izzi was Izzi. He turned aside compliments with self-deprecating humor. The baseball cap he chose to wear on most days was emblazoned with "JCC" for "Jewish Community Center." When asked where he got the cap, he would say, with a smile, "It's my fifteen-million-dollar hat." And much to his chagrin, some of the employees at the center—and a few of Izzi's friends—happily referred to the old Fort Douglas Country Club site as "Fort Wagner."

The first-year program guide showed more than one hundred activities, programs, classes, and celebrations at Fort Wagner—from cooking classes for youngsters to athletic programs for all ages, art and music lessons, tango classes, a bridge club, and family bowling night. When Izzi first looked through the program, he smiled, shook his head, and wondered aloud how they could do it all. The answer, of course, was that without the generosity of I. J. Wagner, "they" could not have done it at all. Izzi Wagner had, indeed, given something back to the community. He had reason to enjoy life. And he did.

10

At Peace with the World ... and Himself

As the twenty-first century began, Izzi Wagner was a man at peace. He was what he was, and he had no desire to be someone or something he was not. There was no pretense in the man. When someone asked him how he was, he was likely to answer, "Old...and glad of it," meaning that being old was preferable to the alternative. As time went on, he struggled a little with short-term memory, but he could always remember a good story to tell, the name of a person he hadn't seen for years, or how the city looked at any given point in the twentieth century...or who picked up the check for lunch.

Financially, Izzi was "comfortable." But there was certainly no large Wagner fortune remaining to be divided when the time came. What little he had not already given away was carefully identified for distribution after his death. He had a few shares of stock in Zions Bank, where he served on the board of directors for so many years, but most of his holdings had been turned over to his favorite projects. Along the way, he picked up the stock options he earned from being a director on several different boards. Those stocks were donated to selected charities, including the Rose Wagner Performing Arts Center and the I. J. and Jeanné Wagner Jewish Community Center. In every case, he bought low and donated high. Interestingly, he never had a broker. He bought and sold stocks on his own and kept the certificates in his safe deposit box. His stock portfolio was never widely diversified. He believed in buying stock in companies he knew, and then holding the stock for long periods. His investment preference was always commercial real estate—not necessarily owning and managing it for long periods, but buying and selling properties as short-term investments.

He received regular retirement payments from at least two boards on which he served and from St. Regis Paper Company—a company long ago swallowed up by larger companies during the merger frenzies of modern U.S. free enterprise (currently Champion Paper Company). He also received a modest income from lease payments on his share of the land under the Salt Lake Marriott Hotel. During the early years of the century, he received regular mortgage payments from at least one of the properties he sold years earlier. A Social Security check arrived every month. (Izzi began paying into Social Security on the day the program was created in 1933. He delayed collecting Social Security payments as long as the law allowed him to put it off.)

Payments came directly to his office. He did not participate in direct-deposit programs because he wanted the hands-on experience of handling his checks. Either Izzi or his secretary deposited the checks in the bank, which was just a few floors down from his office. His safe deposit boxes were also in the same building, but he rarely visited them. He probably knew what the boxes contained, roughly, and he sometimes threatened to "clean them out," but he never got around to it. "Cleaning out" would represent a brush with finality, and he was never ready to confront that possibility. For the same reason, he had closets full of clothes he had not worn in years, and he still held on to much of the clothing that had belonged to Jeanné.

I. J. Wagner had four cars, a high-definition big-screen television set, radio and television in every room of his house, a cell phone, and all sorts of other modern gadgets. But he did not own a computer, and he did not have one in his office. His secretary used an old IBM Selectric typewriter. Izzi said he was too old to learn new skills. The fax machine in his office was old enough to deserve a place at the Smithsonian. Each week, it cranked out several pages of jokes sent to Izzi from a relative in Philadelphia.

The only property he owned was his home, his share of the land under the Salt Lake Marriott Hotel, and the parking lot across from the Rose Wagner Performing Arts Center, from which he received a portion of the parking fees. He drove by every day to see if the lot was full, and he often made small talk with the attendant. (He said the parking lot replaced two bordellos, but the businesses were related, because both depend on short-term "parking." He also said the car-parking business is better than the previous business at the location, because parking cars is legal and is a better bargain for patrons.)

In 2002, the mayor of Salt Lake City decided to install angle parking in the center of Third South, directly in front of Wagner's parking lot. Izzi knew it would cost him a considerable amount of business when drivers chose free or metered parking over leaving their cars in Izzi's parking lot. He called the mayor to express his concerns. The mayor said, "Everyone thinks on-street parking is a good idea, so I don't want to talk about it." Every day, Izzi drove by his parking lot, and so he knew reasonably well how much the center-of-street parking affected his business. The year after installation of the in-street parking, the mayor was running for reelection. He wrote to Izzi asking for a political contribution. Izzi wrote back on a piece of notepaper: "I've already given you more than $60,000." No doubt, the mayor knew Izzi was referring to the losses caused by on-street parking.

Izzi occasionally worried about his resources. He drew up lists of what he had and what he was worth. He sometimes talked openly about giving more away, because he wanted to leave as little as possible. He wanted to minimize his estate, but he also wanted to make sure he left no debts as a result of unexpected illness or other events. He thought he had given enough to the Jewish Community Center. At the same time, he worried every time he heard about an operating deficit at the facility. He talked about doing something for his longtime secretary, Dora Bailey, but he kept putting it off, wondering what to do and how to do it. At times, he doubted his own capacity and wondered if he was making good decisions.

As long as he was able, I. J. Wagner went to his office every day, driving one of his four cars. Actually, he rarely drove the Rolls-Royce, and he did not bother to pay state licensing fees on that car. Breakfast was a sweet roll and a cup of tea. During the day, he talked on the telephone with friends in various parts of the world, and he took care of whatever business may have been pending. His loyal secretary of many years, Dora Bailey, handled the daily office details and made sure he got to his various appointments on time. On most days, Izzi napped on the couch in his office. As the months went by, the nap times grew longer and longer. Almost every day, he went to lunch with friends at Sam Granato's delicatessen—mostly because Sam made his own office available to Izzi and his friends so the lunch hour could be semiprivate. At least two or three times a week, Izzi's lunch companion was his longtime friend Roy Simmons.

On Saturdays, he had lunch at the Salt Lake Country Club with one or two friends. If the weather permitted, lunch was followed by a few holes of golf. One day, Izzi got on the elevator in his office building, and a friend asked if he was still playing golf. "No," Izzi said. "I lost my golf ball." He tried the same line during lunch at the country club a few days later. A table companion excused himself and disappeared for a few minutes. Later, an employee from the pro shop came in and said, "Look, Mr. Wagner. I found your ball." He handed Izzi a golf ball with his name on it.

On Sunday mornings, Izzi had breakfast at a downtown restaurant where a few longtime cronies gathered. He had a number of women friends, and every other week or so he called one of them to invite her to lunch or dinner. "I always ask to see her bank balance before I buy dinner," he said jokingly. On occasion, he took a "date" to the theater, although such outings became less common as the years went by.

The long friendship between Izzi and Roy Simmons continued. When Roy had a small stroke, Izzi worried about him, and when Izzi fell ill, Roy lost some of his own vitality. The depth of their unusual friendship was indicated by a letter Simmons wrote to Wagner in 1969, more than thirty years earlier, thanking Izzi for agreeing to serve on the board of Zions Bancorporation:

> As you know, this corporation means a lot to me and I guess I am more careful in choosing who I want to have with me on this team than any other organization with which I am connected; so I particularly wanted you to be on the board. . . .
>
> You are a great friend Izzy [sic], and I really appreciate the fact because I have often told Tibby [Roy's wife], if anything ever happened to me, I want her to know that you are the man she should rely heavily on to determine what action she should take. Naturally I hope she never has to face this problem, but it is good to have friends like you in case anything ever did happen.

In a shuffle of offices during the remodeling of what is now the Zions Bank Building, Roy Simmons ended up in the office next door to I. J. Wagner. Frequently, Roy dropped in to ask if they were going to lunch together. Izzi said, "It depends on who's picking up the check." And the banter began. Simmons wore a coat and tie and well-shined shoes. Wagner wore a baseball cap, knit golf shirt, cotton pants, and tennis shoes. He said, "I have three tuxedos, twenty suits, and three hundred neckties…and hope I never have to wear any of them again."

Shortly before noon, the two millionaires would climb into Izzi's Cadillac convertible, or whichever car he was driving that day, and go off to lunch. Izzi would often say, "Roy, you're the only Mormon in town with a Jewish chauffeur." The banter continued on the way to lunch. Izzi: "Roy, didn't we own that building once?" Roy: "I think so, but you sold it too soon." Roy: "I hope you paid the insurance on this car." Izzi: "I did, but it doesn't cover passengers."

One summer day in 2003, they went to lunch at Granato's with the convertible top down. As they were finishing lunch, someone rushed in to tell Izzi it was raining, and he had better put the top up on his car. Izzi went out to raise the top, but he couldn't remember how to get it done. He told Roy, "If I drive thirty-five miles per hour all the way back to the office, the rain will go up over the windshield, and we won't get wet." Off they went. Sure enough, the rain flew up and over the pair…until they came to a stoplight. Soon, both men were soaked. As they drove down the ramp into the underground parking garage, Roy said, "I'll send you the cleaning bill for my suit." Izzi responded, "No, you pay it. You have more money than I do. Besides, I picked up the check for lunch."

On another occasion, they were in the Jeep Cherokee. Izzi parked on the street in front of Granato's, and they went inside for a leisurely lunch and talk with friends. When they were ready to leave, Izzi could not find his car keys. He called Dora Bailey and told her to look for the second set of keys in his desk so she could bring them to the restaurant if necessary. (Izzi was meticulous about taking care of his belongings, and so losing his keys was most unusual; still, he was prepared, as always, with a second set of keys at the office.) He then went out to see if he might have left the keys in the car. Sure enough, he could see them through the window, still in the ignition. Then he tried the driver's side door. It was unlocked—also unusual. When he reached for the keys, he found that not only was the key in the ignition, but the ignition was on…and the motor was running. It had been running in idle with the door unlocked on a busy public street for an hour and half. One measure of Izzi's self-assurance was that he was able to tell this story about himself without the slightest embarrassment.

On the wall behind the chair on which Izzi usually sat at the huge table in Sam Granato's office was a sign that duplicated a sign in the parking area at the I. J. and Jeanné Wagner Jewish Community Center: "Reserved for Izzi Wagner." Seated around the big table at various times, one might find a judge, a U.S. senator, a well-known business leader, a young entrepreneur, an old friend of Wagner's, a woman friend, a political consultant, a religious leader, or whoever else happened to be in the neighborhood. Sometimes, the guests included business associates of Sam Granato's—food dealers from the East and West Coasts. Granato always introduced them to Izzi with great respect, and Izzi asked questions about business conditions, or he remembered friends in the area, or he offered compliments. And of course, he always came up with a one-liner or a story to make everyone feel comfortable. The conversations were not quite so serious as they had been in earlier days, but the friendships were deep and sincere.

On Izzi's eighty-ninth birthday, friends arranged a surprise birthday party at Granato's. Guests gathered around long tables set up in the Granato warehouse. They included Izzi's boyhood friend Hank Milano, Roy Simmons and his wife, several leaders from the Mormon Tabernacle Choir organization, well-known sports figures, a Catholic priest, a sister-in-law, a niece from California, politicians, business leaders, attorneys, and various other Izzi fans. As guests consumed lasagna and birthday cake, they told stories about Izzi Wagner or repeated favorite Wagner jokes. A local television station was on hand to cover the event, and a lengthy report appeared on the evening news. Interviewer Chris Vanocur asked Izzi, "Did you know you had so many friends?" Izzi responded, "No. They're here for the free lunch." All his friends laughed; it was just what they expected from Izzi Wagner.

During the first years of the twenty-first century, I. J. Wagner's health was reasonably good for a man his age. He took his own blood pressure almost every day, saw doctors and dentists regularly (sometimes, perhaps, more often than was necessary), and kept himself on a healthy exercise regimen. He never worried about calories, carbohydrates, or fat in his diet.

When his friend Roy Simmons suffered a stroke that markedly reduced his activities, Izzi increased his own exercise regimen. He spent between thirty minutes and an hour every day in the exercise rooms at LDS Hospital or the Jewish Community Center. He favored the treadmills and stationary bikes. Whenever he felt even a slight change in physical health, he called or visited his doctor, Frank Yanowitz, at LDS Hospital. He carried a cane in his car but rarely used it. Sometimes, he complained about being tired, and he worried about forgetting appointments and other obligations.

Even as his own health deteriorated, Izzi continued to be concerned about those in need, especially the homeless and the elderly. "I believe in government subsidies for low-income housing," he said. "We need low interest, long-term loans for housing, especially for the elderly. We have all the money in the world to help other countries. What's wrong with spending a little money on our own people? We spend thirty thousand dollars a year to house murderers, but we have no money to house older citizens who have contributed greatly to this nation."

There is little question that Izzi missed family and friends who had passed away—especially Jeanné. But he didn't dwell on it. Certainly, they played important roles in the many stories he told, but he didn't believe in worrying or in being consumed by events he couldn't change. "If you have a problem and can do something about it, then do it," he said. "If there's nothing you can do about it, then forget it and move on." He did not believe in a heaven or a hereafter. For I. J. Wagner, life was a finite experience that would end at the time of death. Religion was not a part of his life, although he respected those who found comfort in their beliefs, whatever their religious preferences. "There are many religions in the world," he said, "and each one claims to have 'the truth.' I have friends of all kinds. I don't believe one friend is better than another because of his or her religion."

Irving Jerome Wagner was the last surviving member of the Wagner family. Rose Wagner suffered a stroke at the age of seventy-six and died on March 26, 1959. She was visiting Leona in Los Angeles at the time. Izzi arranged for her body to be returned to Salt Lake for burial near her husband, Harry, and her sister, Ethel. Rose had told family members: "I'll be buried next to Ethel. I'll still be living on Fourth Avenue. I won't have to change my address very much."

As long as Izzi was involved with Wagner Bag Company, he kept an office for Rose. Each day, either Izzi or Abe drove Rose from her home in Salt Lake's Avenues district to the office. She began the day by reading two newspapers—a national Jewish paper and the local *Salt Lake Tribune*. For years, she signed company checks, looking carefully at each one and often asking questions. In some respects, she served as the company's internal auditor. In later years, she spent part of each year with her daughter, Leona, in Los Angeles. She genuinely liked to be around others, and she made friends easily wherever she was. She regularly attended synagogue with her friends.

In Los Angeles, she liked to go to the horse races, where she could strike up friendly conversations with strangers. She often rode city buses to the racetrack and back. Leona worried about it, but Izzi told her that Rose never wagered more than five dollars or so, that she enjoyed being on her own, and that the excursions were primarily social. On one occasion, Rose caught the wrong bus on the way home. She ended up in a sometimes dangerous part of Los Angeles. She walked into the nearest establishment—a corner bar. Most patrons turned to look at her as if she were from another planet. But she struck up a conversation and told of her predicament. Before long, one of the patrons walked her to a second bus stop nearby and made sure she got on the correct bus to take her to Leona's Beverly Hills location.

On another occasion, Rose got off the bus at the wrong stop. She decided to walk the rest of the way to her daughter's house. On the way, nature called with some urgency. She saw a house with a swimming pool and a dressing room, so she walked into the yard and used the facility. However, she was a little late, so she washed out her underclothes and hung them on the window to dry. Then she sat down on one of the pool lounge chairs. The woman of the house saw Rose sitting in the chair beside her pool. She rushed out of the house in anger and asked Rose what in the world she was doing in the yard. Rose was one of the most friendly people on earth. In her broken English, she explained her situation, and the two began talking. They became great friends and often had dinner together or went to shows together.

Abe Wagner lived in his mother's house until he was in his middle forties. He then married a woman almost twenty years younger than himself. They adopted two daughters, Robin and Candace. Candace is a talented musician who still lives in Utah. Robin eventually moved to Florida. Izzi remained in contact with both of them. Abe had various roles in the Wagner businesses, although he was never as active or as visible as his brother. Abe's first love was sports—especially baseball. During his youth, he played for a while in a semipro league, and once tried out for a professional team. He made sure that Wagner Company fielded teams in local amateur leagues, and he maintained a company box at the local minor league baseball field. He also enjoyed golf, and he could be seen frequently at the Salt Lake Country Club and other golf courses in the area. Like all the Wagners, Abe was gregarious, and he often circulated about town in tennis shoes, jeans, a sports shirt, a warmup jacket, and a baseball cap, chatting with friends at the barbershop, on a street corner, in a restaurant, or at one of the city's well-concealed "bookie joints."

Like his father, Harry, Abe had more than passing interest in horse racing. Unlike his father, Abe picked winning horses more often than also-rans. He spent a considerable amount of time studying the racing news to learn about horses and their jockeys. He knew where and how to wager on horse races, as well as other sporting events. Abe Wagner died September 22, 2000. He was eighty-seven.

When Leona Wagner reached high school age in the early 1930s, her father had already passed away, the Great Depression was well under way, and Wagner Bag Company was still struggling to survive. In addition, the Wagner house was virtually surrounded by bars, pool halls, sleazy hotels, and houses of prostitution. Rose felt strongly that it was not a good environment for a teenage girl. Rose wrote to her sister Mary in Boston to ask if Leona could stay with her until she finished high school. Leona moved to Boston, where she learned secretarial skills in high school and continued her music lessons under Mary's guidance. After graduation, Leona got a job with a local jewelry establishment. That led to contacts with another jewelry firm in Los Angeles, and she decided to move to the West Coast. There she met a young artist named Burnam Pearlman, and the two were married in 1946. They came to Salt Lake City and moved into a basement apartment in Rose

Wagner's house. Pearlman was a good artist, but the postwar period was not a rewarding time for artists, especially in Utah. Izzi gave him a sales job at Wagner Company, but he had little interest in that line of work. The two moved back to California, where Leona could reconnect to the jewelry business and Pearlman could occasionally sell a painting.

Leona remained a partner in some of the Wagner business ventures, but she did not return to Salt Lake, except for occasional visits, even after her husband died. In 1992, doctors diagnosed a brain tumor. By then, she was retired and living alone in her Beverly Hills apartment. Izzi knew Leona needed full-time care. He investigated a few facilities in Los Angeles, but he was not satisfied with any of them. Besides, he did not like the idea of leaving his sister alone and without family members nearby. Izzi arranged for her to come to Salt Lake City and be admitted to St. Joseph's Villa, a Salt Lake City facility operated by the Catholic church. She died there on February 17, 1993, at the age of seventy-five.

Izzi's health began to deteriorate visibly in the final months of 2003. It troubled him greatly when he forgot events that happened the day before or appointments for the coming day. He began using a cane now and then, and he sometimes skipped his exercise routine.

In late June 2004, someone or something ran into Izzi's Cadillac Allante convertible. He said it happened while he was parked in his parking lot to have dinner at a nearby restaurant, but he could not recall the details of the accident. Salt Lake police had no reports of an accident involving such a car that evening, and so it probably did happen in the parking lot, as Izzi claimed. The car was badly damaged, so much so that the repair estimate almost exceeded the value of the car. Still, Izzi insisted that it be repaired. "It was Jeanné's favorite car," he said, "and I know she would want me to fix it." But repair parts were difficult to obtain, and friends instructed the body shop not to rush the project. Izzi would not drive that car again—or any other car.

In late July 2004, Izzi fell at his home, opening deep cuts on his chin and arm. He could not get up from the floor. Friends rushed him to the hospital, where an MRI revealed that he had apparently fallen several weeks earlier and had ruptured a vessel in or near his brain. Doctors operated to remove the fluids putting pressure on his brain. On one occasion, a doctor told visitors that Izzi probably would not make it through the night. But he did. He cheered up whenever friends dropped by—and many came to wish him well, from Roy Simmons to Hank Milano to the operator of the service station where he bought gas. Sam Granato smuggled in a sandwich now and then (usually enough to feed everyone on duty in Izzi's area). His recovery was slow and sometimes tenuous, but he eventually gained strength and was moved to the same care facility where his sister, Leona, had spent her final weeks. He hated it because he connected it with Leona's death. He ordered many who visited him to "get me out of here!" Late in August, he went back to his home. In those familiar surroundings, his health continued to improve.

Doctors told him he could not drive anymore. He did not like it, and he complained loudly, but he obeyed. He said he had four cars, and none of them worked. He threatened to rent a car. But his threats were mostly empty, since he never acted on any of them. He needed to let everyone know he was still in charge, despite evidence to the contrary. Doctors and friends arranged for someone to be with him twenty-four hours a day, with instructions to drive him wherever he wanted to go.

As he did throughout his life, he came to his office every day, but he limited his time there to three or four hours. He complained a little about being tired and forgetful, but he brightened up when the telephone rang or a visitor arrived. And as always, Izzi Wagner visited his favorite eatery, Granato's, almost every day for lunch. Often, Roy Simmons went along with Izzi. And every day at the deli, friends came by to share stories, listen to the conversation, or simply shake the hand of I. J. Wagner.

In late January 2005, Izzi fell once again at his home. His caretaker helped him to bed. He went to sleep and did not wake up. It was as if he decided that the effort was no longer worth it. Irving Jerome Wagner died at his home on February 1, 2005. The death certificate listed the causes of death as pneumonia and old age. The obituary began: "Irving Jerome 'Izzi' Wagner, 89, died Feb. 1, 2005, in Salt Lake City after a long life and a short illness." In respect of his wishes, there were no funeral services of any kind. A half dozen or so family and friends were on hand for his burial next to his beloved Jeanné and a hundred yards from his mother and father.

Local newspapers published several articles about Wagner and his contributions to the community. Friends sent letters and cards to his office. Business and civic organizations mentioned his passing at their meetings. But perhaps the most meaningful and poignant response was in a letter to the *Deseret Morning News* from Bethany R. Brinton:

> In 1973, in preparation for college, I got a job at Hotel Utah as the cashier in the garage. We had many clients that kept monthly accounts and came in and out each day. The young men that worked in the garage as "runners" for the cars had a few favorites. One individual took great interest in each of us.

His name was Izzi Wagner. He invested in the self-esteem of young people every time he came in and out. He enriched our lives through the time and respect he gave us. He treated us as friends and equals. In every situation, Izzi Wagner gave more than he took.

I left Salt Lake in 1978, taking his influence with me. I returned to Utah in 2003 and was pleased to see that in the Rose Wagner Center, the Wagner Jewish Community Center, LDS Hospital and the University of Utah Medical Center, Izzi Wagner continued to give more to life than he took.

Izzi's many friends held him in similar high regard. A group of them decided to recognize Izzi's departure in a more public manner. As one of them said, "We need some way to say good-bye and establish closure—not so much for Izzi as for ourselves." All were aware of his oft-stated wishes to have no services and no memorial observations. And so they organized a celebration. The original plan was to schedule the event for March 31, which would have been Izzi's ninetieth birthday. However, the Rose Wagner Center was already booked on that date for a naturalization ceremony to grant citizenship to dozens of new Americans. All agreed that Izzi would consider the naturalization event a special birthday gift for himself and a special recognition of his mother's naturalization and her love for the United States. The planning group moved the event to April 1. Some noted that Izzi might find it somehow appropriate that the event be on April Fool's Day.

There was no advertising, and no special announcements were sent out, but on April 1, 2005, several hundred friends gathered in the Jeanné Wagner Theatre at the Rose Wagner Performing Arts Center for an event titled "Celebrating Izzi." The program began with the posting of colors by a police honor guard (representing Izzi's love of the United States and his status as an honorary colonel). Brief remarks were offered by Harris Simmons (representing Roy Simmons and the Simmons family), Elder Robert Hales (representing the LDS Church), Jim Holbrook (Izzi's attorney and friend), Marian Iwasaki (representing the Rose Wagner Performing Arts Center), Judge Ray Uno (representing the Japanese American community), Sam Granato (representing Izzi's mealtime friends), Nano Padolski (representing the Jewish Community Center), and Chief Mac Connole (representing law enforcement officers). Dr. Frank Yanowitz, Izzi's physician, played a jazz piano version of a favorite popular song from the 1950s. Dora Bailey, Izzi's secretary, and Candace Wagner, Izzi's niece, joined two others in a string quartet number. A brief video provided glimpses of Izzi and Jeanné. The program ended with the playing of taps and the presentation of a flag by the police honor guard to

Kay Schott, Izzi's sister-in-law. Remarks were generally lighthearted, as Izzi would have preferred.

After the program, guests moved to the Rose Hall for a buffet lunch featuring Izzi's favorite meatballs from Granato's, "Izzi Dogs" from the Jewish Community Center, and the sweet-and-sour spareribs Izzi often ordered at the Pagoda Restaurant.

The printed program included "The Legacy of I. J. 'Izzi' Wagner":

Izzi Wagner left a legacy of friendship. His friends are everywhere. They are in the highest offices of the land…they wait on tables…they lead worldwide organizations…they pump gas…they play golf at the country club… they wash windows on a high rise. Wherever Izzi went, he found friends. He made all of them happy; he made some of them wealthy. His childhood buddy was a friend for life; his latest office neighbor felt as if he, too, were a life-long friend. Everyone who knew Izzi has a favorite Izzi story—most humorous, some generous, all endearing.

Izzi Wagner left a legacy to honor his mother, his sister, and his wife. The Rose Wagner Performing Arts Center honors their love of the performing arts—dance, theater, music. It stands on the site where Izzi was born, where Rose raised her three children. Inside, the Leona Wagner Black Box Theatre honors Izzi's sister, who persevered as the wife of a struggling artist. In the Jeanné Wagner Theatre, one can easily imagine the star-spangled tap rhythms of Jeanné Doré Rasmussen, the vaudeville hoofer with whom Izzi had a 52-year love affair and a marriage Izzi called "perfect."

Izzi Wagner left a legacy to honor his wife, himself, and his family. The "I. J. and Jeanné Wagner Jewish Community Center" is a testament to Izzi's love of Jeanné, to his love of children, to his love of family, and to his love of human diversity. At his insistence, no one can be denied membership on grounds other than the capacity of the facility to accommodate members. Izzi's eyes sparkled whenever he watched children frolic in the pools…or teenagers compete in the gym…or families participate together in the exercise room…especially if they evidenced racial, ethnic, and religious diversity.

The mood of the event—and the mood of those who knew I. J. Wagner—was captured by one of the participants: "We are here today to celebrate, not to mourn. We celebrate the good times we had with Izzi Wagner…and we celebrate the fact that we were among his friends. In that sense, we are a select group…and for that, we celebrate our good fortune."

Epilogue

THE STORY OF I. J. "Izzi" Wagner does not end with these few words. Neither will it end for many decades to come. His photograph hangs in the Rose Wagner Performing Arts Center, marking the site of the adobe house where he was born. A photo also hangs in the I. J. and Jeanné Wagner Jewish Community Center, where he smiles on thousands of children, youngsters, and adults who pass by on their way to learn, swim, play tennis, exercise, or play basketball. Still another photo is on the long "Hall of Fame" at LDS Hospital honoring many of Utah's most prominent and generous citizens; Izzi liked to point out that his photo hangs next to the photo of Gordon B. Hinckley, president of The Church of Jesus Christ of Latter-day Saints.

Some say Irving Jerome Wagner's "bags to riches" story is a typical American success story. But it is much more. It is the story of twentieth-century Utah. Utah began the century as an isolated, provincial, closed society, where outsiders were treated mostly as separate and unequal. The state ended the century as a cosmopolitan community, where a one-time Jewish rag merchant was not only accepted but also honored as an exemplary native son.

It is the story of a young man who might easily have chosen to live with a chip on his shoulder as a result of the prejudice and discrimination he encountered through most of his life. Instead, he consciously chose to follow the counsel of his mother, Rose Wagner, and live life with a tolerant soul, quick wit, and charitable nature.

It is the story of a man who did not judge others based on social status, religion, wealth, or other criteria. As result, he collected lifelong friends the way most of us collect trivial trinkets.

It is the story of a man whose riches may have come from the bags he sold, but whose richness came from the way he lived.

It is a story that profoundly testifies that what might have been the arrogance of an Irving Jerome Wagner or the pretense of an I. J. Wagner was eclipsed by the straightforward humanity of just plain Izzi.

His life was a metaphor for twentieth-century Utah...and an example for twenty-first-century Utahns.

Guiding Principles

His was a life worth remembering in its own right. It was a life filled with profound examples of ethics, performance, and service. He may have been a self-described agnostic or atheist (depending largely on the person asking), but he sensed the meaning of life and the potential of life far better than some who profess to be guided by religion.

As his life developed, he adopted a set of guiding principles. Some came from his mother, Rose, and his father, Harry. Some came from living in hard times. Many came from his multitude of friends. Some came simply from his honest interactions with life. Among the most important principles guiding Izzi Wagner were the following attributes.

Family

Izzi was devoted to his mother, wife, father, brother, sister, and other family members, even those whose relationship was somewhat removed. He kept in touch with family members all over the world. He helped them when they needed help. He enjoyed their successes, and he suffered with their failures.

Friendship

As his neighbor Jim Holbrook pointed out during the "Celebrating Izzi" event, Wagner believed that friends were vital to personal success on all levels. Friends were necessary ingredients to enjoying life and having fun. Friends were assets to multiply one's own effectiveness. Friends were helpmates in getting important things done. Friends were counselors and advisers. And long-term friendships provided sustaining memories and reassuring continuity to the process of living. He believed that in order to have a friend, one must be a friend. And he did not judge friends according to status, power, wealth, philosophy, or background. His friendships with governors, sena-

tors, millionaires, and church leaders were little different from his friendships with mechanics, waiters, secretaries, and clerks. The two exceptions
were his wife, whom he idolized, and his long-term partner, Roy Simmons,
for whom he held special respect and appreciation.

Humor

Izzi learned from his mother that humor has the power to reduce tensions,
bridge differences, and make friends. He believed that when people laughed
at his jokes, they were more likely to listen to his ideas...that when they remembered his jokes, they were also likely to remember the jokester. For Izzi,
humor—often self-deprecating humor—was a key to opening doors, soften-
ing resistance, eliminating fear, and leveling playing fields.

Integrity

Izzi's integrity was not complex. His word was his bond. His handshake was
his contract. He set his own standards, and if he failed to meet those standards, he blamed only himself. He was his own man, making his own decisions. He did not easily relinquish control over his affairs, and he did not seek
control over the affairs of others. He was not motivated by power or the need
for approval. He believed that success is achieved not by taking advantage of
others but by treating others fairly so they will want to deal with you again.
He believed in the goodness of people, and when others failed to live up to his
expectations he regarded them as exceptions, not examples.

Generosity

Izzi believed that every success included a measure of good fortune; no one is
solely responsible for his or her position in life, whether it be financial, social,
emotional, or physical. Therefore, according to Izzi, one should, first, be
grateful for each success and, second, be willing to help others succeed. Since
the difference between one person's success and another person's failure may
be a bit of good luck, it was not fair in Izzi's mind to judge one person better
or worse than the other based on wealth, position, or title.

Responsibility

To Izzi, responsibility was part of a two-way interaction. If a customer
bought a product with certain expectations, it was Izzi's responsibility to
see that the expectations were met or exceeded. If Izzi wanted trust from
a friend, it was Izzi's responsibility to return the trust. If the nation, state,
and city provided opportunities for success, it was Izzi's responsibility to be

a good citizen. He was always the first in line at his voting place. He paid his taxes without complaint. He supported political candidates with words, actions, and contributions. He gave time and wisdom to numerous volunteer boards and committees. He championed causes he felt would improve the community. He volunteered for military service when he could have avoided it, placing himself in great danger. To Izzi, these were the responsibilities of citizenship. The responsibilities of business, friendship, and daily living were equally important.

Tolerance

Izzi did not like the word *tolerance,* because it implies effort in order to tolerate those different from oneself. For Izzi, no effort was needed. He accepted everyone equally, as if there were no differences. He grew up during a time of racial discrimination. He experienced it, but he never learned to practice it. He did not believe in religion, but over the years, he attended all manner of churches at the invitation of friends. He said he found good people in all of them. He enjoyed good-natured debate about belief systems, but he did not ridicule any of them. Former Salt Lake City mayor Ted Wilson, a longtime friend of Wagner's, called him "an icon of inclusion, of entrepreneurship, and of community building."

The list of I. J. Wagner's guiding principles could certainly be expanded, and everyone who knew him would probably develop a different list. This man who sometimes seemed so straightforward and simple was, in fact, very complex.

And like all human beings, he had his faults. Once the trust of friendship was broken, he did not forgive easily. When Jeanné died, a couple with whom Izzi and Jeanné had been close for many years failed to acknowledge her death with a visit, a phone call, or a card. Izzi never forgave them. He could not easily accept praise without returning a sarcastic comment intended as humor. Some found such responses difficult to understand. He welcomed friends, but he also erected a distinct personal-space barrier that no one could cross (with the exception, perhaps, of Jeanné).

Stories circulated about Izzi being tightfisted. Many of the stories were started by Izzi himself. Most of the stories were wrong. For instance, someone circulated a story about how he refused to upgrade a group of houses he supposedly owned in Salt Lake's Avenues section. But there is no evidence that he ever owned residential property in the area, except the houses in which he lived.

Still, Izzi Wagner's detractors were few, and his admirers were many. Those who knew him will not soon forget him.

Major Contributions

The city will not soon forget I. J. Wagner either. Nor will those who live in Salt Lake City in the years ahead. Much of what he did may have come about without him, but Izzi was the catalyst, the advocate, the leader, the conscience. He made it happen more quickly, and he insisted on higher standards than others may have allowed. He wanted the city to be better than it had been during his life. He did his homework. And as Governor Cal Rampton said, he was tenacious; he did not give up. Among Izzi's contributions are the following:

- Rose Wagner Performing Arts Center—Salt Lake County's most-used performance venue
- I. J. and Jeanné Wagner Jewish Community Center—a recreation and learning center serving children and adults of all races, creeds, and backgrounds
- Wagner Industrial Park—Utah's first and most successful industrial park
- Salt Palace Convention Center—the state's leading generator of convention and tourism activity
- Salt Lake International Airport—a modern, well-run transportation facility that generates economic activity for the state
- Downtown sign ordinance—a downtown free of billboards and signs overhanging the sidewalks
- Removal of rails on Second West—without the railroad tracks, Second West became a traffic artery, an extension of the downtown business community, and a street across which the Salt Palace Convention Center could grow
- Second West tunnel under the convention center—the tunnel permits vital north-south access, even more important since the closing of Main Street at South Temple
- Improved health care—special facilities or rooms at LDS Hospital, University Hospital, and Salt Lake Regional Health Center (formerly Holy Cross Hospital)
- Additional downtown parking—parking across from the Rose Wagner Center; on the block bordered by Main Street, Second South, West Temple, and Third South; and elsewhere
- Strengthened zoning regulations at all levels—making Salt Lake and its environs more coherent, more functional, and more attractive

- Less tension among those from diverse races, creeds, and religions—partially from his example and partially from the organizations he encouraged and supported

Izzi was only one man, but he was one man who cared. He was one man who had a vision for his city. He was one man who took action when he thought action was needed. He was one man who would not give in to prejudice or discrimination. He was one man who made a difference. And that may be the greatest legacy of his "bags to riches" journey: I. J. "Izzi" Wagner made a difference.

Index

Page numbers in *italics* refer to photographs.